Routledge Revivals

The Value Dimension

The essays in this edited collection, first published in 1986, focus on important debates surrounding the central Marxian problem of the transformation of values into prices. The collection brings together major contributions on the value theory debate from the decade prior to the book's publication, and assesses the debate's significance for wider issues. Value theory emerges as much more than a technical relation between labour time and prices, and the structure of the capitalist economy is scrutinised. This is a relevant and comprehensive work, valuable to students, academics and professionals with an interest in political and Marxist economy.

The Value Dimension

Marx versus Ricardo and Sraffa

Edited by Ben Fine

Routledge
Taylor & Francis Group
REVIVALS

First published in 1986
by Routledge and Kegan Paul Ltd

This edition first published in 2013 by Routledge
2 Park Square, Milton Park, Abingdon, Oxon, OX14 4RN

Simultaneously published in the USA and Canada
by Routledge
711 Third Avenue, New York, NY 10017

Routledge is an imprint of the Taylor & Francis Group, an informa business

Publisher's Note
The publisher has gone to great lengths to ensure the quality of this reprint but points out that some imperfections in the original copies may be apparent.

Disclaimer
The publisher has made every effort to trace copyright holders and welcomes correspondence from those they have been unable to contact.

A Library of Congress record exists under LC control number: 87109334

ISBN 13: 978-0-415-83760-6 (hbk)
ISBN 13: 978-0-203-78354-2 (ebk)
ISBN 13: 978-0-415-83853-5 (pbk)

The Value Dimension

Marx versus Ricardo and Sraffa

Edited by
Ben Fine

Routledge & Kegan Paul
London and New York

First published in 1986 by
Routledge & Kegan Paul Ltd
11 New Fetter Lane, London EC4P 4EE

Set in 11/12 pt Plantin
by Columns of Reading
and printed in Great Britain
by T.J. Press (Padstow) Ltd,
Padstow, Cornwall

British Library Cataloguing in Publication Data

The Value dimension : Marx versus Ricardo and Sraffa.—(Economy & society)
1. Value
I. Fine, Ben II. Series
338.5'21 HB201

ISBN 0-7102-0766-2

Contents

A cynic knows everything of price and nothing of value.
with apologies to Oscar Wilde.

We have developed a passion for formulae which mitigate facts and obscure issues.
Lord Horder, *Obscurantism*, Conway Memorial Lecture, Watts & Co. London, 1938, p. 6.

CHAPTER 1

Introduction

Ben Fine

It is normal for an introduction to an edited collection to engage in a broader literature survey, to explain the criteria of selection and to summarize and give a guide to the pieces that have been included. I have not attempted to do any of these, although some are partially covered in passing. Instead, I have attempted to construct a potted history of the debate over the period concerned, giving some explanation of why the contributions came as and when they did. For this reason, I presume some knowledge on the part of the reader of what the transformation problem is and of some of the issues which are raised by it. To a large extent, even at an elementary level, this is the subject matter of the readings included here, so that a return to this introduction may be warranted after a reading of the text.

Any such history as intended here, is bound to contain a heavy element of subjectivity and bias. It is as if a minor character in a play is responsible for a review of it. The scenes in which the character appears are necessarily going to figure more prominently and other scenes, whatever their importance, may pass unobserved. Like a play, it will be argued in this introduction that the transformation problem is open to alternative interpretations and presentations – according to the way in which the relationship between production and exchange is understood and which aspects of this relationship are the subject of attention. To see it as the search for and discovery of a definitive solution to a well-defined problem, the calculation of prices as the Sraffian or post-Sraffian interpretation would have it, is only one construction of the transformation. But it is not the only one (although it has, from different viewpoints, been central to much recent debate); if it were, it would be a simple matter to rehearse the solution, even with varying interpretations, for each new generation of economists and the play need never grace the stage of original research nor original context again.

The setting

From the late 1960s onwards there was a considerable growth of interest in Marxism within the western academic world. Following the student activism of the immediately preceding period, the general liberalization of life-styles amongst the young and the expansion of university and other higher education, teaching and research posts became open to a new breed of academic Marxists. But the traditions that it found available within the existing literature were far from satisfactory as the capitalist world economy moved into recession in the early 1970s. Whilst there were Marxist theoretical journals of considerable sophistication, most notably *New Left Review* published in the UK, these were remarkable for the lack of articles on economic matters, whether theoretical or empirical. In the United States, the world of political economy was dominated by a single text, *Monopoly Capital* by Baran and Sweezy. As has been increasingly realized in retrospect, this book contained many theoretical and empirical weaknesses. But most significant for our purposes is that it essentially rejected Marx's value theory, substituting a theory of potential surplus in its place. This reflected an explicit dependence of Baran and Sweezy on the role of the lack of effective demand (under-consumption) as the underlying contradiction of modern capitalism.[1] For this a value theory in itself, let alone one based on labour time, is redundant.[2] Accordingly, there was little here on which a new generation of political economists could hone their analytical powers.

In the UK, a growing challenge to orthodox neoclassical economics was perceived to be contained in the Cambridge critique of capital theory. In its details, this involved an attack on neoclassical one-sector growth and distribution theory and, for some, by implication from the work of Sraffa (1960), an attack on neoclassical theory as a whole.[3] The Cambridge critique constructed a theory of prices and distribution (the wage–profit relation) by reference to 'production conditions' (input–output coefficients) alone and without reference to demand (subjective preferences as expressed by utility).

This solution to the determination of prices and profits from given production conditions was, then, originally intended as the basis for a criticism of the neoclassical orthodoxy. And it has proved to be such and has even given rise to a more positive alternative in the school of post-Keynesian economics, which emphasizes aggregate macroeconomic relations, monopolization, class-based distributional struggle and other common sense realities of the modern economy in contrast to the orthodoxy.[4] But the determination of prices and profits within the Cambridge critique has also proved to be the basis on which to launch an attack on Marx's value theory under the rubric of the transformation problem to which it is perceived to be offering a correct solution. Not surprisingly, the originators of the Cambridge critique, with the exception of Sraffa himself, had no particular commitment to Marxism and the person, Joan Robinson, with whom the critique and its popularization is most closely associated, had always been a critic of Marx's value theory and the propositions derived from it.[5]

Meanwhile, the flag of Marxist political economy had been held aloft, particularly by Maurice Dobb and Ronald Meek. For the former, in his academic writings, the labour theory of value figured very much as a tool with which to create both a sociology of capitalist exploitation (as opposed to bourgeois welfare economics) and as a means to uncover the laws of motion of capitalism (as opposed to the dominant stream of neoclassical/ Keynesian economics). In the first instance, this was a return to the 'natural right' of labourers to the full fruits of their work, a moral that had been basic to the Ricardian socialists.

Second, Dobb's view implied there existed *the* labour theory of value, based on the labour time required to produce a commodity (labour embodied). In this, the labour theory of value of Ricardo is identical to that of Marx. Indeed, Dobb referred to the Ricardo-Marx labour value theory, something which, in the light of recent literature ought now to be impossible, as we shall see. So, in his hands, the labour theory of value became an analytical tool which might be useful for some purposes (which would differ between Ricardo and Marx) but which, in principle, might not be useful for others.

Subsequently, particularly in the context of the transformation problem, many were to argue that in practice the labour theory of value was at the very least useless and even erroneous. This became true of Meek, as a result of which much of his work, distinguishing Marx's labour theory of value from that of his predecessors, drew little (sympathetic) reading.

Value form

An early and cogent criticism of the Dobb–Meek position was provided by Pilling (1972)*.[6] Whatever its limitations,[7] it was to provide a model for one of the two strands in the first phase of the debate around value theory and the transformation problem. As such, it had a number of crucial features. First, as has been made clear, a distinction was to be drawn between the labour theory of value of Marx and that of Ricardo. The failure of writers such as Dobb to make this distinction, despite their sympathy to Marx, was something shared in common with bourgeois critiques of Marx which (particularly around the transformation problem) became unanswerable. Not surprisingly, then, these bourgeois criticisms were found to have been embraced by Dobb and Meek and Marx's transformation found wanting. Inevitably, those who failed to distinguish Ricardo's and Marx's theories of value did so by imposing the former's on the latter's.

Second, emphasis was placed upon the unique character of Marx's method. Here, reference was made to the distinctions between and/or the relationship between form and content, essence and appearance, the qualitative and the quantitative, historical specificity and logical abstractions, and dialectics and contradictions. Third, this was closely tied to the object of study – value theory. Where Ricardo and his followers employed a simple concept of labour embodied, a mental construct with or without useful purpose, Marx derived the labour theory of value from the workings of commodity-producing society itself, as a consequence of social relations between producers. From here, a discourse was derived which explored the relations between use value and exchange value, value and price and concrete and abstract labour. These were quite notable for their absence in the works of Ricardo and his conscious or unconscious followers.

They were to become the focus for analysis, leading to the fourth characteristic of one strand of the early contributions to value theory – the interrogation of the texts of Marx and, on occasion when it suited, those of other writers of the past such as Rubin (1973) and Rosdolsky (1977). This is not surprising given the previously observed lack of a continuing trend of literature faithful to and developing Marx's own contributions. It led to an ethos of *Capital* reading groups whose existence became expressed socially in the creation of new journals, the most important of all for this purpose in the UK being *Capital and Class* or the *Bulletin of the Conference of Socialist Economists*, as it was then known. But equally, the debates found their way into other journals such as *Economy and Society* which had itself been created by the wave of interest in Marxist theory.

The result was that very little attention in this strand was paid to the quantitative aspects of the transformation problem. Focus was placed on the opening chapters of Volume I of *Capital* and the series of texts by Marx, such as the *Grundrisse*, that had led up to it. To a large extent, even Marx's own treatment of the transformation in Volume III of *Capital* warranted little attention since it was not concerned to establish the social, historical and logical relation between value, as created in production, and its form of existence in exchange. It was more or less presumed that the conceptual solution to this problem carried with it as a corollary the quantitative relation between value and price with or without amendment to Marx's own contribution. Far more important, however, was the extent to which the solutions to the transformation based on Sraffa by his followers set aside these qualitative considerations.

The quantity of price

For the Sraffians, the other major strand in the first phase of debate, the concentration on the value-form, was irrelevant to their purpose of deriving a numerical solution to the transformation problem. Their point of contact with Marx was an immediate confrontation with Volume III of *Capital*, as if all that came before was of no relevance to their immediate and self-contained object of study, the derivation of equilibrium prices. This was so even if the significance of Marx's analysis of other matters, such as how production develops under capitalism or how capitalism is established, was considered enormous. But Marx's analysis here was seen to be quite independent of the transformation and of the value theory that posed it, to the extent of Steedman (1977) ultimately arguing that 'Marx's value reasoning – hardly a peripheral aspect of his work – must therefore be abandoned, in the interest of developing a coherent materialist theory of capitalism', p. 207.

Unfortunately for the generation of debate, the opponents to the followers of Sraffa focused little on what came after the opening chapters of Volume I, concerned with the value-form. There was a different terrain within *Capital* on which the two sides were engaged. Indeed, for the Sraffians, most of the discussion of the value-form was, in Ian Steedman's description, 'obscurantist'. Nonetheless, with an ever weakening grip on and an ever weakening will to hold hands with Marx's own contribution, the Sraffians still felt it necessary to claim that they were dealing with the qualitative side of the question: that, for example, the use of homogeneous embodied labour presumed the assumption of concrete labour reduced to abstract labour[8] and that Sraffa was consistent with Marx's method in all but the details.[9] In retrospect, these claims read rather weakly, not only in terms of their own intrinsic content in the light of a developing understanding of the unity of Marx's contributions within *Capital*, but also by reference to the continuing development of the Sraffian school in which the derivation of mathematical results from well-defined models has all but eliminated anything other than a passing reference, often negative, to the works of Marx.

Two features stand out from the Sraffian strand (and stand against Marx). The first is that it is an equilibrium analysis in the standard neoclassical meaning of the term. The attempt is to obtain equilibrium prices from given conditions of production (and there is much else besides from neoclassical theory, such as optimizing behaviour by individuals in response to market prices, as Steedman (1977) makes clear, once an agency of profit equalization is introduced). The significance of this is that it defines the nature of the transformation problem to be solved and, consequently, the nature of the solution. Second, the Sraffians conflate 'causation' with 'calculation', an aspect which is concealed to a large extent by the common use of the term 'determination' in the two different senses to express both causation and calculation. The significance here is the interpretation of determination which is put upon what is already a heavily circumscribed context in which the transformation is located. This can all be made clearer by a brief examination of the results claimed by the Sraffians.

With given production conditions, generally an input–output matrix, both values and prices and profits, subject to wages, can be *calculated*. But prices and profits cannot be *calculated* from the corresponding values. Hence, it is argued that values are irrelevant in the *causation* of prices and profits and are thereby rendered redundant. Here, there is a clear slippage between what causes prices to be what they are and what allows them to be calculated. Because I can measure and calculate the level of rainfall, this does not imply any understanding of the causes of rainfall. By the same token, to claim that technology etc. determines prices, and values do not, simply because prices can be calculated from technology and not from values, is irrelevant to the causal status of values, certainly until we know at least what determines technology to be what it is.[10]

Steedman (1977) provided an implicit answer to this criticism in so far as he argued that capitalists respond to prices perceived on the market, rather than unknown values, in choosing technology for profit-maximizing behaviour. This is but a reflection of the orthodox assumptions that inform the Sraffian analysis – of an economics based on the market behaviour of atomized individual capitalists, *except* where capital and labour confront each other as classes in a distributional struggle. But it is equally symptomatic of the divorce between Sraffians and those dependent on analysis of the value-form. For the latter, market behaviour and the evolution of technology are themselves the more concrete and complex consequence of underlying value (and class) relations just as are prices. Consequently, the Sraffians had made explicit their false perception of value theory through their treatment of the transformation problem but they had not addressed themselves to *Marx's* labour theory of value.

In short, the rupture between the Sraffians and the theorists of the value-form was multi-faceted. Each strand subscribed to a different method, each addressed a different problem, making little if any contribution to that of the other side, and each engaged on textual terrains that were not only distinct but which were also separated by the vast majority of both Volumes I and II of *Capital*. At the time, the situation was described as a dialogue of the deaf (even if it was hardly a dialogue of the dumb).

Value-form and price quantity

This phase in the debate was brought to a close in the intellectual sense by the remarkable paper by Gerstein (1976)*. He achieved what appeared to be impossible – a stance firmly within the value-form strand but a quantitative answer to the transformation problem. His paper contained little of originality when taken apart piece by piece – his solution to the transformation, for example, had its origins in a paper of Seton (1957) and on others before – but it did provide a complex synthesis of the preceding literature. His exposition of the relation between abstract and concrete labour was linked to the notion of an economic structure linking production to exchange, with values and prices being reconstructed at ever greater levels of complexity.

The presence of the Althusserian school at the height of its influence is plain to see. It served to set aside the models and Ricardianism of the Sraffian strand. In addition, Gerstein's paper is littered with a wealth of unexplored observations that are seen as drawing relevance from his analysis, ranging from the role of fixed capital, money and the distinction between the organic and value compositions of capital at the economic level through to the role of domestic labour, the mode of production, the state and class interests both at more complex and more general levels of analyses.

But, at the end of the day, Gerstein offered a solution to the transformation problem from within the value-form strand. 'Marx's approach is inherently dynamic and has little in common with the static equilibrium models that underly both vulgar economy and neo-Ricardianism. Still, it is important for Marxists to recognise . . . the quantitative connections.' He was not, however, true to the implications of his words. For the solution offered clearly lies within the bounds of static equilibrium and is dynamic only in the sense of allowing the reproduction, through the economic structure, of that equilibrium. The values and prices of production yielded are, in principle, immortal in Gerstein's solution just as they are in the Sraffian case.

Where the two differ is that Gerstein takes values and applies transformation coefficients to them to obtain prices of production. A set of simultaneous equations results that can be solved. For Sraffians, this is not so much wrong (or not a matter of logic to use their vernacular) as irrelevant and superfluous, as we have previously mentioned. Their transformation is both more direct and cleaner. But, as Gerstein observed, this is a matter of mathematics and this cannot resolve the principles of political economy involved. For him, Seton 'conclusively ended the debate about the mathematical factors involved'. As the mathematics allowed prices to be calculated in relation to values, the latter could not be rejected as a causal element to put the point in the terms used earlier.

Here Gerstein is relying on the principle of the neutrality of mathematics in constructing causality or, to put it negatively, the fallacy of deriving causality from the process of calculation. It is a point that has been made by Dobb (1973): equations set A equal to B, no more and no less. It cannot be deduced that A causes B nor that B causes A without some external assumption, whether this is made explicit or not. But, as Fine (1982) has argued, this does not go far enough in comprehending the role of equations. For they inevitably carry with them a more or less explicit economic structure by the very nature of the variables (concepts) that are brought into equality with each other or not. In a sense, the Sraffians were well versed in rejecting this observation, for their polemical battle cry was always: 'Never mind my concepts, do you or do you not accept my logic [by which is meant mathematics]?' – to which the answer has to be in the affirmative (but I do not accept your concepts).

But what the mathematics of both Gerstein and the Sraffians had in common was the construction of an equilibrium set of prices of production, however much Gerstein might have suggested otherwise. In particular, the prices of inputs and of outputs are taken to be equal. This both rules out dynamics and limits the extent to which (changing) conditions of production can determine conditions of exchange and distribution. It also leads Gerstein to the same conclusion as the Sraffians, although more mildly put, that Marx 'goes astray' in his own solution. Thus, although Gerstein bases his conceptual, qualitative argument on the complex unity in structure of reproduction through production, exchange and distribution, his quantitative argument collapses this structure and unity.

Gerstein's approach leaves him with a symptomatic difficulty which we discuss by way of digression. The solution that he proposes is only unique for the determination of relative rather than absolute prices of production. To go a further step to absolute prices requires the choice of a numeraire or normalization as Gerstein terms it. Again, for him, the choice is not one of mathematics but of political economy, although why the choice arises and has to be made at the proximate level of analysis is not questioned within his own frame of reference. A related but different point is that the normalization can only arrive, in general, at an equality between total value and total price or between total surplus value and total profit but not both (as in Marx's transformation). Gerstein's choice within political economy is for the equality between price and value but his argument is, of necessity, forced and arbitrary. The whole episode also contradicts a basic starting point of the value-form strand, but it requires the measurement of value against price, whereas the two are seen as qualitatively different and consequently cannot be quantitatively measured against each other. From this perspective, without the irrelevant detour of the transformation problem, the aggregate conditions are tautologies, since total (surplus) value in its form of exchange value must equal total (profit) price.[11]

Whilst Gerstein's paper had the effect of partially healing the rupture between the two strands of thought (even if leaving a long scar of equilibrium analysis), debates within the two strands have continued to the present day.[12] But other issues within value theory were the subject of debate, quite apart from the transformation problem, and these reflected and reacted back upon each other. The most important issues concerned the distinction between productive and unproductive labour and the nature and validity of the law of the tendency of the rate of profit to fall. In a survey of and contribution to the literature, Fine and Harris (1979) relied heavily on Gerstein's contribution to classify schools of thought as neo-Ricardian or fundamentalist across these and other issues, whilst offering an alternative. But the method of doing so was by reference to the dynamic and structured relations between production, distribution and exchange and the equilibrium element within Gerstein's approach was absent except in posing a solution to the transformation problem.

Value and rent

These developments in value theory 'outside the immediate transformation problem' were to have delayed, but important, repercussions, precisely because they dealt with values in the context of accumulation. In a paper on rent, following that of Ball (1977), Fine (1979)* (and Ball (1980)* in debate with Fine (1980a)*) attempted to unravel the mysteries of Marx's theory of agricultural rent from his extensive but unsystematic writings on the subject. To do so, and to explore the effects of landed property on accumulation as much as the quantitative determination of rent, it proved necessary to specify more closely the structures of value determination both within sectors as well as between sectors and to link these to the accumulation process. In this way, an analysis could be made of the ways in which landed property might intervene to obstruct or promote these processes and structures of accumulation. Differential rent was tied to competition within a sector.

Differential Rent I was seen to arise out of the process of value formation in the absence of changes in the conditions of production, except through the movement of capital on to lands of differing quality. Differential Rent II was also located in terms of competition and value formation within the sector, but it involved intensive accumulation. Finally, absolute rent was constructed on the basis of competition between sectors, in the context of the flow of capital into and out of agriculture, a process intimately connected with the formation of prices of production, distorted in this instance by the presence of landed property and its effects on accumulation and *hence* on distribution and prices rather than on the latter two alone, directly and as a monopoly element.

The results of some of these contributions to rent theory, and their confrontation with the existing literature, whether sympathetic to Marx as for Murray (1977), for example, or less so, as in Clarke and Ginsburg (1976), are reproduced in this volume. What is significant is that they necessarily confronted the processes of value and price formation in the context of accumulation, that is with changing values in general, and competition between capitalists. Accordingly, the relation between value and price had to be seen as dynamic and changing. To yield a quantity of rent as appropriated surplus value, the relation between value and price had also to be structured in relation to individual values of production within a sector, value for the sector as a whole and the realization of these values in exchange as prices.

The intimate relation between this and the transformation problem is transparent. Indeed, rent and landed property add complications but, in doing so, provided a stimulus to probe the structures and processes connecting production to distribution and exchange. In looking at absolute rent, Fine attempted to do this by stressing the importance of the distinction between the organic and the value compositions of capital.

The structure of value relations

This distinction had played a crucial role in Fine and Harris's (1979) interpretation of the law of the tendency of the rate of profit to fall. It both examined the changing conditions of production (values) during the accumulation process and linked these to the relation between production and exchange. The dynamics involved necessarily made equilibrium impossible as an organizing tool of analysis.

These themes were taken up specifically in Fine (1983a)* in the context of the transformation problem. It was observed that Marx specifically defined and referred to the organic composition in treating the transformation and that this tied the analysis to the implications for prices of production of changing technology alone. By contrast, the whole weight of literature had concerned itself with the transformation in terms of the value composition, in practice if not in terminology, so that it had dealt with the formation of prices from the perspective of both production and exchange. It had only been able to do so through an equilibrium analysis, i.e. where input and output prices were equal and predetermined by predetermined technology (values).

In an independently written paper, Carchedi (1984)* developed a similar approach at greater length by situating the transformation within the structures and processes of capitalist production and circulation. Here, as Marx makes clear in a number of places, the prices of production and average rate of profit are already formed prior to the re-entry of capital into the sphere of production. They are the basis, together with the operation of productive capital, for the formation of the subsequent prices of production and rate of profit and are not determined simultaneously with them. In this way, the transformation has been moved away from a static equilibrium analysis of the economy as a whole. Instead, it has been located in terms of a partial process, linked to production and in a contradictory unity with other processes, such as the formation of prices and profitability in exchange even as underlying values are transformed by the accumulation of capital.

This interpretation also removes a textual anomaly in the works of Marx, one which had reached extremes within the literature. For rather than the transformation being an immediate corollary of the value-form or of the production of surplus value by capitals of unequal composition, both readily analysable within Volume I of *Capital*, it becomes immediately linked to the contradictions unravelled in the law of the tendency of the rate of profit to fall (in which the contradictions between production and exchange are analysed by reference to the changing organic composition of the transformation problem and the value composition that it becomes through exchange).

The debates over productive and unproductive labour also led to a clarification of the formation of value, not in the narrow sense of the relation between production and exchange, but in understanding the formation of value within production itself. For the Sraffians, value was created by labour irrespective of the conditions under which it was organized as long as it ultimately, and possibly indirectly, entered exchange. Thus, teachers, welfare workers and domestic labour could all be sources of (surplus) value through the creation of value in the form of labour power. This approach followed from a static analysis of the effects of such labour on the input-output matrix used to calculate prices and profits.

The alternative was to see production in terms of a number of sharply delineated social relations of production, not only in the classical Marxist sense of distinguishing one mode of production from another, and not only in the sense of distinguishing capitalist and non-capitalist production within a single mode of production or social formation. Rather, even with value production, there were different forms of organization of the labour process whether it be simple commodity production or, for surplus value production, the distinction between the real and formal subordination of labour to capital. These developments were particularly stimulated by the response to the work of Braverman (1974) and led to a new wave of literature concerning the labour (for commodities, the value-producing) process. Inevitably, this involved much more than a study of technology. It embraced the methods of control, and struggle over them, within the sphere of production, as well as their connections with wider economic relations, vertical and horizontal integration, monopolization, etc.

The historical transformation problem

Thus, from a whole series of different points of view, the subject matter of the transformation problem was being considered. Whether it be the law of the tendency of the rate of profit to fall, the role of landed property, productive and unproductive labour or the anatomy of the labour process, the relationship between the spheres of production and exchange were under interrogation. This also formed the basis of a dispute over the historical transformation problem.[13] Ostensibly, this concerned whether a time existed in the past when commodities exchanged at their values so that, if so, and given the presumed contemporary exchange of values at prices of production, a transition between exchange at values and exchange at prices of production must have occurred, that is, the historical transformation. The complicating issues raised by Fine for the debate, and for the historical and even for the contemporary record, was that the historical transformation had first to recognize and identify the different types of value production. In this light, the transformation problem seemed only pertinent to that stage of development of capitalism for which the tendency of the rate of profit to be equalized operated.[14] This, in turn, in Marx's theory was precisely the stage of the developed credit system, of machinofacture and of the real subordination of labour to capital.[15]

Ricardo versus Sraffa

As should be abundantly clear, the development of the value-form strand yielded a substantial weight of criticism of the conceptual content of neoclassical and of Sraffian economics as a by-product of the defence of Marx's value theory against its identification with the value theory of Ricardo. In particular, the theory of commodity fetishism, itself a corollary of value-form analysis, pointed to the reification of economics in the hands of both neoclassicals and Sraffians. For the latter, there was the tendency to cornify or, more exactly, to standard commoditify the economy. Such was the general character of the Sraffians, but it was particularly prominent in the treatment of value as an unproblematical calculation of labour embodied which had the effect of creating the Ricardo–Marx value theory.

But this characteristic of the Sraffians also extended to their interpretation of the works of Ricardo quite independently of their relation to the works of Marx. In this, the Sraffians had something of a command position since Sraffa had edited Ricardo's works. Looking down on Ricardo from this vantage point, it is not surprising that the evolution of his work should be seen in terms of its relation to the Sraffian model. Whilst this was challenged from a more distant neoclassical viewing tower, seeking the germs and genes of supply and demand analysis,[16] it was only challenged from within the Marxist perspective at a relatively late date. Faccarello (1982)* questioned Sraffa's interpretation of Ricardo prior to his commitment to value theory based on labour time and Fine (1983)* extended it to the Sraffian interpretation of the Ricardian value theory problem and its solution. Meanwhile, a parallel debate between the Sraffians and the neoclassicals took place over the same ground,[17] ultimately casting doubt on the Sraffian interpretation, without thereby abandoning the field to their rivals.[18]

Concluding remarks

As has always been recognized, the transformation problem and the positions adopted on it, have far-reaching implications for economics beyond the narrow confines of the relation between value and price. We hope to have shown that the matter goes a little further – that the transformation problem has itself to be constructed and can, in principle, embrace the subject matter of what might otherwise be considered to be separate from it, even if within the scope of its implications. As this review has illustrated, the transformation can be viewed in a number of different ways, each with a differing content and reflecting the isolation for analysis of one or more aspects of the relations between production and exchange within the capitalist economy. Because the capitalist economy, to use White's (1985) term, is a 'cascade' of relations and processes, the transformation necessarily chooses some aspects to examine at the expense of others, and also choses to relate them to each other in particular ways. The validity of these differing views and what they include as well as what they exclude is open to dispute. But each view should be able to posit how it is to relate the elements that are absent to the elements that are present. Not just production, distribution, exchange, value and price, but also accumulation, and changing conditions of production.

The Sraffian strand might be seen as collapsing the contradictory unity of these aspects into a simultaneous equilibrium. By doing so, they inevitably see any alternative as partial, incomplete (failing to transform inputs, for example) or simply defying the rules of (their) logic. On the other hand, their solution is partial to equilibrium (harmony between production and exchange) and fixed conditions of production, for example, for which there does indeed appear to be no role for a value theory based on labour time. It also appears to close off further analysis of the transformation and its implications in anything other than a more complicated, through combining more factors, input–output equilibrium.[19]

But, if otherwise, the transformation is open to a greater or lesser terrain of interpretation, what are the future territories on which it might be explored? There is one obvious direction of analysis which remains severely underdeveloped – the role of money. This has not been absent from the existing literature on the transformations. For the Sraffians, it has often proved to be one of the sectors, a commodity money whose unit price sets the absolute price level to accomplish normalization. However, in this context, and more broadly, the Marxist theory of money has been developed little beyond the comparable position occupied by the value-form strand in its early days. The qualitative aspects of money and its functions have been derived, although they remain controversial, but the situation of money in the structure and processes of capitalist circulation remains underexamined – in much the same way that the structures and processes of value creation were absent in the early days of the transformation debate.

This leaves an urgent task to be accomplished, for it would shed light, from a Marxist perspective, on the changing contours of the international financial system, an area of analysis where Marxism has not significantly moved much beyond description and narrative. It might be argued that the transformation problem, with or without money, can cast little light upon these concrete and complex developments, since it is an abstract, theoretical question. This is contradicted by the significant but subtle and scarcely observed influence that the transformation problem and related value theory debates have had on the directions of empirical research. From an analysis organized around the levels of demand (under-consumption) and the levels of wages (distributional profit squeeze), attention has turned to the restructuring of capital – internationally through multinationals, through state intervention, in the production process through new technology and/or command structures, through new divisions of labour within and between sectors, etc. In this, demand and distribution play a role but it is not exclusive and determining. No doubt these developments and the urgency of the need to analyse them were brought into sharp relief by the end of the post-war boom. Nonetheless, through the transformation problem, some theoretical elements were available to confront the analytical task.

Notes

* This denotes that the above mentioned article appears in this volume.

1. For the most elegant statement and development of the theory of monopoly capitalism on the foundations provided by Baran and Sweezy (and Kalecki), see Cowling (1982) and Sawyer (1982). For a critique, see Fine and Murfin (1984).
2. This has been argued by Weeks (1982).
3. For the most comprehensive account of the Cambridge critique, see Harcourt (1972) and for an emphasis on its limitations as an assault on neoclassical economics, see Fine (1980).
4. See, for example, the contributions to the *Journal of PostKeynesian Economics*.
5. See Robinson (1953/4) which emerges as a very weak contribution in the light of debates over the transformation problem and other aspects of Marx's economics.

6. For a more direct presentation of his own views, see Pilling (1980). See also the debate between Meek (1973) and Pilling (1973).
7. Supportive criticism is to be found, for example, in de Brunhoff (1973) and Itoh (1980).
8. See Hodgson (1974).
9. See Steedman (1977).
10. The argument of this paragraph is given at greater length in Fine (1982).
11. For a similar argument, see Itoh (1980).
12. Within the value-form strand, see Elson (1979) and more recently Gleicher (1983) and (1985) and Eldred (1984). The value-form strand engages on the formal, mathematical terrain of the Sraffians by examining exchange as a binary relation. See Ganssmann (1981)* and Krause (1982). Sraffian contributions have been numerous, building various mathematical models to accommodate a variety of factors. Steedman *et al.* (1981) gathers together contributions from both strands. See also the special issues of *Science and Society* of 1980 and 1984/5 and of the *Review of Radical Political Economy*, 1982.
13. See Catephores (1980)* and Fine (1980b)*, following Appendix 4 of Fine (1979)*.
14. As a passing comment, it can be observed that this *tendency* has more often been seen as an *assumption* within the literature, in parallel with neoclassical economics, reflecting the extent to which the transformation problem has been connected to the problematics of equilibrium.
15. Elsewhere, Fine (1985) has brought the same observation on the different types of value production to bear on another transition – to socialism – in the context of the role of the law of value under socialism.
16. See Hollander (1979).
17. See Garegnani (1982) and (1983) and Hollander (1983).
18. See Rankin (1984).
19. This is explicit, for example, in the work of Steedman (1977).

References

Ball, M. (1977) 'Differential Rent and the Role of Landed Property', *International Journal of Urban and Regional Planning*, vol. 1, no. 3.

Ball, M. (1980)* 'On Marx's Theory of Agricultural Rent – a Reply to Ben Fine', *Economy and Society*, vol. 9, no. 3.

Baran, P. and Sweezy, P. (1966) *Monopoly Capital*, Monthly Review Press: London.

Braverman, H. (1974) *Labour and Monopoly Capital: the Degredation of Work in the Twentieth Century*, Monthly Review Press: New York.

de Brunhoff, S. (1973) 'Marx as an A-Ricardian: Exchange Value and Money at the Beginning of "Capital" ', *Economy and Society*, vol. 2.

Carchedi, G. (1984)* 'The Logic of Price as Values', *Economy and Society*, vol. 13, no. 4.

Catephores, G. (1980)* 'The Historical Transformation Problem – a Reply', *Economy and Society*, vol. 9, no. 3.

Clarke, S. and **Ginsburg,** N. (1976) 'The Political Economy of Housing', *Kapitalistate*, Summer, no. 4/5.

Cowling, K. (1982) *Monopoly Capitalism*, Macmillan: London.

Dobb, M. (1973) *Theories of Value and Distribution since Adam Smith*, Cambridge University Press: Cambridge.

Eldred, M. (1984) 'A Reply to Gleicher', *Capital and Class*, 13.

Elson, D. (ed.) (1979) *The Representation of Labour in Capitalism*, CSE Books: London.

Faccarello, G. (1982)* 'Sraffa versus Ricardo: the Historical Irrelevance of the "corn-profit" model', *Economy and Society*, vol. 11, no. 2.

Fine, B. (1979)* 'On Marx's Theory of Agricultural Rent', *Economy and Society*, vol. 8, no. 3.

Fine, B. (1980) *Economic Theory and Ideology*, Edward Arnold: London.

Fine, B. (1980a)* 'On Marx's theory of Agricultural Rent – a Rejoinder', *Economy and Society*, vol. 9, no. 3.

Fine, B. (1980b)* 'On the Historical

Transformation Problem', *Economy and Society*, vol. 9, no. 3.
Fine, B. (1982) *Theories of the Capitalist Economy*, Edward Arnold: London.
Fine, B. (1983)* 'On the Economics of Ricardo and Sraffa', *Economy and Society*, vol. 12, no. 2.
Fine, B. (1983a)* 'A Dissenting Note on the Transformation Problem', *Economy and Society*, vol. 12, no. 4.
Fine, B. (1985) 'On the Political Economy of Socialism: Theoretical Considerations with Reference to Non-European and European Experience', in D. Banerjee (ed.), *Marxian Theory and Studies on the Non-European World*, Sage Publications, forthcoming, an expanded version of 'Marx on Economic Relations under Socialism', in B. Matthews (ed.), *Marx 100 Years On*, Lawrence and Wishart: London, 1983.
Fine, B. and **Harris**, L. (1979) *Rereading 'Capital'*, Macmillan: London.
Fine, B. and **Murfin**, A. (1984) *Macroeconomics and Monopoly Capitalism*, Wheatsheaf: London.
Ganssmann, H. (1981)* 'Transformations of Physical Conditions of Production', *Economy and Society*, vol. 10, no. 4.
Garegnani, P. (1982) 'On Hollander's Interpretation of Ricardo's Early Theory of Profits', *Cambridge Journal of Economics*, vol. 6, no. 1.
Garegnani, P. (1983) 'Ricardo's Early Theory of Profits and its "Rational Foundation": a Reply to Professor Hollander', *Cambridge Journal of Economics*, vol. 7, no. 2.
Gerstein, I. (1976)* 'Production, Circulation and Value', *Economy and Society*, vol. 5, no. 3.
Gleicher, D. (1983) 'A Historical Approach to the Question of Abstract Labour', *Capital and Class*, winter, no. 21.
Gleicher, D. (1985) 'A Rejoinder to Eldred', *Capital and Class*, no. 24, Winter.
Harcourt, G. (1972) *Some Cambridge Controversies in the theory of Capital*, Cambridge University Press: Cambridge.
Hodgson, G. (1974) 'Marxian Epistemology and the Transformation Problem', *Economy and Society*, vol. 3.
Hollander, S. (1979) *The Economics of David Ricardo*, Heinemann: London.
Hollander, S. (1983) 'Professor Garegnani's Defence of Sraffa on the Material Rate of Profit', *Cambridge Journal of Economics*, vol. 7, no. 2.
Itoh, M. (1980) *Value and Crisis: Essays on Marxian Economics in Japan*, Pluto Press: London.
Krause, U. (1982) *Money and Abstract Labour*, Verso-New Left Books: London.
Meek, R. (1973) 'Reply to Pilling', *Economy and Society*, vol. 2.
Murray, R. (1977) 'Value and Theory of Rent: Part I', *Capital and Class*, no. 3.
Pilling, G. (1972)* 'Law of Value in Ricardo and Marx', *Economy and Society*, vol. 1.
Pilling, G. (1973) 'Reply to Meek', *Economy and Society*, vol. 2.
Pilling, G. (1980) *Marx's 'Capital': Philosophy and Political Economy*, Routledge & Kegan Paul: London.
Rankin, S. (1984) 'The Wage Basket in Ricardo's "Essay on Profits" ', *Cambridge Journal of Economics*, vol. 8.
Robinson, J. (1953/4) 'The Production Function and the Theory of Capital', *Review of Economic Studies*, vol. 21.
Rosdolsky, R. (1977) *The Making of Marx's 'Capital'*, Pluto Press: London.
Rubin, I. (1973) *Essays on Marx's Theory of Value*, Black Rose Books: Montreal.
Sawyer, M. (1982) *Macroeconomics in Question: the Keynesian and Monetarist Orthodoxies and the Kaleckian Alternative*, Wheatsheaf: Brighton.
Seton, F. (1957) 'The "Transformation Problem" ', *Review of Economic Studies*, vol. 24.
Sraffa, P. (1960) *The Production of Commodities by Means of Commodities*, Cambridge University Press: Cambridge.
Steedman, I. (1977) *Marx after Sraffa*, New Left Books: London.
Steedman, I. *et al.* (1981) *The Value Controversy*, Verso-New Left Books: London.
Weeks, J. (1982) 'A Note on the Underconsumptionist Theory and the Labour Theory of Value', *Science and Society*, Spring, vol. XLVI.
White, R. (1985) Thesis submitted for the PhD in Economics, The American University, Washington, DC.

CHAPTER 2

The law of value in Ricardo and Marx

Geoffrey Pilling

Abstract

A statement of Marx's law of value and the place which it occupies in the structure of his economic studies. A critique of the treatment of the law of value as found in the work of several writers—principally Maurice Dobb and Ronald Meek. The implications of this critique: an examination of Ricardo's method in the light of *Das Kapital*. The wider implications of the issues discussed for Marxist scholarship.

There can be little doubt that for academic economists at least, the main object of their attack against Marxism continues to be its theory of value. This is as true of Marx's 'friends' (such as Joan Robinson and many of her colleagues in the Cambridge School) as it is of his 'enemies'. We do not propose to answer all these attacks. This would be impossible in the confines of a single paper; in any case most of them have failed to advance on those issued by Böhm-Bawerk more than seventy years ago.

Instead, we intend to restate as simply as possible the essential features of this law and the place it occupied in Marx's work as a whole. In the light of this statement we wish to suggest that fundamental errors have been committed particularly by English writers, many claiming to write as Marxists, in their treatment of this law. Finally we intend to examine these errors in the light of Marx's relationship to classical political economy, and in particular to Ricardo.[1]

The best statement which Marx made about his law of value—an account which Lenin advised all students of *Capital* to consult carefully—is to be found in his famous letter to Dr. Kugelmann of July 11, 1868. We reproduce the critical passage and then offer some comments on it.

> . . . Even if there were no chapter on 'value' in my book, the analysis of the real relationships which I give would contain the proof of the real value relation. The nonsense about the necessity of proving the concept of value arises from complete ignorance both of the subject dealt with and of the method of science. Every child knows that a country which ceased to work, I will not say for a year, but for a few weeks would die. Every child knows too, that the mass of products corresponding to the

> different needs require different and quantitatively determined means of the total labour of society. That this necessity of distributing social labour in definite proportions cannot be done away with by the *particular form* of social production but can only change the *form it assumes*, is self evident. No natural laws can be done away with. What can change, in changing historical circumstances, is the *form* in which these laws operate. And the form which this proportional division of labour operates, in a state of society where the interconnections of social labour is manifested in the *private exchange* of the individual products of labour, is precisely the *exchange value* of these products. The science consists precisely in working out *how* the law of value operates. So that if one wanted at the very beginning to 'explain' all the phenomena which apparently contradicted the law, one would have to give the science *before* the science. (Marx, 1934, pp. 73–4)

In our view this is an extremely important passage and in a sense the rest of this paper will be a commentary on the ideas which we feel are implicit in it. Marx evidently wished to stress one basic idea—the historico-relative character of all the categories of political economy. We mean this in the sense that for him none of the categories met with in political economy—such as 'production', 'division of labour', etc.—can be understood except in their relations to the specific mode of production of which they formed a part.

'The categories of bourgeois economy . . . are forms of thought expressing with social validity the conditions and relations of a definite, historically determined mode of production viz., the production of commodities' (Marx, 1961, p. 76).[2] But this recognition of the relative nature of economic categories—a recognition which the theory of historical materialism required—did not mean however that there were not features common to many if not all modes of production. This was inevitable in that all societies had this much in common: that they involved some mechanism for the allocation of social labour between the various branches of economy. Socialist society will be no different in experiencing this universal need. However, and this is crucial, the *form* which this mechanism takes differs widely from society to society. The differences depend ultimately upon the structure of the productive relations and it was to be one of Marx's chief preoccupations to establish —in opposition to the vulgar school—the dependence of 'distribution' on 'production'.

Having made clear the precise nature of this task, Marx shows that the *specifica differentia* of the capitalist mode was the dominant position achieved within it of commodity production, and the transformation of the category 'labour' into the category 'labour power'. Given this, how was the allocation of social labour between the different branches effected? It was effected, answered Marx, only through the exchange of commodities as equivalents, through their exchange values. And, as we shall see, this category 'exchange value' was but the phenomenal form of 'value'. For Marx, in other words, the law of value reflected the only possible, indirect, mechanism whereby social labour could be distributed in a commodity producing society. *The law of value reflects the specific social relations which operate under commodity (and particularly capitalist commodity) production, and under these conditions alone.* Speaking of socialist economic organisation, Engels said 'The people will arrange everything very simply, without the intervention of the much-famed law.' (Engels, 1962, p. 423.)[3]

In his letter to Kugelmann, Marx wished to draw his friend's attention to another point which will particularly concern us in this paper—namely the fact that capitalism was also unique in another sense in that the value relation (a social relation) appeared as a relation between *things. Capital* is concerned, that is, with both quantitative problems (the exchange ratios prevailing between commodities) and qualitative problems (that behind these quantitative ratios stood social relations). In exchanging commodities men were in fact exchanging their labour. For Marx, the attachment of social relations to things was no 'illusion'. For under capitalism the social relations between the labour of individuals constituting society could only manifest themselves, or *appear as* the relations between objects of material wealth. These appearances were, as Marx puts it, 'necessary appearances'.

> A social relation of production appears as something existing apart from individual human beings, and the distinctive relations into which they enter in the course of production appear as the specific properties of a thing—it is this perverted appearance, this prosaically real, *and by no means imaginary mystification* [emphasis added, GP] that is characteristic of all social forms positing exchange-value. (Marx, 1971, p. 49)

Or again

> '. . . the relations connecting the labour of one individual with that of the rest appear, not as direct social relations between individuals at work, *but as what they really are* [emphasis added, GP] material relations between persons and social relations between things.' (Marx, 1961, p. 73)

A very important result flowed from this conception of appearances as *necessary* appearances: they could only be destroyed by overthrowing the economic categories which sustained them. Marx did not see his task merely as one of stripping away the illusions of capitalism, to reveal things 'as they really were'. This conception is indeed implicit in all those treatments of *Capital* which seek to reduce its method to a variety of sociological 'model building'. Thus one prominent writer puts the matter this way in discussing his requirements for such a 'model': 'But to permit any full quantitative statements to be made, such governing dimensions or entities to which the price-variables are connected must be related in a way which enables them to be reduced to a common term.' (Dobb, 1940, p. 11.) For him, Marxism is superior in an 'operational' sense in that 'labour' provides such a constant to which all the other entities in his model can be reduced.

For Marx, no such task presented itself. His aim was not to *reduce* all the phenomena of the system (such as the structure of prices) to the determination of value by labour-time, but on the contrary one of *explaining* these phenomena by demonstrating how they could be reconciled with the operation of the law of value. Hence his scorn for all those intent on 'proving' the law of value, rather than seeking to find out how it *operated.*

While not anticipating Marx's solution to this problem, this much can be said: the entire method of *Capital* is based upon the conception that the thing in itself (in this case 'value') *can* only present itself through its contradictory opposite, its appearance (to continue with our illustration, 'exchange-value' is the form of appearance of 'value'). In other words, Marx rejected Kant's separation of the 'thing in itself' from its 'appearance' in favour of Hegel's method. The task of Marx's critique of political economy was *not* one which involved him finding a 'constant' in terms of which everything could be quantified but of establishing the laws of mediation through which the 'essence' of phenomena manifested itself as 'appearance'. 'Hence law is not beyond Appearance, but is *immediately present* in it; the realm of laws is the quiescent counterfeit of the existing or appearing world.' (Hegel, 1929, p. 133.) As we shall see, while Ricardo grasped the nature of the problem facing political economy his method prevented him from arriving at a satisfactory solution to it.

Marx, we have suggested, traces the many links between 'essence' and 'appearance', demonstrating the necessary nature of the latter. This is why he is able to write 'The discovery [of the determination of the magnitude of value by labour-time] while removing all appearance of mere accidentality from the determination of the magnitude of the value of products, yet in no way alters the mode in which this determination takes place.' (1961, p. 75.) In other words, only a re-organisation of society can abolish fetishism: 'The life process of material production, does not strip off its mystical veil until it is treated as production by freely associated men, and is consciously regulated by them in accordance with a settled plan.' (1961, p. 80.) Or as he notes a little earlier after the discovery by science of the component gases of air, the atmosphere itself remained unaltered. (1961, p. 74.)

So far we have elaborated a number of points which are implicit in the letter to Kugelmann. To state matters from a different angle: Marx intended to remind his friend of what he had already said nine years earlier with the publication of the *Critique*—that the 'guiding thread' for his work was the materialist conception of history. This was the theory which started from the proposition that the social relations of production form the 'real foundation' of society on which arose a political, legal, etc. 'superstructure.' Specifically, Marx set himself the task over the three volumes of *Capital* of tracing out the manifold interconnections between the social relations of production (under capitalism, the reflection of which is to be found in the category 'value') and all the other phenomena within the system, including the class struggle. As we shall discover, this implied a method entirely opposed to that of Ricardo, as Marx's letter already suggests.

It is now our intention, this preliminary statement having been made, to show that many of Marx's aims and methods have been seriously mis-represented by the majority of commentators who would wish to be designated 'Marxist economists'. We can start with the case of the leader in this field, Maurice Dobb. He opens his major theoretical work in the field of value theory with a chapter entitled 'The Requirements of a Theory of Value'. (Dobb, 1940, Ch. 1) Immediately he presupposes a method alien to that of Marx; we have already argued that the analysis of 'value' cannot be disembodied from a work the aim of which was to 'lay bare the law of motion of modern society'. If Dobb has in mind *Marx's* value theory (as against that of Ricardo for example) then the concern of the chapter would seem to be misplaced. For our only answer would consist of an exposition of the value analysis as developed in *Capital.* If on the other hand Dobb has in mind a *general concept* of value (as indeed the remainder of the work shows him to have) he is guilty of starting from an abstract concept and not as Marx insisted we must, from an examination of the process of social labour as it appears in 'modern society'. Marx evidently had this type of error in mind when he replied to the charges of A. Wagner; this latter had accused him of 'illogicality' in 'splitting the concept of value into exchange value and use value'. Marx said 'Above all I do not start from "concepts" thus not "from the concept of value". What I start from is the simplest social form in which the product of labour in the present form of society presents itself; and this is "commodity".' (Marx, 1972, p. 50.) Marx is here pointing out to Wagner and others that he started as a materialist from 'real active living men' and not as an idealist who starts always from 'concepts'. In this respect Dobb is firmly in the camp of Wagner, against Marx.

Similarly, when Ronald Meek writes a book 'to try and build some sort of bridge between Marxian economists and their non-Marxian colleagues' and sets out to convince Mrs. Robinson that Marx's value theory 'was good sense' (1956, p. 7) his task is as ill-conceived as Dobb's starting point—the comparison of the 'adequacy' of 'models'—is wrong. Marx's avowed aim—of exposing the ever-sharpening contradictions of a particular mode of production—is one necessarily abandoned by vulgar economy. We need only recall, that for Marx, if not Meek, '1830 sounds the knell of scientific bourgeois economy'. If we do accept this judgement, then we are forced to the inescapable conclusion that 'modern economics' with which Meek is so keen to forge links, cannot have a theory of *value*, 'adequate' or otherwise. It was Marx's point that with the emergence of the working class, increasingly consciously ranged against the capitalist class and its political economy, the latter inevitably degenerated into shallow apologetics for the existing order, ultimately to become a branch of technology. All modern 'price theory' (it still occasionally masquerades as a 'value theory') derives from the category 'utility' or the relationship between 'wealth' (for Marx the aggregate of use values) and the 'individual consumer'. The point about such theories is that because they are ahistorical they are necessarily asocial. For 'individuals' *always* confront 'nature' whatever the mode of production; because such theories concern only the individual's relationship with nature and not with his fellow man they are devoid of social content. Thus it is impossible that 'economics' can have a category 'value' which, we insist, is not a 'thing' but a social relation. Yet running through the work of many of those who would wish to 'defend' Marx or 'praise' him is the conception that they have a rival value theory to answer. Dobb writes of 'the two major value theories which have contested the economic field' (1940, p. 12) and proceeds to suggest that both (he means of course the 'labour' theory and marginal utility analysis) meet his formal requirements of 'adequacy': 'Quite a number of theories of value can be derived with no means of choice between them except their formal elegance.' And in a later work he repeats this view in even stronger terms (Dobb, 1955, *passim* but particularly pp. 110–11). In the same fashion, Meek accepts Pareto's and Böhm-Bawerk's utility analysis as constituting an alternative value theory to that of Marx which he seeks to defend (1956, ch. 6). Both these writers wrongly see their task as merely exposing the penumbra of approbation with which these theories surround capitalism. Put another way, the mistake they both make is to fail to see the significance of the profound distinction which Marx and political economy—however unclearly in this latter case—drew between 'wealth', the sum of material objects and *value*, a social relation specific to capitalism.

This is not a minor point of difference with these writers. For it is closely connected with a number of equally erroneous conceptions which they hold about value theory. Dobb, for example, has tried to answer the question: Why did Marx choose labour as the basis for his value theory? Why not choose capital or land as the category in terms of which everything else is computed? Here is the answer:

> In the case of land or capital, clearly there were serious practical objections to taking them as a basis: difficulties which would

> have exceeded any of those which were charged against the labour theory. . . . Acres are more dissimilar than man-hours of labour. In the case of capital there was the more crucial objection that it was itself a value, depending upon other values, in particular upon profit to be earned. (1940, p. 18)

These, apparently were insurmountable difficulties. Thus labour is chosen! Thus the labour theory of value! In a sense we cannot analyse the nature of the answer which Dobb provides for his own question. *For it is in the very posing of the question that the fundamental error is committed.* With good reason did Lenin on one occasion speak of 'the so-called "labour" theory of value'. (Introduction to Marx, 1934) We must repeat—Marx is concerned with an analysis of the social relations of production and his work never strays outside of these limits. Man's social relations under capitalism appear only through the relations between 'things' (commodities). Leaving aside their particular properties as use values—which Marx says is an area of concern appropriate to commerce—their one common quality is that they are products of abstract labour, the quantitative measure of which is *time*. In other words, the category 'value' is one entirely subordinate, in both a logical and historical sense, to the commodity. As Dobb would have it, Marx 'chose' labour—a subjective act—because it enabled him to solve certain 'practical' problems. 'The statement which the labour theory implied' we are told 'was that the exchange-values bore a certain relation to the output and using up of human energies and in so doing provided a term which gave some meaning to the distinction between a gross and net product and to the concept of surplus, and a criterion for differentiating one type of income from another.' (Dobb, 1940, p. 22)

Here a number of issues are raised, all of them of great importance for a correct interpretation of Marx's work. First we see Dobb moving directly in the direction of Ricardo with the emphasis he places upon questions of *distribution*. We need to recall that it was *Ricardo*, not Marx, who defined the task 'To determine the laws which regulate this distribution [of the social product between rent, profit and wages] as the principal one facing political economy.' (Ricardo, 1953, p. 55)[4] In following Ricardo, Dobb is playing into the hands of all those, from Bernstein onwards, who have falsely accused Marx of 'using' his value theory to 'prove' the existence of exploitation under capitalism. But was the quantitative problem—that of the distribution of the social wealth between the classes which constituted capitalist society—Marx's main preoccupation? It was not. A surplus over and above the needs of immediate consumption is inevitable and necessary in all but the most primitive societies. Value theory merely reflects the particular form, within capitalism, of this more general relation.

This leads us to another matter, also implied in this same quotation—

that Marx's value theory can in some sense be empirically 'verified', unlike the value theory of marginal utility analysis. A recent and widely-read textbook states

> The neo-classical theory [This refers to the theory formulated by Jevons in England and Walras, Menger, Pareto and others on the Continent in the last quarter of the nineteenth century—GP] is not only divorced from social reality as a whole. It is also divorced from the practical reality of everyday life. The labour theory can be demonstrated empirically, even if only in the sense that, in the last analysis, all the elements of the cost of production of a commodity tend to be reduced to labour, and to labour alone, if one goes back far enough in the analysis. (Mandel, 1968, p. 716)

Dobb echoes this point when he writes: 'It seems clear, from the nature of its subject matter and the type of statements which it required to make, that an economic theory must be quantitative in form; the determining relation or relations which figure in the equational system should be capable of expression in terms of quantitative entities in the real world.' (1940, p. 11) But what, we must ask of those who share this standpoint, are these 'quantitative entities in the real world'? If the phrase has any meaning it must refer to categories such as 'price', 'rate of profit' 'rate of interest' etc. It deals, that is, with the realm of *appearances* to which the vulgar school is exclusively confined, the realm where reign supreme 'equality and Mr. Bentham'.

Specifically, we can ask Dobb: how do you propose to 'measure' or quantify 'capital' or 'socially necessary labour time'.[7] For Marx, capital, we again have to repeat, was a social relation, the means of production in a specific social form—confronting the sellers of labour power as an alien, coercive power. In the same way, how may we 'calculate' the quantity of socially necessary labour time incorporated into a commodity? As we have said, this latter is but the quantitative equivalent of Marx's abstract labour which as a category cannot appear empirically within the capitalist system. In any case, the exchange value of any commodity does not depend upon the productivity of the labour in the branch of economy in which it has been produced; it reflects the productivity of labour on a social scale. In dealing with 'microscopic' entities we are forced to consider phenomena of a 'macroscopic' dimension. In other words, no one commodity can be abstracted from the totality of commodity production; as we shall see, Ricardo's false method of abstraction forced this erroneous view upon him. Society, not Mr. Mandel, can be the only accountant of socially necessary labour time.

It is clear that the last few matters we have briefly considered are not isolated questions which flow from a series of 'particular' mistakes. For they all involve a distortion of Marxism in the general direction of positivism. Mandel, for example (*op. cit.*, p. 716) makes this clear when he suggests that one aspect of the superiority of the Marxist value analysis lies in the fact that businessmen, albeit unconsciously, actually price their products according to the labour theory of value. Sweezy also takes this position when he writes: 'Marx's value theory thus has the great merit, unlike some other value theories [he here incidentally accepts that there can be rival value theories to that developed by Marx out of his critique of classical political economy] of close correspondence to the actual accounting system of capitalistic business enterprise.' (1946, p. 63) Dobb makes essentially the same point, if from a slightly different angle, when he states: 'An economic law or tendency must state the possibility of some actual course of events occurring' (1940, p. 29), and earlier 'The ultimate criterion [for the "adequacy" of a theory] must be the requirement of practice: the type of question which one requires to answer, the purpose of the inquiry in hand' (p. 8). Here we have only a thinly disguised form of *instrumentalism*, the method which selects its categories, not according to their congruence with historical and social forces but simply by virtue of their ability to sustain predictions 'in the real world'.[5]

It was positivism, we must remember, which falsely decreed that the only 'real' sciences were those dealing with natural phenomena: 'real' in the sense that they alone were exact enough to make predictions. But Marxism involves the view that the future evolution of events can be 'predicted' only to the extent that the material and social world consists of a series of fixed quantities. But the entire method of *Capital* is based on entirely the opposite view—that 'quantity' ('commodity' for example) is constantly in process of transformation into other quantities and qualities ('money' to continue with our example) and thence into new quantities and qualities ('capital' in this case); this method further insists that far from being automatic, such transformations occur only under definite historical and social circumstances, which must be established by science. Marx also made clear that because the capitalist system is fundementally an anarchic one—that is, cannot be subjected to *a priori*, conscious regulation—each law of the system asserts itself as a 'blindly working average' as he makes clear in connection with the law of value.[6] Given that this is so, the predictability of future events cannot be dealt with in the peremptory manner Dobb and others would have us believe.

To cite but one case. In what sense can Marx's law of the falling rate of profit enable us concretely to predict the future course of capitalist development? Its author certainly made no such claims on its behalf. In formulating this law of tendency, he wished to draw attention to the fact that (a) the rate of profit was the regulator of the entire accumulation process and (b) that this very process was profoundly contradictory and must lead to periodic crises. But he never pretended that the precise *forms* taken by such crises could be predicted, nor even their exact magnitude or timing. As Marx makes clear in many places in *Capital*, each crisis was in a sense unique, determined by the whole past process of capital accumulation; it was therefore obligatory to examine each crisis in its concreteness and not by means of some simple formulae. Precisely *because* capitalist social relations were antagonistic—that is based upon the struggle of classes whose historical interests were diametrically opposed, that is qualitatively different—no predictions of a concrete nature about the evolution of economic categories was possible. More precisely, in connection with the movement of the rate of profit, Marx made clear that he was stating a general *law of tendency*, which, as in all cases, inevitably produced 'counter-acting' forces to its operation which modified its functioning in important respects. These included the strength and determination of the working class, the 'weight' of which could in no sense be known beforehand in that it depended upon both objective and subjective forces, amongst which had to be numbered the role which a knowledge of this law would have within the organised working class movement.[7] Here Marx, was, in effect, warning against the old mechanical materialism which thought that the world could be understood in a purely *contemplative* manner.

These distortions of Marx's method are doubly important because they also involve, in our view, another danger. This is the tendency to reduce Marxism to the level of 'political economy' particularly in the latter's Ricardian form. We wish therefore briefly to review Marx's attitude to his predecessors in the classical school in order to establish what we consider to be the fundamental break which his work represents with this school. Marx's studies in the history of political economy provide no mere 'appendix' to *Capital*; in every sense *Theories of Surplus Value* must be considered as the final volume of *Capital*, as indeed Marx intended it to be. For contained in the *Theories* is a detailed examination of the evolution of the categories 'value' and 'surplus value' as reflected in the work of the principal French and English economists. But this work should not be taken as 'history' in the conventional sense; it was intended as Engels at one point notes to provide 'a detailed critical history of the pith and marrow of Political Economy, the theory of surplus value, and develops parallel with it, in polemics against predecessors, most of the points later investigated separately in their logical connection in the manuscripts for Books II and III.' (Preface to Marx, 1957) Marx writes this work always 'critically', from the vantage point that is of his own theory (historical materialism), just as the anatomy of the ape must be studied from the standpoint of its higher, further development, in man. He is interested not merely in tracing the origin of his own ideas, in paying his intellectual debts, as it were. Nor is he interested only in exposing the limitations of the classical school—of which he was fully conscious. He aims, throughout the *Theories*, to probe the contradictions in the writings of Smith, Ricardo, etc., because he sees in them only a 'purer', more abstract and therefore heightened expression of the real economic contradictions of the capitalist system which was their real underpinning.

It is from this standpoint that the work of Ricardo is judged, in an all-round fashion. Marx never saw his problem as one merely of correcting the 'distortions' in Ricardo's work, nor of analysing capitalism, in a naive manner, from the 'standpoint of the working class'. Indeed, as anyone acquainted with the *Theories* will know, Marx was always insistent upon drawing attention to Ricardo's great 'disinterestedness' (objectivity) as against the special pleading of Malthus—that 'shameless sycophant' 'that bought advocate of the ruling classes' as Marx contemptuously dubs him. But Marx stresses always that Ricardo's sincere insistence that the needs of production should be placed above the sectional claims of any class (herein lay the 'disinterestedness' of this rich financier) coincided with the needs of the rising capitalist class only in that period when the bourgeoisie had every interest in the further development of the productive forces. With the emergence of the modern working class, the most decisive of all the productive forces, this progressive interest was finished and scientific political economy died. That is why the period around 1830 spells for political economy its 'final crisis'; Ricardo's doctrines become the basis, albeit in a confused and unsatisfactory manner, for the political economy of Utopian Socialism.

What were the main periods which Marx discerns in the history of political economy up to its ignoble collapse in the first quarter of the nineteenth century? While Petty can be regarded as the founding father of the science, French Physiocracy represents the first true school in political economy. The writers who formed this school grasped that forms of production were *physiological* forms, arising out of the necessities of production and independent of will and politics. Seeing value in production, the school then proceeds to trace the connections between production and circulation. The weaknesses of Physiocracy was that 'production' was still seen concretely and not abstractly, for according to Quesnay and his followers, labour on the land was alone productive of value. But this limited view, a reflection of the limited stage reached in the evolution of the eighteenth century French economy, was nonetheless decisive for the future analysis of the capitalist system. For the contradictions at the heart of Physiocracy arose essentially from its attempt to explain feudalism from a more consistently bourgeois point of view.

The *Wealth of Nations* marks a new leap forward in that it sees 'labour in general' as value-creating. It was from this time onwards that political economy could be placed upon a much firmer theoretical basis. But again, Marx sees the material basis for the advance which Smith's work constitutes. The category 'abstract labour' which Smith correctly sees as forming the basis of value was an expression of the economic categories which were being created by the development of the class struggle; for here was reflected a society where the organic bond between an individual and his labour was in the process of violent rupture. Smith's indifference to the particular type of labour when considering value—his real point of criticism against Physiocracy—implied the existence of highly developed varieties of concrete labour, none of which was predominant.

But, as in the case of Physiocracy, so now with Smith: his advance in theoretical understanding was severely limited and necessarily so. He was a 'transitional' figure in every sense. This was particularly so in the fact that his work continues the classificatory and descriptive emphases of his British predecessors—as seen most clearly in Petty's *Political Arithmetic*—and the more abstract approach which was to be found in Ricardo's writings some fifty years later. The matter can be put this way: Smith was on the one hand concerned with a search for those abstract laws which would accurately express the innermost workings of capitalism as a system—hence the importance for his work of the concept of the 'hidden hand'. This side of his work—which Marx refers to as its 'esoteric' element is seen in his famous phrase 'It is not from the benevolence of the butcher the brewer or the baker that we expect our dinner but from their regard to their own interest'. On the other hand Smith's work contains also a considerable 'exoteric' element, that is a concern not for the inner-structure of phenomena, but for their outward manifestations. Many examples of this naive 'duality' of which Smith was unaware, could be drawn from the *Wealth of Nations* and elsewhere. But it is seen most clearly in his conception that the law of value only holds in a 'rude and primitive' state of society, and must be abandoned once 'modern' society is reached. Smith was thus guilty of allowing immediate impressions of competition between the branches of economy to intrude into and ultimately overthrow his basic theoretical starting point.

In this respect, Ricardo's work involved a significant advance. We should in any case remember that he first took up the study of political economy as a result of the feeling of dissatisfaction he experienced with the theoretical and practical answers provided by the *Wealth of Nations*. For Marx, his work represents a decisive attempt to establish political economy as an *abstract science* dealing with the laws which governed the workings of the capitalist system. Ricardo, in effect, insists that the science can no longer operate with 'description' on the one hand and 'analysis' on the other. It must, starting with its basic principle—the determination of value by labour time—make all the outward appearances of the system 'answerable' to it.

This advance in method, what Marx at one point calls 'Ricardo's great service to the science' can be judged by an examination of the latter's *Principles*. This work, consists, in its third edition, of thirty two chapters; the essential theoretical matters are however given in the first two—the rest consist of elaborations or applications of principles enunciated at the start of the work. How does Ricardo proceed? He starts with a statement of the determination of value by labour time which is much less ambiguous than that to be found in Smith. In the next sections he takes up a number of questions—the movement of relative wages between different branches of economy, the varying structure of capital between the different sectors, etc. Of each he asks: to what extent do they overthrow or force the modification of the law of value as already stated? We give, as an example of this procedure, the opening paragraph of the section dealing with rent: 'It remains to be considered whether the appropriation of land, and the consequent creation of rent, will occasion any variation in the relative value of commodities, independently of the quantity of labour necessary to production.' (1953, p. 67) He thus tries to 'hold fast' to the law of value, whereas Smith had concluded as we have noted, that it had to be rapidly abandoned in the face of the immediate appearances of the emerging economic system.

Thus it can be said that Ricardo posed correctly the problem facing political economy. Hence for Marx the 'great theoretical satisfaction' afforded by the earlier chapters of the *Principles* as against the 'diffuse and meandering' work of Smith. The whole bourgeois economic system was based firmly upon one law and all phenomena which seemed to conflict with it were examined in its light. Here the clue to the real meaning of the English adage 'It's the exception that proves the rule'; for Ricardo, after neatly setting forth the law of value 'demonstrates that this law governs even those bourgeois relations of production which contradict it most decisively.' (Marx, 1971, p. 60)

Here, however, Marx's praise for Ricardo's great historical achievement ends. Each advance in political economy can be seen as a 'criticism' of previous writers—Smith of mercantilism; Ricardo of the *Wealth of Nations*, etc. But Marx's attitude towards Ricardo cannot be seen as in any way analogous. For each of the writers who preceded Marx accepted that the laws of the capitalist system were akin to the laws of nature. As we have seen this was Marx's main objection to their work which he sees as the source of its ultimate break-up.

But it was an objection directly tied in with another: a recognition that empiricism dominated the method of classical economy. In this connection the central role which Marx ascribed to Locke should not be forgotten: '. . . his philosophy served the basis for all the ideas of the whole of subsequent English political economy.' (1969, p. 387) Again: 'With all later bourgeois economists, as with Adam Smith, lack of theoretical understanding needed to distinguish the different forms of economic relations remains the rule in their coarse grabbing at and interest in the empirically available material.' (1969, p. 92)

All Ricardo's weaknesses reflect this empiricism and resolve themselves into this: that while he starts correctly from the law of value he attempts *immediately* to deal with all the phenomena which conflict with this law. Hence Marx's reference to the 'faulty architectonics' of his work. What is lacking in the *Principles* is any treatment of the process of *mediation* by which the 'forms of appearance' in bourgeois society are connected to the source of their origin, the law of value.

This makes it imperative to highlight the differences between Ricardo's method and that of Marx, as reflected in the structure of *Capital*. While Ricardo feels obliged to take up all the phenomena which appear to overthrow the law of value in the very opening chapters of his work, Marx only comes to deal with the realm of 'appearance' with the opening of the *third* volume, after an exhaustive study of the fundamental processes of production and circulation. Marx explains his procedure at the very opening of this third volume and we reproduce the key passage from the first chapter:

> In Book I we analysed the phenomena which constitute the *process of capitalist production* as such, as the immediate productive process, with no regard for any of the secondary effects of outside influences. But this immediate process of production does not exhaust the life span of capital. It is supplemented in the actual world by the *process of circulation*, which was the object of the study in Book II. In the latter, namely Part III, which treated the process of circulation as a medium for the process of social reproduction, it developed that the process of capitalist production taken as a whole represents a synthesis of the process of production and circulation. Considering what this third book treats, it cannot confine itself to a general reflection relative to this synthesis. On the contrary, it must locate and describe the concrete forms which grow out of the *movements of capital as a whole*. In their actual movement, capitals confront each other in such concrete shape for which the form of capital in the immediate process of production, just as its form in the process of circulation, appear only as special instances. The various forms of capital, as evolved in this book, thus approach step by step the form which they assume on the surface of society, in the action of different capitals on one another, in competition, and in the ordinary consciousness of the agents of production themselves. (Marx, 1959, p. 25)

Here Marx explains that the process of movement to the realm of appearances cannot be an immediate one. All the manifold links, missing in Ricardo, have to be established between the outward form of things and their inner source. For Marx, this was precisely what he had in mind when he suggested to Kugelmann that the problem was to establish *how* the law of value operates. So when the realm of appearances was finally reached, they were not considered as isolated, disembodied, phenomena, as in the vulgar conception, nor were they merely counterposed to their source, the law of value, as in classical economy. They were now grasped as *necessary appearances*, contradictory, opposite, manifestations of definite, historically determined social relations of production. To take one illustration of this method: at one point Marx writes of the transformation of value and price of labour power into the form of wages:

> This phenomenal form, which makes the actual relation invisible, *and indeed shows that direct opposite of that relation* [emphasis added—GP], forms the basis of all the juridical notions of both labourer and capitalist, of all the mystifications of the capitalist mode of production, of all its illusions as to liberty, of all the apologetic shifts of the vulgar economists. (1961, p. 540)

We must now indicate the connection between Ricardo's faulty abstractions (Marx calls them 'violent' at one point) and the grave errors which he made on all the questions of political economy which left his work open to ready attack by his opponents. This question cannot be systematically dealt with; we shall merely indicate some important issues. In the first place, Ricardo failed to see that under capitalism, prices could never coincide with values, but were transformed into 'prices of production' around which prices in turn oscillated, according to the fluctuations of supply and demand.[8] Because Ricardo tried *directly* to reduce all prices to values (and this is the method of procedure that writers like Dobb would have us adopt) he ended up, as Marx shows, with a false theory of *rent*, a serious matter in his case as it constituted the corner-stone of his system. Ricardo tried *directly* to uphold the law of value; this forced him to deny the possibility of *absolute* rent (rent on the least fertile land) and he focused his attention exclusively on the movement of *differential rent* (rent earned on land of varying fertility). Marx, in his critique of Ricardo, establishes the possibility of absolute rent, by demonstrating the indirect operation of the law of value, *via* prices of production.

Ricardo also consistently confused the generic category, surplus value, with one of its specific forms, profit. This resulted from his faulty conception of capital, which he saw only in its immediately available form as 'stored up labour'. This in turn stemmed from his wrong understanding of the relation between the source of a category (in this case surplus value) with its various forms of appearance (rent, interest, profit). Marx shows in Volume I of *Capital* that surplus value is created in the sphere of production, in the antagonistic relations between wage labour and capital. It is subsequently divided between the three classes who live on this surplus according to definite and objective laws, but laws which are only analysed at a later stage. Not that this procedure could be reversed, by moving from the realm of appearance back to essence, as Marx makes clear:

> The transformation of surplus value into profit must be deduced from the transformation of the rate of surplus value into the rate of profit, not vice versa. And in fact it was rate of profit which was the historical point of departure. Surplus value and rate of surplus value are, relatively, the invisible and unknown essence that want investigating, while rate of profit and therefore the appearance of surplus value in the form of profit are revealed on the surface of the phenomenon. (1959, pp. 42–43)

Because Ricardo wrongly identified the category 'profit' with the more general category 'surplus value' he wrongly concluded that the rate of profit could only change if the value of wage goods changed—in other words, and using Marx's terms, only if the rate of surplus value altered. Marx rejected this conclusion. By dividing capital into *variable* capital (that portion of capital advanced in the form of wages) and *constant* capital (that portion expended on raw materials, heat, light power, machinery, etc.) Marx was able to arrive at his category the 'organic composition of capital', the ratio of constant to variable capital. This was placed at the centre of his theory of capital accumulation, and the potential breakdown associated therewith. Here indeed was a revolutionary development. The only possible barrier to the further development of the productive forces which Ricardo's work had allowed was associated with *agriculture*. Ricardo had assumed that what Marx scornfully termed the 'so-called law of diminishing returns' operated in agriculture; the working of this law would ultimately, said Ricardo, force up the price of corn which would in turn lead to an increase in wages and produce a tendency for the rate of profit to decline—a prospect which sent shivers down the spine of the millionaire banker.[9] Hence the need for a 'heavy class struggle' against the landed interest if this ominous tendency were to be checked. Marx was able to show, however, that there were forces quite *internal* to the accumulation process which provided potential sources of breakdown; he was thus able to reject all 'explanations' of capitalist crisis which relied upon the importation of 'outside' factors—in Ricardo's case from the sphere of agriculture which Marx recognised was rapidly becoming a force increasingly subordinate to industrial capital. Marx went on to show that with the 'progress of industry' there was an inexorable tendency for the rate of profit to decline through a tendency for the organic composition of capital to rise. (We should recall, however, what was said above about the possibility of this tendency being modified in its operation.)[10]

But the inadequacies of classical economy were revealed most clearly and fundamentally in its analysis of the commodity. It is this question which we now wish to deal with in that it will enable us to highlight some of the criticisms we have already made of the treatment of the law of value. We have seen that classical economy had noted the distinction between the value of a commodity and its use value. But it had singularly failed to grasp the implications of this distinction, which for Marx was to provide the key for his entire analysis. Marx commences with an analysis of the commodity both because the commodity is the basic expression of the relations between man and man in capitalist society and secondly because the development of commodity production was a necessary pre-condition for the development of capitalist social relations. As we know, Marx went on to show that these two aspects of the commodity were reflected in his distinction between *concrete labour* and *abstract labour* (the source of use values and exchange values respectively). This examination of the two-fold nature of labour contained in the commodity was, according to the author of *Capital*, 'the point on which a clear comprehension of Political Economy turns' (Marx, 1961, p. 41), just as the confusion of Ricardo and others on this question constituted the 'weak point' of the classical conception. Marx explains the importance of the distinction when he writes 'Tailoring, if one considers its physical aspect as a distinctive productive activity produces a coat [a use value—GP] not the exchange value of the coat. The exchange value is produced by it, not as tailoring as such but as abstract universal labour, and this belongs to a social framework not devised by the tailor.' (Marx, 1971, p. 36) Here Marx wishes to stress that, unlike the classical school, he not only sees labour as the *measure* of value, but as its *substance*.

In the first chapter of *Capital* we find the following observation 'It is one of the chief failings of classical economy that it has never succeeded, by means of its analysis of commodities, and in particular their value, in discovering the form under which value bears exchange value' (p. 80). Commenting on Petty in an earlier work he says: 'His case is striking proof that recognition of labour as the source of material wealth by no means precludes misapprehension of the specific social form in which labour becomes the source of exchange value.' (1971, p. 54)

Let us look more closely at the manner in which Marx investigates the nature of the commodity. In his *Marginal Notes on Wagner* mentioned above he tells us

> I analyse this [the commodity] and indeed, first in the form in *which it appears*. Here I find that on the one hand it is in its natural form a *thing of use*, alias a *use-value*, on the other hand *a bearer of exchange-value*, and in this respect itself 'exchange-value'. Further analysis of the latter shows me that exchange-value is only a '*phenomenal form*', an independent mode of representation of the *value* contained in the commodity. (1972, p. 50)

Hence, accurately speaking Marx was 'wrong' as he himself recognised:

> when at the beginning of this chapter, we said, in common parlance, that a commodity is both a use-value and an exchange-value [for] . . . a commodity is a use-value or object of utility, and a value. It manifests itself as this two-fold thing, that it is, as soon as its value asserts an independent form—viz, the form of exchange value. It never assumes this form when isolated but only when placed in a value or exchange relation with another commodity of a different kind. When once we know this, such a mode of expression does no harm; it simply serves as abbreviation. (1961, p. 60)

The most generalised value form taken by commodities was of course the *money form* (one coat = £2). *Marx seeks, in his analysis of the value form, to trace the genesis of this money form from the internal structure of the commodity and to demonstrate its further development in the form of capital.* 'Here however, a task is set us, the performance of which has never been attempted by *bourgeois* economy, the task of tracing the genesis of this money-form, of developing the expression of value implied in the value-relation of commodities, from its simplest, almost imperceptible outline, to the dazzling money-form.' (Marx, 1961, pp. 47–8)

In general, Marx was once more showing the origin of all the 'appearances' within the capitalist system and at the same time pointing to the basis for their overthrow. Thus he explains that the contradictions within a single commodity (as a unity of a use-value and a value) are necessarily overcome only through the relations between two commodities in what Marx calls the 'accidental' or 'elementary' form (one coat = 20 yards of linen). 'Hence the elementary form of value of a commodity is the elementary form in which the contrast contained in that commodity, between use-value and value, becomes apparent.' (Marx, 1961, p. 61)

Here are two crucial points. First, the category value *can* only appear as *exchange-value*; the two cannot be torn apart, as some imply they can when they argue that the category 'value' could continue to exist in socialist economy while its form of appearance, exchange-value would disappear.[11] Second, and connected with this point, Marx insists that 'exchange-value' arises from the category value, and not vice versa. 'Our analysis has shown that the form and expression of the value of a commodity originates in the nature of value, and not that value and its magnitude originate in the mode of their expression as exchange-value.' (Marx, 1961, p. 60) Here we have seen one aspect of the different conception of Marx from the later vulgar economy which taught that exchange could be examined quite independently of the relations of production.

Marx now subjects the 'elementary' form to detailed examination.

He discusses the three 'peculiarities' of the form '20 yards of linen (the relative form) = one coat (the equivalent form)', when he examines the role of the equivalent. 'The first peculiarity that strikes us . . . is this . . . use-value bears the form of manifestation, the phenomenal form of its opposite, value . . . the second peculiarity . . . is that concrete labour becomes the form under which its opposite, abstract human labour, manifests itself . . . a third peculiarity . . . namely that the labour of private individuals takes the form of its opposite, labour directly social in its form. (Marx, 1961, pp. 56–8)

Next we see how this accidental form leads to the 'expanded' form along with the development of capitalism. This is given by '20 yards of linen = one coat or 10 lbs of tea, or 40 lbs of coffee', etc. This form brings out what was only implicit in the accidental form 'It becomes plain that it is not the exchange of commodities which regulates the magnitude of their value; but, on the contrary, that is the magnitude of their value which controls their exchange proportions.' (Marx, 1961, p. 63) But this expanded form suffers from grave 'defects' in that it is an incomplete form—the creation of every new commodity lengthens the chain and thereby furnishes the material for a fresh expression of value. Hence out of these contradictions arises the 'general' value form one coat, 10 lbs of tea, 40 lbs of coffee, etc. = 20 yards of linen). This points the way for the emergence of the money form which is in fact identical with this general form except that gold now replaces the linen of our example. Thus has Marx traced the series of logical-historical transitions from the commodity form to the money form. Hence he is able to end this section (the third section of the opening chapter, Marx 1961) thus: 'The simple commodity-form is therefore the *germ* [emphasis added, GP] of the money form.' The riddle of money is solved:

> Money is a crystal formed of necessity, in the course of exchange, whereby different products of labour are practically equated with one another and thus by practice converted into commodities. The historical and progressive extension of exchange develops the contrast latent in commodities, between the use-value and the value. The necessity of giving an external expression to this contrast for the purpose of commercial intercourse, urges on the establishment of an independent form of value, and finds no rest until it is once and for all satisfied by the differentiation of commodities into commodities and money. (Marx, 1961, p. 87)

Only now is Marx able to understand the mystery of the commodity form which is treated in the famous section: 'The Fetishism of Commodities and the Secret thereof.' He explains, after his investigation of the elementary form of value and its further development, that under capitalism: (a) the equality of human labour is expressed not as this equality but in the form of distinctly different commodities such as linen and overcoats; (b) the quantity of social labour time congealed in each commodity is not expressed in a direct comparison of time but in the *indirect* phenomenal form of equal quantities of value; (c) relations of people take the necessary appearance as relations between things; (d) the social character of labour, that is, its relation to total human output, appears as something else, as the value relation of a multitude of commodities to one universal equivalent (money).

Having established the genesis of the money form, Marx then shows how this can, under certain historical circumstances, lead to the emergence of *capital*. 'Value . . . suddenly presents itself as an independent substance endowed with a motion of its own . . . money in process as such, capital.' This transition is reflected in the circulation schema which Marx discusses; under simple commodity production we have C—M—C (commodities-money-commodities) but under capital M—C—M (money-commodities-money). In the former we see that means of circulation, as a means of purchasing what one needs; in the latter it is turned into its opposite—now the owner of the means of production uses money to buy what he does *not* need to augment his capital, the driving force of production.

As we have several times said, the transitions involved in the movements from 'commodity' to 'money' were historical as well as logical movements. Marx makes this clear when examining the various value forms:

> It therefore follows that the elementary value-form is also the primitive form under which a product of labour appears historically as a commodity, and that the gradual transformation of such products into commodities, proceeds *pari passu* with the development of the value-form.' (1961, p. 61)

But these developments should be not conceived of in a mechanical way; one can say that 'capital' is 'latent' within the 'commodity'. However, it is only under certain objective conditions, the outcome of long historical processes, that this potential can be realised. The circulation of commodities and the existence of money in one or other of its functions can and has pre-existed capitalism by many hundreds of years. It is quite otherwise with capital.

> The historical conditions of its existence are by no means given with the mere circulation of money and commodities. It can spring to life only when the owner of the means of production and subsistence meets in the market with the free labourer selling his labour-power. And this one historical condition comprises a world's history. Capital, therefore, announces from its first appearance a new epoch in the process of social production. (Marx, 1961, p. 170)

Why did Marx spend so much time on the problem of value. We should recall that this question finds much fuller treatment in *Capital* (1867) than it does in the *Critique* (1859) and was revised no less than four times, with the help of Engels, Kugelmann and others, between this latter date and 1872. He did so precisely because he wished to establish the link between the internal structure of the commodity and the heightened expression of the contradictions within the commodity form in the form of capital. Here was a decisive break with classical economy; because this latter had ignored the value form (in turn a reflection of its acceptance of capitalism as a 'natural' mode of production) it had failed to comprehend either the nature of money or of capital.[12] For classical economy, money was merely a means of overcoming the difficulties of barter; many of the early Utopian Socialists, criticised in *Theories of Surplus Value* had betrayed a similarly naive conception when they had proposed the abolition of money while retaining commodity production, equivalent to attempts, commented Marx, to retain Catholicism without the Pope. Similarly, as we have already noted, for Ricardo, capital was never seen as a social relation but merely as accumulated labour. Hence for Marx a presentation of the real nature of capital—not a thing but rather a definite social production relation—involved him in a *critique* of political economy.

Unless we accept the links between 'commodity'—'money'—'capital' then the unity of Marx's thought is immediately ruptured and a fatal blow struck against historical materialism. We must repeat: Marx did not aim merely to demonstrate the exploitation of the working class—it can be said that this is implicit in Ricardo and certainly brought out by the Ricardian socialists long before Marx embarked upon his economic studies. Nor did Marx wish only to show that this exploitation was *endemic* to the system. What he had to establish was the manner in which the tendency to develop the productive forces came into increasing collision with the social relations of production. In other words, he had to show the relation between the contradictions of the accumulation process and the social relations of production, the basic expression of which was to be sought in the analysis of the relations between commodities. It was central to Marx's method to trace inner, undeveloped contradictions to their fullest expression. Speaking of the ever-increasing division of labour under capitalism he notes, '. . . the historical development of the antagonisms, immanent in a given form of production, is the only way in which that form of production can be dissolved and a new form established.' (1959, p. 488)

Specifically: we do not accept that there is a separate Marxist 'theory of capitalist crisis' if this is taken to mean that the analysis of capitalism's contradictions can in any way be considered apart from the results of these contradictions as revealed in the process of capital accumulation. In this important respect, we must state that once more what might be called the 'Dobb school of political economy' is considerably inadequate. Not only do these writers fail entirely to deal with the question of the form of value,[13] but we actually find Dobb positively supporting those classical views which Marx was at pains to reject. Thus he writes, speaking of classical economy, 'money could be neglected in the determination of exchange values, so for the same reason could the "amount of demand" be regulated as a factor determining the processes of production and exchange'. (1940, pp. 42–3)

Equally serious is the manner in which this same group of writers has placed a rigid line between their exposition of 'crisis theory' and 'value theory'. Because of this, they must tend in the direction of some variant of Keynesianism. This latter theory starts from the conception of 'effective demand' (borrowed in its essentials from Malthus) treated in isolation from the structure of production. Sweezy's latest work (Baran and Sweezy, 1966) is almost purely Keynesian in form.[14] Meek similarly accepts this division between what is conventionally viewed as the 'micro' as against the 'macro' problem when he attempts at one point to explain the relative lack of any creative work in the area of value theory in terms of the fact that the attention of Marxists has necessarily been turned on to other, 'theoretical problems (e.g. the problem of the "breakdown" of capitalism) which are of more direct and immediate relevance to the policy of the working class movement.' (Meek, 1956, pp. 202–3)

At one blow, the unity of Marx's conception is broken and large concessions to vulgar economy are made. For here we see not merely a move in the direction of Keynes. There is also a tacit admission that whatever the strengths of 'Marxist political economy' (and from the argument of this paper, it should be clear that this is a category that cannot be accepted) vulgar economy may be better able to analyse microscopic, short-run phenomena. This indeed has long been the explicit standpoint of a trend amongst Marxist commentators led principally by the late Oscar Lange. Once more the implications of this position are not confined to purely theoretical matters. For it implies that some form of marriage may be arranged between Marxian analysis and neo-classical 'price theory' (how there can be a price theory in the absence of a value theory is never explained) in the solving of 'economic problems' in all 'industrial societies' which are increasingly brought together by the imperatives of planning and state regulation of economic affairs.[15] Such ideas are only variants on the spurious sociological 'convergence' theory, a theory owing everything to Max Weber and nothing to Karl Marx.

The logic of many of the various positions we have analysed in the course of this paper has demonstrated the crucial importance of a correct understanding of Marx's value theory and the implications of any distortions which lead it, via empiricism, in the direction of Ricardo, that is back to political economy. But it is not enough merely to show that Marxism cannot be reduced to some form of sociological 'model building'. We must go on to establish, against some increasingly fashionable ideas, that the completion of Marx's critique of political economy and his writing of *Capital* would have been impossible without the profoundest grasp of the Hegelian dialectic. We hope that on another occasion this problem can be considered in much greater detail than has here been possible.

Notes

1. 'Once and for all may I state, that by classical Political Economy I understand that economy which since the time of W. Petty, has investigated the real relations of production in bourgeois society, in contradistinction to vulgar economy which deals with appearances only . . . confines itself to systematising in a pedantic way and presenting for everlasting truth, the trite ideas held by the self-complacent bourgeoisie with regard to their own world, to them the best of all possible worlds. . . .' (Marx, 1961, p. 81) It should be pointed out that it is not only those writing as Marxists who confuse Ricardo with Marx. Thus Schumpeter tells us that 'His [Marx's] theory of value is a Ricardian one' and of course 'Everybody knows that this theory is unsatisfactory'. (1959, pp. 23–4) A more recent writer is equally typical when he speaks of 'the labour theory of value which Marx takes over from Adam Smith and Ricardo'. (Giddens, 1971, p. 46)

2. Cf. '. . . M. Proudhon, mainly because he lacks the historical knowledge, has not perceived that as men develop their productive faculties, that is, as they live, they develop certain relations with one another and that the nature of these relations must necessarily change with the change and growth of the productive faculties. He has not perceived that *economic categories* are only the *abstract expressions* of these actual relations and only remain true while these relations exist. He therefore falls into the error of the bourgeois economists who regard these economic categories as eternal and not as historic laws for a particular historical development, a development determined by the productive forces.' (Marx & Engels, 1956, p. 45)

3. This remark by Engels has occasioned considerable controversy and we therefore feel obliged to comment upon some aspects of it. Engels, in the section in *Anti-Dühring* from which it is taken, clearly wishes to stress that whereas the distribution of social labour takes place *indirectly* within capitalism, that is through the exchange of commodities, under socialism this distribution will be achieved *directly*, in that sense 'simply'. Hence Engels should not be taken to mean that economic planning would represent no problems. Socialist economy would, for instance, need to arrange that a proportion of its output was used to maintain and extend the means of production. But this 'overproduction' of the means of production would take a form quite opposite to that under capitalism 'This sort of overproduction is tantamount to control by society over the material means of its own reproduction. *But under capitalist society it is an element of anarchy!*' (Marx, 1957, p. 469) Thus we cannot mechanically translate the reproduction schema of the second volume of *Capital* into the analysis a socialist society.

On the more substantial point concerning the disappearance of the law of value under socialism. It was of course Joseph Stalin who terminated the discussion which had long continued in the USSR with his edict that the law of value did indeed continue to operate within Soviet economy, albeit in 'modified' form. This pronouncement still continues to form the basis for official Soviet thinking in this area. Stalin's statement threw writers like

Meek into considerable difficulties. It was clearly in conflict with Marx's explicit statements that the law of value was a reflection of economic forces operating *only* under commodity production, and would disappear with socialism—which involved the elimination of such forms of production. On the other hand Stalin had also pronounced that the USSR was, by the 1930s, already 'socialist'. The real theoretical point is this: we have to distinguish, as Marx does in his letter, between 'economic laws' and 'natural laws'. Under capitalist commodity production, and under this form of production alone, the need to distribute labour in definite proportions takes the form of the creation of *values*. In other words, the labour process can take place only through the value creating process.

As we have already implied, Engels' statement can be supported by many drawn from Marx's own writings. In his *Critique of the Gotha Programme* (Marx & Engels, 1962, pp. 22–3) he states: 'Within co-operative society based upon the common ownership of the means of production, the producers do not exchange their products. Just as little does the labour employed on the products appear here *as the value* of these products, as a material quality possessed by them, since now, in contrast to capitalist society, individual labour no longer exists in an indirect fashion but directly as a component part of the total labour.' It is also often forgotten by those who wish to counterpose Engels' 'wrong' formulations to the 'correct' statements made by Marx that the whole of *Anti-Dühring* was read by Engels to Marx, partly written by the latter and published with his full knowledge. (Engels, 1962, p. 14)

4. It might seem that there is a paradox here. For on the one hand Ricardo defined the subject matter of political economy as one concerned primarily with the questions of distribution. It was this emphasis upon distribution which implicitly exposed the contradictions between the classes; thus while for Marx, Ricardo remained 'that most stoical opponent of the working class' for others, like the American Carey ('Mr. Ricardo's system is one of discords') he was denounced as the 'father of communism'. Yet Marx many times also sees Ricardo as the economist of *production, par excellence.* But as he explains (Marx, 1971, pp. 200–1) this apparent contradiction only arose because Ricardo had 'instinctively treated the forms of distribution as the most precise expression in which the factors of production manifest themselves in a given society'. Yet Dobb's emphasis, when dealing with Marx's value theory is wrongly placed on distribution. Equally mistaken is Meek when he says: '. . . all economists, whether classical, Marxian or modern, have been largely concerned with the laws governing the distribution of the national cake between the main social classes.' (1955, p. 232) For Marx, this was positively *not* his 'main concern'. What he did show was that relations of distribution and exchange cannot be understood 'in themselves' but only as a reflection of definite *social relations of production.* It almost goes without saying that vulgar economy treats 'production' and 'distribution' as discrete sectors. It was John Stuart Mill who made of this distinction a virtue; for him the laws of (capitalist) production were immutable while the laws of distribution might be capable of some modification in their operation. This trite idea later formed the basis for Fabian economics.

5. We can see how close Dobb, Mandel and others are to the most vulgar pragmatism when we read in Milton Friedman—amongst the most prominent apologists of instrumentalism—'. . . the only relevant test of the validity of a hypothesis is comparison of its predictions with experience' (1953, pp. 8–9) and speaking of the 'adequacy' of hypotheses he says 'Whether they are sufficiently good approximations for the purpose in hand [is a

question we can only answer by] seeing whether the theory works.' (1953, p. 15) For Marx, in opposition to this conception, his categories were not 'chosen' according to pragmatic criteria, but were historical and social in character. Thus the category 'labour power' (the ability to work) was not arbitrarily 'selected'; it was a commodity brought into being by the process of class struggle, in the manner described by Marx in the sections of *Capital* dealing with the forcible separation of the English peasantry from its land and its transformation into a class of wage labourers.

6. 'The vulgar economist has not the faintest idea that the actual everyday exchange relations can *not be directly identical* with the magnitude of value. The essence of bourgeois society consists precisely in this, that *a priori* there is no conscious social regulation of production. The rational and necessary asserts itself only as a blindly working average. And then the vulgar economist thinks he has made a great discovery when, as against the revelation of the interconnection, he proudly claims that in appearance things look different. In fact, he boasts that he holds fast to appearances, and takes it for the ultimate. Why, then, have any science at all?' (Marx, 1934, p. 74)

7. See Marx, 1959, Chs. 13–15.

8. For the 'transformation problem' and its 'solution' see Marx, 1959, pp. 152–70.

9. Having defined the rate of profit as uniquely determined by the rate of surplus value to variable capital (p′ = s:v), Ricardo confined his discussion of changes in the rate of profit to a debate about changes in the value of labour power. Having accepted the infamous 'principle of population' as formulated by Malthus, which by pronouncing the supply of labour infinitely elastic assumes wages constant at subsistence level, Ricardo proceeded to limit the debate about the value of labour power to the question of the productivity of agricultural labour. He believed—also accepting the 'law' of diminishing returns—that agricultural productivity would decline over time and thus, by forcing up wages, bring about a reduction in profits. Hence his dictum: 'the interest of the landlord is always in opposition to that of every class in the community'.

10. The basic idea runs as follows; as capital accumulates, there is a tendency for the constant element (c) within the total capital to increase as a faster rate than the variable portion (v). The organic composition of capital is the ratio of constant capita to variable capital (c:v). If the rate of profit is represented by the relationship of surplus value (s) to total capital (c + v), then, if the ratio c:v is rising, the ratio s: (c + v) must tend to decline on the assumption that there is no increase in the rate of exploitation, s:v.

11. A. Hussain (1972, pp. 35–9) takes this position in attempting to show that Engels was wrong in the statement we quoted from *Anti-Dühring* above. He suggests, specifically, that Engels was guilty of confusing 'value' with its phenomenal form 'exchange-value'. We have already argued that there is a necessary connection between 'value' and its mode of appearance, which Marx shows is a function of the nature of the commodity itself. Hence his insistence on the primacy of the commodity as against any 'concept of value'. Second however, how does Hussain reconcile his position with Marx's insistence that the law of value of necessity can only operate in an unplanned, blind, way? It is from this understanding that Marx sees that 'value' and 'price' must diverge, a divergence demanded by the very law of value itself. Now if we accept that socialism involves not the blind, but the *conscious* regulation of production (that is, socialism involves the production of wealth, of use values, not the production of 'values') then the law of value ceases to hold in such a mode of production.

12. 'The gentry the economists have hitherto overlooked the extremely simple point that the form 20 yards of linen equals one coat is only the underdeveloped basis of 20 yards of linen equals £2 and that therefore the *simplest form of commodity*, in which its value is not yet expressed as a relation to all other commodities but only as something *differentiated* from the commodity in its natural form, *contains the whole secret of the money form* and with it, in embryo, of all bourgeois forms of the product of labour.' (Marx, 1956, p. 228)

13. A notable exception is Blake, 1939.

14. In this work (Baran and Sweezy, 1966) we find virtually no reference to the theory of value in a study which purports to deal with the structure and dynamics of capitalism. Instead modern oligopoly 'price theory' is accepted without question and an almost purely Keynesian, underconsumptionist view of economic crisis elaborated. With the benefit of hindsight it is now possible to discern many of the seeds of this position in Sweezy's earlier and still popular work (Sweezy, 1946) where again a near-Keynesian view of the functioning of capitalism is presented and no link whatsoever established between the exposition of value theory and the rest of the analysis.

15. A decade after the publication of his study of value theory which this paper has criticised (Meek, 1956) Meek had moved to precisely this position. In a later work (Meek, 1967) he had constructed extremely firm bridges towards the vulgar school. For now he was arguing for a reconciliation between Marxism and what no doubt he would earlier have called 'bourgeois economics'.

References

Baran, P. A. and **Sweezy,** P. M. (1966) *Monopoly Capital: An Essay on the American Economic and Social Order*. New York: Monthly Review Press.

Blake, W. J. (1939) *An American Looks at Karl Marx*. New York: Cordon Company.

Dobb, M. H. (1940) *Political Economy and Capitalism: Some Essays in Economic Tradition*. London: Routledge.

Dobb, M. H. (1955) *On Economic Theory and Socialism*. London: Routledge.

Engels, F. (1957) Preface to **Marx,** 1957.

Engels, F. (1962) *Anti-Dühring*. London: Lawrence and Wishart.

Friedman, M. (1953) *Essays in Positive Economics*. Chicago: University of Chicago Press, Chicago.

Giddens, A. (1971) *Capitalism and Modern Social Theory: An Analysis of the writings of Marx, Durkheim and Max Weber*. London: Cambridge University Press.

Hegel, G. W. F. (1929) *The Science of Logic*. London: Allen and Unwin.

Hussain, A. (1972) 'Marx's Notes on Adolf Wagner', *Theoretical Practice*, 5, pp. 18–39. **Lenin,** V. I. (1934) Introduction to **Marx,** 1934.

Mandel, E. (1968) *Marxist Economic Theory*, Volume 2. London: Merlin Press.

Marx, K. (1961) *Capital*, Volume 1. London: Lawrence and Wishart.

Marx, K. (1957) *Capital*, Volume 2. London: Lawrence and Wishart.

Marx, K. (1959) *Capital*, Volume 3. London: Lawrence and Wishart.

Marx, K. (1969) *Theories of Surplus Value*, Part 1. London: Lawrence and Wishart

Marx, K. (1972) 'Marginal Notes on A Wagner's Lehrbuch der politischen Okonomie' Introduced by A. Hussain *Theoretical Practice* 5, Spring 1971.

Marx, K. (1971) *Contribution to the Critque of Political Economy*. Edited, with an Introduction by M. H. Dobb. London: Lawrence and Wishart.

Marx, K. (1934) *Letters to Kugelmann*. New York: International Publishers.

Marx, K. and **Engels,** F. (1956) *Selected Correspondence*. London: Lawrence and Wishart

Meek, R. L. (1955) 'Professor Cole on Marxian Economic Theory', *Marxist Quarterly*, Vol. 2, No. 4, October 1955.

Meek, R. L. (1956) *Studies in the Labour Theory of Value*. London: Lawrence and Wishart.

Meek, R. L. (1967) *Economics and Ideology: Studies in the Development of Economic Thought*. London: Chapman and Hall.

Ricardo, D. (1953) *Principles of Political Economy and Taxation*. Edited, with an Introduction by P. Sraffa, in collaboration with M. H. Dobb. London: Cambridge University Press.

Schumpeter, J. A. (1959) *Capitalism, Socialism and Democracy*. London: Allen and Unwin.

Sweezy, P. M. (1946) *Theory of Capitalist Development*. London: Dobson.

CHAPTER 3

Production, circulation and value:

the significance of the 'transformation problem' in Marx's Critique of Political Economy

Ira Gerstein

Abstract

The Marxian transformation problem is usually thought of as bridging the transition from 'essence' (value) to 'phenomena' or surface (prices). This paper shows that such a conception is incorrect. The transformation is actually between two theoretical levels of the construction of the economic region of the capitalist mode of production. The first of these levels is *production in itself (Capital,* Volume I), while the second is the complex unity of production and circulation (*Capital*, Volume III). This theoretical construction is complicated for two reasons: (1) despite the fact that production is the dominant instance, the social relationships of commodity production appear only in circulation; (2) circulation categories appear *implicitly* even at the level of *production in itself.*

These considerations establish the transformation problem at the heart of a correct conception of the capitalist mode of production, Thus the sharpest distinctions between neo-Ricardianism, vulgar Marxism and Marxism can be drawn here. In particular, it is shown that a correct appreciation of the transformation problem proves the inadequacy of an instrumentalist conception of the state since, at least in this area, bourgeois class interest arises only at the level of class and is not the sum of individual interests (even over a subgroup of the class).

Finally, the transformation problem itself is reviewed in detail. Mathematical results are separated from the essentials of the problem which are shown to lie in the correct choice of normalization, a choice that insures the transformation will actually be from value to modified value and not from value to price.

I Introduction: Marxism, classical political economy and vulgar economics

There has been recently a growing awareness that the dominant economic models of the postwar period must be rejected. This awareness is marked by a search for theories that will better take into account and explain the realities of the contemporary capitalist world economy; realities that include, to name only a representative few, monetary crises, inflation, increased levels of unemployment, and more open international capitalist competition, as well as the growing political strength of communist parties and a not yet completed series of political realignments working out the new power relations that were made manifest by the defeat of the United States in Southeast Asia.

The need for new theoretical understanding is felt on both sides of the class struggle, by defenders of capitalism and by critics who would overthrow it, as each seeks to ground political strategies in the context of events that do not fit comfortably into formerly accepted paradigms. For the bourgeoisie the hegemony of bourgeois ideology is vital. Vast financial and institutional resources are available to create and maintain a coherent and practical ideological framework with which to view the world. The nature of the capitalist mode of production dictates that economic theory be the linchpin of this ideology. When this aspect of ideology begins to crack, its reconstitution is a matter of urgent necessity. The most coherent and institutionalized attempt to carry out this reconstitution, on a basis that it is hoped will be better able to comprehend the contemporary world, is found in the neo-Ricardian attack on the neo-classical synthesis.[1]

The search for new approaches on the left has been less sharply focussed, the major reason being the relatively low level of class struggle that has existed in the theoretical realm. This, itself, is related to the overall state of the class struggle, as well as, more specifically, to the disorienting and corrosive effects of the existence of bourgeois ideology within the left. To the extent that there has been a dominant model for the left in the postwar period (at least in the United States), it is the tendency put forward by the journal *Monthly Review*, its publishing house Monthly Review Press, and given popular form in Baran and Sweezy's *Monopoly Capital*. This work stems from neo-Keynsianism as much as from Marx's critique of political economy and as such it must be rejected. However, it has much more to say that is of value than does the neo-classical synthesis, and, as a result, a left critique of it is bound to be more muted and subtle than is the neo-Ricardian critique of the neo-classical school.[2] It is the point of view of this paper that the starting point of the radical reconstruction of economic theory must be those elements of Marx's theory that break decisively with bourgois thought and ideology.

Of course, if a return to Marx is to be part of a convincing analysis, it must amount to more than a return to the mechanistic positions of the Second and Third Internationals, which themselves did not break sufficiently with bourgeois ideology.[3] In part, it was their rejection of dogmatic and undialectical readings that enabled Baran and Sweezy to provide an interpretive framework that appealed to a great number of people in the 1960's. What is needed is a theory that breaks decisively with *all* forms of bourgeois ideology. For this a careful and searching appraisal and reconstitution of Marx's critique, in a form that can be used in the conditions we find ourselves in today, must be undertaken.

A curious parallel thus emerges. For the left the renewal of economic theory involves a critical rejection of recent models in favor of a return to Marx's critique of political economy. For bourgeois theory it implies a similar rejection of postwar formalism in favor of a return to Ricardo.

The return to Marx, on the one hand, and to Ricardo, on the other hand, is not all that surprising. If we expand the perspective somewhat it is possible to see the mid-1960s as the termination of 100-some-odd years of capitalist expansion, rather than simply as the end of the anomalous post-World-War-II period. This is not meant to raise the false issue of the 'final crisis,' but it does imply that a significant boundary has been crossed. It will be possible to argue convincingly for such a periodization only after more information is in, and more theoretical work is done, including the reconstitution of the critique of political economy. However, as a preliminary assumption it makes sense to view both the neo-classical synthesis and the Marxism of the Second and Third Internationals, as, on the whole, attempts to conceptualize a successful, secure, and expansive capitalist world system. Baran and Sweezy represent a transitional tendency in this perspective. With the passing of this period of capitalist success, whose existence, it must be admitted, was neither forseen nor expected by either Marx or Ricardo, it makes sense to look once again at the period before the onset of what Marx termed 'vulgar economy.'[4]

In short, the period of vulgar economy had a 100-to 150-year existence, coinciding with the period in which the capitalist mode of production was established and secure. Vulgar economy produced elegant formulations and justifications for the bourgeoisie, and rather defensive and dogmatic ones for the proletariat.[5] In neither case was the surface of reality penetrated to any significant degree. That the usefulness of these theories has now passed is signalled by the growing search for a new political economy on the part of sectors of the bourgeoisie, and for a new critique of political economy on the part of the left.

The fact that the critique of vulgar bourgeois economy takes the form of neo-Ricardianism poses special problems of Marxism, problems that are magnified by the relatively advanced and coherent state of current neo-Ricardianism. For it must not be forgotten that Marx's *Capital* was itself a critique of Ricardo, whom Marx treated not as a vulgar economist but as the highest representative of classical political economy. Both neo-Ricardianism and Marxism are opposted to vulgar economics as it has developed over the past 150 years. That is their unity. However, in as much as they are each opposed to the other, as Marx was to Ricardo, the line between them must be clearly drawn. Not to do so would be to treat Marx as simply another representative of classical political economy, which is, in fact, precisely the tack that both the neo-Ricardians and the vulgar bourgeois economists take.[6]

One of the aims of this paper is to discuss systematically the differences between Marxism, on the one hand, and vulgar economy, both bourgeois and Marxist, and neo-Ricardianism, on the other hand. Although clarifying differences is important for its own sake, it is also a contribution to a more important task—developing revolutionary theory. What is needed, at bottom, is an adequate conception of the object of Marx's *Capital*, that is, of the economy in the capitalist mode of production. The most promising framework within which to do this is that suggested by Althusser and developed by him and his coworkers. In this framework the capitalist mode of production is conceived of as a structural combination of its economic, political, and ideological levels or regions (the number of these levels is subject to modification and deepening), the structure as a whole being determined in the last instance by the economic, and maintaining itself through a process of reproduction. Further, the levels themselves are structures in dominance. In particular, the economic structure is a combination of production, circulation, consumption, etc., the level of production being dominant.[7]

The specific differences between Marxism and the various other trends discussed above are located concretely in the different ways that they conceptualize the articulation between circulation and production, circulation being the form taken by distribution in the capitalist mode of production. Articulation refers to the precise connection between two levels or structures. Its specification is a specification of the type of complex unity exhibited by the total structure of which the structures in question are levels. Thus, to specify the articulation between production and circulation means to construct the complex unity of the economic level, which is the object of *Capital*.[8] That this is the place in which basic differences are located is not at all surprising. The fundamental aspect of any theory of the economic level is its conception of the constitution of that level—that is, the object of the theory. Theories will naturally differ most radically on exactly this point, while at other levels differences can be masked by ideological and superficial similarities of terminology that obscure the difference in their object.

The category that links production and circulation is 'value'. It is, at the same time, the simplest and most difficult of Marxist concepts. The second section of this paper is devoted to developing the nature of value and exposing certain misconceptions of it. In particular, in the first part of this section I outline how value provides the articulation of production and circulation. The concrete form this articulation takes is known as the 'transformation problem'. Section III is a detailed study of this somewhat obscure, but in this context crucial, aspect of Marx's theory.

This understanding of the place of the transformation problem is not conventional. Even though it has been the center of a running controversy between Marxists, on the one hand, and neo-Ricardians and vulgar economists, on the other hand, that has flared up and died down several times in the past 75 years, the transformation problem has never been seen as a problem of developing the categories that link production and circulation, and so as fundamental in constructing the object of political economy. Thus the aims of this paper are three-fold: in the first place, to enter the debate between the various theoretical tendencies; to do this by, in the second place, clarifying the different nature of their objects at the level of their conceptions of the economic structure; and finally, to concretize this conception by interpreting the transformation problem as the bridge between production and circulation, and presenting a detailed discussion of the Marxist solution to it, a solution that can be obtained, it should be noted, only in the context of this interpretation.

II Marx's theory of value

Although it is conventional to use the phrases 'labor theory of value' and 'Marx's theory of value' as if they were interchangeable, this formulation involves errors that inevitably push Marxism toward vulgar economy and Ricardianism. In the first place, it implies that there was a 'labor theory of value' before Marx. While it is true that the classical political economists often seem to be struggling toward such a theory, and that they use parts of it, albeit inconsistently, it is also true that none of them was able to formulate a consistent and coherent labor theory of value meant to apply to the capitalist mode of production.[9]

Adam Smith's discussion of the labor theory of value was limited to a (mythical) precapitalist period in which everyone owned their own tools and exchanged their products on the market. 'In that early and rude state of society which precedes both the accumulation of stock and the appropriation of land, the proportion between the quantities of labor necessary for acquiring different objects seems to be the only circumstance which can afford any rule for exchanging them for one another.' (Smith, 1965: 46) However, as Paul Samuelson is only too happy to point out, 'Adam Smith lingered in his "early and rude state" with its undiluted labor theory for only a page. Turn the page and Eden is left behind.' (Samuelson, 1971: 404) Smith then enters a world in which 'stock has accumulated in the hands of particular persons.' (Smith, 1973: 48) In this capitalist world the labor theory of value as he originally formulated it no longer holds and Smith abandons it completely. In any event, it was not a theory of value in the first place but a theory of exchange ratios; and Smith substitutes for it a factor theory of exchange ratios in which prices are *composed* of wages plus profits plus rent. One of the purposes of Marx's own analysis was to lay bare the ideological basis of this factor theory to which he referred sarcastically as the 'trinity formula.'[10]

Ricardo attempted to maintain Smith's labor theory of exchange in the presence of capital. He did this by making the obvious observation that, 'Not only the labor applied immediately to commodities affects their value, but the labor also which is bestowed on the implements, tools, and buildings, with which such labor is assisted.' (Ricardo, 1965: 13) This emendation by Ricardo is correct. However, as he himself notes, *it refers to the means of production simply as physical objects and not as capital*; that is, the fact that the means of production are owned by Smith's 'particular persons' is irrelevant to Ricardo's value theory (though not, of course, to his distribution theory, which is thus separated from his value theory).[11] This conceptual separation of value and distribution, based on an understanding of the means of production as simply physical objects, remains the central feature of contemporary neo-Ricardianism.

Now it is true that Marx carried this theory further, to a consistent conclusion, by taking into account the fact that means of production are always capital in the capitalist mode of production. He did this in his solution to the problem of the formation of the general rate of profit; this is, by his introduction of the transformation problem. However, to see only this aspect of Marx's theory is to make it merely a continuation of classical political economy and Marx the last of the classical political economists. In fact, Marx completely reoriented the object of inquiry. The distinction between the 'labor theory of value' the development of which has just been outlined, and 'Marx's theory of value', lies at the level of the conception of the nature of value.

It is this distinction that enabled Marx to break with the object of classical political economy and so validates his work as a critique of political economy, rather than as 'Marxist' political economy.[12]

For Ricardo there is nothing problematic about the labor that creates the value of commodities. It is labor—nothing more need be said. But for Marx,

> As regards value in general, it is the weak point of the classical school of Political Economy that it nowhere, expressly and with full consciousness, distinguishes between labor, as it appears in the value of a product and the same labor, as it appears in the use-value of that product. (Marx, n.d.: 84n)

That is, *the value of a commodity is not to be identified with the concrete labor that produces the commodity*, for example, the labor of soldering, or welding, or printing, or assembling, or any of the hundred-thousand other useful activities that produce or contribute to the production of commodities. This concrete labor 'appears in the use-value' of the commodity.

If value is not created by concrete labor, which was the conception of all of the classical political economists when they thought about it at all, then what labor does create it? Marx terms the value-creating aspect of labor *abstract labor, and emphasizes that it has a purely social reality*,

> . . . all are reduced to one and the same sort of labor, human labor in the abstract . . . When looked at as crystals of this social substance, common to them all, they are—Values. (Marx, n.d.: 46)

This distinction between concrete labor and abstract labor leads Marx to his critique,

> [Political Economy] has never once asked the question why labor is represented by the value of its product and labor-time by the magnitude of that value. (Marx, n.d.: 85)

The reason that Political Economy did not ask this question is that it could not conceive it. Seeing only concrete labor, and identifying it with value, makes value a natural rather than a social category. Only the understanding that value is created by abstract labor allows one to ask why abstract labor exists. And only this question allows the historical query: What is the origin of abstract labor and what is its future?

Marx emphasized the importance of his notion of the two-fold character of labor. He wrote to Engels in 1867 that,

> . . . the best points in my book are: 1) *the two-fold character* of

> labor, according to whether it is expressed in use-value or exchange-value. (*All* understanding of the facts depends upon this.) It is emphasized immediately, in the *first* chapter . . . (Marx and Engels, 1965: 192)

Indeed, the title of the second Section of Chapter I of *Capital*, Vol I is, 'The Two-Fold Character of Labor Embodied in Commodities.'

Now it is very easy to understand concrete labor. We see it around us and perform it ourselves every day. However, abstract labor is a much more difficult concept.

> Turn and examine a single commodity, by itself, as we will, yet in so far as it remains an object of value, it seems impossible to grasp it. If, however, we bear in mind that the value of commodities has a purely social reality, and that they acquire this reality only in so far as they are expressions or embodiments of one identical social substance, viz., human labor, it follows as a matter of course, that value can only manifest itself in the social relation of commodity to commodity. (Marx, n.d.: 54)

The points made in this passage are essential to understanding Marx's value theory. The most important one is that *it is precisely the social nature of abstract labor that makes it invisible in the process of production, which in the capitalist mode of production takes the form of an individual activity*, for the process of commodity production is not *directly* social. Thus, while concrete labor can be seen directly, abstract labor appears only in its effects. 'The progress of our investigation will show that exchange-value is the only form in which the value of commodities can manifest itself or be expressed.' (Marx, n.d.: 46) This is, as Marx indicated, the key to 'all understanding of the facts.'

An immediate consequence of the peculiar nature of abstract labor is that while Marx's theory of value is a theory of price *formation*, it is not directly a theory of prices. Ricardo's theory of value, on the other hand, is a theory of price because he identifies abstract labor and concrete labor. Here the substance of value can be measured in the process of production, and thus relative prices can be determined directly. Paradoxically, in this way Ricardo loses the concept of value completely. His is a labor theory of price and not a labor theory of value.[13]

The reason that Marx's theory of value is not a theory of price is that *there is no way to reduce observable concrete labor to social abstract labor in advance, outside of the market which actually effects the reduction.* This observation is the central feature of Marx's concept of value. The reduction of concrete labor to abstract labor in the market is prior to the problems involved in the determination of socially necessary labor time and in the reduction of skilled labor to simple labor. Even assuming that a worker is working at socially average productivity, the reduction of concrete labor to abstract labor must still be made, and can only be made, in the market. This may account for Marx's apparently cavalier treatment of the reduction of skilled labor to simple labor, which has disturbed many readers of *Capital*, Vol I. The translation from a particular concrete labor to abstract labor must take place in any event. No mechanical rules can be given in advance for making this reduction. In fact, this reduction is the basic element in the articulation of production and circulation. Of course, when the process of reproduction runs smoothly certain relationships become crystallized and producers can take the value of their product into account before the action of the market takes place. The reduction from skilled labor to simple labor is merely a further part of this process, and Marx was justified in treating it as he did, commenting, 'Experience shows that this reduction is constantly being made.' (Marx, n.d.: 51)

The statement that Marx's theory of value is not a theory of price may be construed in two ways–one weak and the other strong. The weak sense would be that value theory can predict prices, but that Marx was not (and by implication Marxists should not be) interested in this aspect of the problem. The strong sense is that *in principle* Marx's theory of value cannot be used to obtain prices. It is this strong version of the statement that is the case. Knowing that the substance of value is abstract labor does not help, for abstract labor can be *observed* in only one place–the market–where its palpable reality takes the form of money. As Marx says, 'Value, therefore, does not stalk about with a label describing what it is [i.e., abstract labor–I.G.] ' (Marx, n.d.: 79) Abstract labor as such can be 'measured' only when it takes the independent form of money, a form that poses it against the bodily form of the commodity in which it is embodied.

However, it will not do to separate the qualitative and quantitative aspects of Marx's theory too sharply.[14] While abstract labor cannot be observed in the process of production where it is actually expended, appearing (in another form) only in exchange, it is not merely a mental construct. It has a social nature and so has a social reality;

> The fact that the specific kind of labor is irrelevant presupposes a highly developed complex of actually existing kinds of labor, none of which is any more the all-important one . . . The fact

> that the particular kind of labor employed is immaterial is appropriate to a form of society in which individuals easily pass from one type of labor to another, the particular type of labor being accidental to them and therefore irrelevant. Labor, not only as a category but in reality, has become a means to create wealth in general, and has ceased to be tied as an attribute to a particular individual. This state of affairs is most pronounced in the United States, the most modern form of bourgeois society. The abstract category 'labor,' 'labor as such,' labor *sans phrase*, the point of departure of modern economics, thus becomes a practical fact only there. (Marx, 1972: 210).[15]

The precise connections between this social reality of abstract labor and the quantitative aspect of Marx's theory are, however, not specified clearly and remain a problem in his work. A remark made by Sowell in his book on the classical political economists may be pertinent here. He distinguishes between two types of theories, those which explain *states of being*, and those which explain *changes*. For the classical political economists, and for Marx as well, the task of theory was understood to be the latter, that is, to explain changes. For example:

> In terms of the Marxian theory of history, economics might explain very little of why families exist—instead of there being a wholly atomistic society or one in which people clustered in ways unrelated to biological kinship—and yet explain very much of why families have changed in the way they have from one century to another. (Sowell, 1974: 129)

Thus, a major problem for Ricardo was to understand the effect that changes in wages would have on profits and prices. Marx was concerned with, among other things, the effect of changes in the productivity of labor on the rate of profit and accumulation. And, of course, Marx was interested in the development of abstract labor. Although concrete labor cannot be identified with abstract labor, Marx generally restricts himself to talking about changes in the parameters of concrete labor. Changes in the length of the working day, in the total work force, and in the intensity of labor, although they refer directly to the description of concrete labor are presumably correlated with changes in the magnitude of abstract labor expended. On the other hand, a change in labor productivity alone, that is, an increase in produced use-value with no change in concrete labor, does not change the magnitude of expended abstract labor. In this way Marx's theory finds its quantitative dimension.

These remarks are only preliminary. *Capital* must be read carefully with the above principle in mind. However, I believe it is safe to say that the useful quantitative results stemming from Marx's critique of political economy will apply to the explanation of changes and the effects of changes. This program is hindered to some extent by Marx's vocabulary which does not always reflect this emphasis consistently.[16] Nevertheless, Marx's approach is inherently dynamic and has little in common with the static equilibrium models that underly both vulgar economy and neo-Ricardianism. Still, it is important for Marxists to recognize that the quantitative connections have not yet been made in a completely satisfactory way. Much work remains to be done in this area.

To return to the main thread of the discussion, let us look more closely at the reason behind the fact that abstract labor cannot be observed in the process of production. The capitalist mode of production, as a commodity mode of production, is characterized by the fact that production is an independent activity of individual producers who produce products for the purpose of selling them in the market. Considered in its productive aspect alone, such a mode of production does not *appear* to be social. Indeed, in a sense it is not social because no social relationships are established between the producers in the process of production. It is only when products are brought to the market that actual social relationships are established between the producers. It is for this reason that abstract labor, which has a purely social reality, is not observable in the *isolated* act of production (despite the fact that it is expended and value is created there), appearing only in the process of exchange and circulation in which the actual social connections are made. Marx says this, in fact, quite explicitly. It is hard to see how he could be misunderstood:

> As a general rule, articles of utility become commodities, only because they are products of the labor of private individuals or groups of individuals who carry on their work independently of each other. The sum total of the labor of all these private individuals forms the aggregate labor of society. Since the producers do not come into social contact with each other until they exchange their products, the specific social character of each producer's labor does not show itself except in the act of exchange. In other words, the labor of the individual asserts itself as a part of the labor of society, only by means of the relations which the act of exchange establishes directly between the products, and indirectly, through them, between the producers. (Marx, n.d.: 77–78)

This brings us right to the heart of Marx's theory of value. At issue is the general relationship between production and distribution, and the form that relationship takes in the capitalist mode of production. As to the former, Marx wrote,

> A distinct mode of production thus determines the specific mode of consumption, distribution, exchange and the *specific relations of these different phases to one another.* Production *in the narrow sense,* however, is in its turn also determined by the other aspects. (Marx, 1972: 205)

In other words, 'production is the decisive phase,' (Marx, 1972: 204) in a structure in which the other levels, distribution and consumption, have relative autonomy and exercise their own determinations. To move beyond these general observations, the articulation of these phases in a specific mode of production must be constructed. In this process of articulation categories established at one level of analysis are 'transformed' into new categories, or at least given new meanings. (See, for example, Althusser and Balibar, 1970: 223, 268) In fact, this is precisely the significance of the 'transformation problem.' It is a member of a much larger category, the transformation of meanings and categories attendant upon the increasingly complete specification of a structure. In this case the structure is the economic level of the capitalist mode of production, the category is value, and the specification corresponds to considering distribution (circulation, exchange) in a complex unity with, and dominated by, production.

The unique feature of the articulation of production and circulation in the capitalist mode of production has already been brought out above. It is that despite the fact that production is dominant (as in any mode of production), circulation establishes the social connections between the agents of production. This paradoxical situation gives rise to a series of effects summed up in the concept of commodity fetishism and the observation that everything appears inverted in competition. *The major inversion is taking circulation as the dominant level because it is the most accessible and apparently distinguishing level of the capitalist mode of production.* This is the root source of commodity fetishism and of most incorrect understandings of the nature of value. It is evident that this error is inherent in the structure of the capitalist mode of production and is not simply 'a mistake'. It was to avoid this problem that Marx introduced the, at first apparently meaningless, distinction between value and exchange-value. Value is the social category produced in the process of production; its form of appearance in exchange is exchange-value.

Marx begins *Capital* with 'A Critical Analysis of Capitalist Production,' (the subtitle of Volume 1). He starts this way because production is always the dominant aspect of the economic region. Thus its structure must be established first. Circulation, however, is present implicitly in its effects even at this stage of the analysis. The implicit presence of non-dominant structures in the analysis of dominant structures, even before the non-dominant structure is analyzed (or can be analyzed), is characteristic of structural combination, and distinguishes it from model building. In the case of the combination of production and circulation in the capitalist mode of production this characteristic has special salience. Value could not even be talked about if the forms of its appearance were not specified. Even more, the social nature of value demands that circulation be present implicitly at the point of its creation in the individual act of commodity production. As was the case for abstract labor, this is not merely a theoretical construct but corresponds to social reality in commodity modes of production. The producer must take into account the probable result of exchange, even in the act of production. Thus commodities can be produced only after exchange has become sufficiently generalized,

> This division of a product into a useful thing and a value becomes practically important, only when exchange has acquired such an extension that useful articles are produced for the purpose of being exchanged, and their character as values has therefore to be taken into account, beforehand, during production. From this moment the labor of the individual producer acquires socially a two-fold character. (Marx, n.d.: 78)

It is this structure, the dominance of production requiring that it be the focus of the first part of the investigation, the absence yet implicit presence of circulation at this stage, in a situation in which the nondominant aspect, circulation, provides the linkages that realize the social nature of production, that creates the major barrier to an adequate conceptualization of the capitalist mode of production. If this conceptualization were to be schematized in terms of Marx's *Capital* the result would be as follows. In Volume 1 production alone is considered, with, however, the qualification that circulation is present implicitly in its specific effects (i.e. value). Volume II considers circulation itself. Volume III is not simply the addition of production and circulation, but is the construction of their unity as an articulated complex structure. The difference between the two points of view is that in the second key categories of production are changed (transformed) between Volumes I and III. For the remainder of this paper references to Volume III, or simply to circulation, always refer to the unity of production and circulation in this sense. (For a detailed exposition of the articulations of *Capital* see Establet, 1973)

A major difference between Marxism, neo-Ricardianism, and vulgar Marxism is located in their different conceptions of the articulation of production and circulation. Marxism maintains the relationship outlined above. Both neo-Ricardianism and vulgar Marxism separate the two realms. Neo-Ricardians take a simple unity of production plus circulation to be a correct description of the economic level. Specifically, they view production as a natural phenomenon, and put the total content of social relationships, rather than simply their establishment, into circulation. As the theoretical basis of reform movements neo-Ricardianism leads only to considerations of distributive justice, leaving production relationships unchanged. Thus it supports various types of reformist positions that do not question the underlying basis of capitalism as a mode of production.

Vulgar Marxists, on the other hand, make the opposite mistake. Vulgar Marxism fetishizes production *per se*, and views circulation as a mere epiphenomenon of it. *Thus the dominant instance is mistaken for the entire structure.* Vulgar Marxism may be revolutionary in intent, but lacks an adequate theoretical underpinning for these intentions. It does not comprehend the nature of social relationships because it cuts itself off from the sphere in which they are realized. Ultimately then, this tendency, too, inevitably leads in a reformist direction because it cannot take effective action to realize its own goals.

Value links production and circulation in the capitalist mode of production. It is produced in the process of production but appears in circulation. Since it is the transformation problem that makes the linkage explicit by transforming the category of value from its meaning at the level of production alone to its meaning at the level of the unity of production and circulation, the differences between Marxism, vulgar Marxism, and neo-Ricardianism are epitomized in their different approaches to the transformation problem. Neo-Ricardians focus on it, only to sever production from social relationships entirely by constructing a simple unity in which production is understood technically and the transformation problem itself is treated simply as a problem of mathematical economics. They interpret the necessity of transformation as a rejection of the dominance of production relations in the structure of the economic level, by treating the transformation as being one from an inadequate *model* of economic reality in which circulation categories are ignored to a more realistic one in which they are dominant. Vulgar Marxism, on the other hand, tends to ignore the transformation problem completely, preferring to remain at the safe level of Volume I. The confrontation between neo-Ricardianism and vulgar Marxism is thus, not surprisingly, a sterile one. It is between two incorrect conceptions of the construction of the unity of production and circulation, and so cannot be resolved.[17]

-ii-

If one error, common to neo-Ricardianism and vulgar Marxism, is to treat value as observable in production, and the theory of value as a theory of price, thus confusing production and circulation, then a second error, again common to both tendencies (and again with a characteristic difference) is to treat the theory of value as mainly a proof of capitalist exploitation. In the concept of surplus value the emphasis is placed upon the adjective–*surplus* value.

The neo-Ricardians make this connection via Ricardo's proof, updated by Sraffa (1960), that total profits and total wages vary inversely. This is taken to be the total content of the theory of surplus value. The point is not to deny the validity of the Ricardian theorem under the conditions for which it has been proven. However, as we shall see, it does not come close to exhausting the content of Marx's use of notion of surplus value.[18]

Vulgar Marxism, too, takes the theory of surplus value to be a proof of capitalist exploitation. However, the different stances taken by vulgar Marxism and neo-Ricardianism of the relationship between production and circulation lead to different (mis)understandings of the nature of the exploitation. The neo-Ricardian emphasis on circulation results in the use of exchange categories to describe exploitation. Thus they emphasize the inverse relationship between profits and wages rather than the connection between surplus value and the value of labor power. Vulgar Marxism remains at the level of abstract production. It sees only the relationship between individual capitalists and individual workers since the social phenomena built up in the process of circulation remain unavailable to it. This emphasis seriously undercuts the desire to build up a class description of social events. In particular, by focusing on that aspect of exploitation which occurs at the level of individual capitalist versus individual worker (or factory-wide collective worker) it cannot explain such basic structures as, for example, the state, imperialism, fascism, all of which require an understanding of the capitalist mode of production as a whole. In addition, and for the same reasons, by remaining at the abstract level of production in itself, it is impossible to construct a scientific theory of consumption or ideology, which is clearly necessary if a strategic perspective for the advanced countries is to be developed.

The exploitation argument is sometimes taken a step further. Not only is the theory of value seen as a theory of exploitation, it is combined with the notion of 'natural right' and expanded into the moral demand that the laborer (or, more generally, labor) receive the full product of his (its) labor. The roots of this idea are located in Locke's notion of the right to property flowing from labor. Thus it is basically a bourgeois conception. The so-called Ricardian socialists of the early 19th century attempted to turn it against the bourgeoisie but could only do so in the interest of another property-owning class, petit-bourgeois artisans.[19]

Marx was particularly opposed to the appearance of these ideas within the working-class movement. When commenting on the draft program of the German Workers' Party, the Gotha Program, which opened with the statement,

> Labor is the source of all wealth and all culture, and since useful labor is possible only in society and through society, the proceedings of labor belong undiminished with equal right to all members of society

he responded with two arguments. First,

> Labor is *not the source* of all wealth. *Nature* is just as much the source of use values (and it is surely of such that material wealth consists!) as labor . . . (Marx and Engels, 1968: 319)

The reference to use value alludes to the dual nature of the commodity. Although it is the sole source of *value*, labor is not the sole source of *use value*. The formulation of the Gotha Program confuses the two. Thus it cannot be the basis for an attack on surplus *value*. It leads, rather, to demands for a more equitable distribution of the product. This formulation mounts no challenge to the capitalist mode of production.

In the second place, Marx writes,

> The bourgeoisie have very good grounds for falsely ascribing *supernatural creative power* to labor; since precisely from the fact that labor depends on nature it follows that the man who possesses no other property than his labor must, in all conditions of society and culture, be the slave of other men who have made themselves the owners of the material conditions of labor (Marx and Engels, 1968: 319)

That is, an emphasis on labor as the only productive (of use value) factor leaves out means of production, whose private ownership is characteristic of the capitalist mode of production. These considerations explain the neo-Ricardian predilection to treat constant capital as past (dated) labor. (See, for example, Bortkiewicz, 1952; Sraffa, 1960; Steedman, 1972)

-iii-

The interpretations of Marx's theory of value that have just been discussed, a theory of price, on the one hand, or a theory of exploitation, on the other hand, barely scratch the surface of the content he attributed to it. Marx was not interested in how capitalism worked for its own sake, but wanted 'to lay bare the economic law of motion of modern society . . .' (Marx, n.d.: 20) The notion of value lies at the heart of this project, for Marx attributed centrality to the *form* and not simply the *fact* of exploitation:

> The specific economic form, in which unpaid surplus-labor is pumped out of direct producers, determines the relationship of rulers and ruled, as it grows out of production itself and, in turn, reacts upon it as a determining element. Upon this, however, is founded the entire formation of the economic community which grows up out of the production relations themselves, thereby simultaneously its specific political form. It is always the direct relationship of the owners of the conditions of production to the direct producers—a relation always naturally corresponding to a definite stage in the development of the methods of labor and thereby its social productivity—which reveals the innermost secret, the hidden basis of the entire social structure, and with it the political form of the relation of sovereignty and dependence, in short, the corresponding specific form of the state. This does not prevent the same economic basis—the same from the standpoint of its main conditions—due to innumerable empirical circumstances, natural environment, racial relations, external historical influences, etc., from showing infinite variations and gradations in appearance, which can be ascertained only by analysis of the empirically given circumstances. (Marx, 1971a: 791-92)

I have cited this passage at length because it is one of the clearest general indications of the content of Marx's theory of history, that is, the science of historical materialism.[20] It fills out and modifies the sketch given in the well-known 1859 Preface in which Marx wrote less specifically of the 'relations of production [constituting] the economic structure of society, the real foundation, on which arises a legal and political super-structure and to which correspond definite forms of social consciousness.' (Marx, 1972: 20) The somewhat open notion of 'relations of production' in the Preface is thus specified in *Capital* to consist, at least in part, of the 'specific economic form in which unpaid surplus-labor is pumped out of direct producers.'

Marx specified the content of the concept of 'relations of production' further:

> Whatever the social form of production, laborer and means of production always remain factors of it. But in a state of separation

> from each other either of these factors can be such only potentially. For production to go on at all they must unite. The specific manner in which this union is accomplished distinguishes the different economic epochs of the structure of society from one another. (Marx, 1967: 36)

This passage appears in the context of a discussion of the conditions for the generalization of commodity production. Marx thus linked this generalization (a market or circulation phenomenon) to a particular change in the relationships of production, namely the complete transformation of labor power into a commodity and hence the introduction of a new category, the *value* of labor power. (For a detailed discussion of this point see Althusser and Balibar, 1970)

Marx's use of the category of value is thus unique. He conceived of it as the central category with which to unravel the law of motion of the capitalist mode of production. Fundamental to this project is the category of surplus value where the emphasis is placed on the noun—surplus *value*, for this is the form in which the surplus is pumped out of the direct producers in the capitalist mode of production. In order that this form be dominant it is necessary that labor power itself become a commodity, that is, have a value. Thus the concept of value properly understood is the most central expression of the relations of production specifically characteristic of the capitalist mode of production.

Marx's own results using this scheme were many; this is not the place to analyze them in detail. They range from the prediction of the progressive centralization and concentration of capital, to the homogenization of labor, to the crisis-prone character of capitalism, to the falling rate of profit, and, of course, to a theory of the growth of consciousness and the origin of revolutionary change. Some of these have been borne out historically, others may be partial. It remains true, however, that if we are to remain within Marx's analytical framework, value is the category that must be the basis of study of the laws of development of the capitalist mode of production.

As argued above, such an analysis cannot stop with the conception of value obtained from Volume I of *Capital*. The correct links between production and circulation must be grasped in order to develop the category of value to the point where it can play the central role ascribed to it. At the same time, of course, the articulation of the capitalist mode of production will be clarified, since developing the laws of motion of a mode of production takes place through an understanding of its complex structured existence. Thus the two roles of value turn out to be the same. Value is the category that links production and circulation, while it is, at the same time, the form in which the surplus is pumped out of direct producers.

From this point of view the transformation problem is hardly a formal mathematical exercise of little intrinsic interest, as the neo-Ricardians would have it; rather, it moves to center stage. (May, 1949, 67; Robinson, 1950: 361) A correct understanding of the transformation problem is necessary (although only a first step) in reconstructing Marxist theory after 100 years of its subordination to bourgeois ideology.

III The Transformation Problem

i The 'Contradiction'

In simplest terms the transformation problem arises from the fact that while in Volume I Marx treats commodities as if they exchange at prices equal to their exchange values, it turns out that this is incompatible with the formation of a general rate of profit.[21] The argument is as follows:

The value of any commodity has a structure. In the first place, there is the new value created by the expenditure of the labor that is socially necessary to produce the commodity. A certain number of workers work a certain amount of time in the process of production. Their concrete labor produces the use value of the commodity while the abstract labor expended is the substance of the newly created value, whose magnitude is the amount of abstract labor expended. This would be all there was to it if it were not for the existence and use of means of production: tools, raw materials, machinery, fuel, buildings, etc., which were themselves produced as commodities and so are values. If the process of producing the final commodity is thought of as an extended one, in which the means of production are themselves produced as intermediate steps, then the labor time socially necessary to produce them (i.e., their value) is seen to be labor time expended upon the production of the final commodity. Thus the value of the means of production is simply transferred to the final product, either all at once if the item is completely used up, or piece by piece if, as for example is the case with a machine, the item is used up only after several production cycles. This latter situation is referred to as fixed capital.

The value of any commodity then is composed of two parts. One part is the *preserved and transferred* value of the means of production; its magnitude is fixed by the value of the means of production and has nothing to do with the process of producing the new commodity (assuming that the machines, etc. have been used 'properly'). Value from this source is *transferred* from the means of production to the final product. For this reason Marx refers to the means of production as constant capital. New value is not created here; the sum of value before and after the production process has taken place is the same. Only the location of this value has changed. Before the production process, it is in the form of means of production; afterwards, in the form of the final product.

The second part of the value of the product is the new value created by the direct labor of production. The total of this value produced in a single working day clearly varies directly with the length of the working day. It also varies with the intensity of labor, and considered in its social totality, with the number of employed workers. For these reasons Marx describes this part of the value as the product of variable capital; that is, labor power is variable capital when it is purchased by a capitalist for use in capitalist production. In terms of the distinction between concrete labor and abstract labor, that is the dual nature of labor, abstract labor is the substance of the newly created value, while concrete labor preserves and transfers the value of the means of production. Of course these are not two separate processes, but are aspects of a single labor process.

The newly created value too has a structure. For capitalist production does not use simply labor, but wage labor. That is, labor power is a commodity whose value, like that of any other commodity, is the amount of abstract social labor necessary to produce it.[22] Now the value of labor power, the time necessary to 'produce' the laborer (or, more accurately, reproduce the labor force—recall the social nature of value), bears not immediate quantitative relationship to the value created by that laborer in the process of production. This value is determined by the length of the working day, the intensity of labor, and the conversion of a particular concrete labor to abstract labor. Thus the newly created value itself has two parts. The first part is equal to the value of labor power, and replaces it in the product. The second part is the remainder. It accrues to the capitalist as surplus value.

Putting these considerations together, the value, w, of any commodity can be written in the following form:

$$w = c + v + s \qquad (1)$$

where

c = the transferred value of the constant capital;
v = the value of labor power;
s = the surplus value.

Of course, $(v + s)$ is the newly created value and $(c + v)$ is the capitalist's advanced capital, the money laid out to start production. The value w may be thought of as the value of a single unit of a particular commodity or of several units.

Marx assumes that, in general, the ratio s/v, which he calls the rate of exploitation or the rate of surplus value, is the same for all workers. The argument is as follows. The value of labor power is the same for all workers because it is the abstract labor time needed to produce those commodities needed to reproduce the laborer. By definition of the social nature of value this does not vary from worker to worker.[23] On the other hand, s is the difference between this value and the length of the working day, at given intensity, assuming that the reduction from concrete to abstract labor is the same for all workers. Now, since work has neither meaning nor dignity under capitalism, despite the attempts of bourgeois ideology to convince people otherwise, perfectly 'free' wage labor will search for the shortest working day with lowest intensity. Furthermore, this is not merely a passive search but is part of the content of the class struggle at the economic level, which, for example, establishes a 'normal' (i.e. fixed and uniform) working day. Under these conditions all workers produce the same amount of surplus value, and so the rate of exploitation is uniform. Perhaps it would be more accurate to assert that there is a *tendency* in the capitalist mode of production toward equalization of the rate of exploitation.[24]

Now this tendency appears to be incompatible with another tendency of the capitalist mode of production, that of the equalization of the rate of profit. The essence of the capitalist mode of production is capital's search for profit. No capital can be satisfied unless it produces the highest profit possible, and on this basis capitalist competition takes place. This competition is not limited to intrabranch competition between producers of identical or substitutable products, but proceeds across branch lines. It is competition not for the consumer's dollar but for the highest profit rate. The result of this general competition is an equalization of the rate of profit—all capitals receiving the same rate of profit—and so establishing the general rate of profit, which as with all market phenomena must be thought of as the center of innumerable fluctuations.[25]

The conflict is as follows. The capitalist, according to the analysis expressed in Eq. (1) obtains an amount of value over and above his advances of (c + v) equal to s. Since prices have been assumed to equal exchange value these quantities may equally well be thought of as amounts of money. Then s is the capitalist's profit, (c + v) his capital outlay.[26] The rate of profit, r, is then given by the ratio of profit to investment

$$r = s/(c + v) \tag{2}$$

Rearranging the terms of this equation gives,

$$r = \frac{s/v}{1 + c/v} \tag{3}$$

Since the rate of exploitation, s/v, is the same for all workers independent of industry, it follows that r will be uniform only if c/v, the ratio of constant capital to variable capital, is the same for all industries. But c/v is the value measure of the amount of means of production per worker. There is no reason to expect it to be invariant to the type of production. The chemical industry, for example, uses far more complex and costly machinery and far fewer workers proportionately than does, say, the textile industry.[27] The conclusion is inescapable that there is a conflict between an analysis based on Marx's theory of value and a characteristic feature of the capitalist mode of production, the formation of a general rate of profit.

There is a less technical and perhaps more illuminating way of arriving at this conclusion. Surplus value arises from new labor and not from the means of production whose value is preserved and transferred to the final product without undergoing any change in magnitude. But this is seemingly in contradiction with everyday capitalist reality. It would appear to be to the capitalist's advantage to increase his labor force, the source of surplus value, relative to his means of production. In fact, exactly the opposite takes place. The tendency of capitalism is to increase the means of production relative to living labor, which is thus in contradiction to 'rational' behavior according to the law of value. To the capitalist it appears as if profit springs from total capital, rather than from living labor.[28] It is this observation, in fact, that gives plausibility to factor theories that ascribe productive power to capital, as opposed to the labor theory of value which denies that capital can create new value except in its form of variable capital. Factor theories thus take the point of view of the individual capitalist, which explains the fundamental role played by the notion of the 'firm' in neoclassical theory.

ii Marx's Solution

Smith and Ricardo effectively gave up in the face of this contradiction. Smith abandoned the labor theory of value, and Ricardo retreated into inconsistencies when faced with problems that touched on the equalization of the rate of profit. Marx's solution to what, in fact, is only an apparent contradiction, is based on his understanding of the relationship of value, production and circulation as discussed in Section II above. The value theory on which the above discussion has been based is the theory of Volume I, in which production is treated explicitly and in abstract isolation. Circulation is treated only implicitly to the extent that production, even in abstaction, requires concepts of circulation and exchange. Production of commodities, considered abstractly in this sense, does not allow any differentiation between capitals on the basis of the use values of their products, because use value is relevant only in exchange. What concerns the capitalist as an abstract producer is that his commodity be a use value for some purchaser (this is the implicit appearance of exchange). The particular use value is important only to the purchaser. Thus the process of capitalist production, abstracted from circulation, is a process of value production alone. Since value is a socially produced substance, the product of any given capital considered at this level can only be thought of as a fraction of the total social capital.

The formation of a general rate of profit depends upon and results from the action of capitalist competition; in other words, on the explicit consideration of circulation and exchange. Thus there is no 'contradiction' between the theory of value and the existence of the general rate of profit, for they are concepts that belong to theoretical constructions of a different order. The theory of value belongs to the level of production, considered in abstraction, and the general rate of profit to the level of the complex unity of production and circulation. *The question then is not how to reconcile the two sides of a contradiction, but how to move or 'transform' from one level of analysis to another.*

The basis for Marx's procedure has been established in the preceeding analysis. He argued that the introduction of circulation individuated the capitals that had been considered previously only as fractions of the total social capital, but that it could not affect the total social capital itself. Thus, according to Marx, the total social capital continues to undergo self-expansion, and an analysis at the level of Volume I is correct because circulation cannot add anything at this level. In particular, the formula for the value of a commodity, Eq. (1), continues to hold, but now only for the total social capital.[29] If this is the case then the rate of profit for the total social capital is correctly given by,

$$R = S/(C + V) \tag{4}$$

where upper-case letters have been used to refer to total surplus value, total constant capital, and total variable capital, which are assumed to be the sum of the respective individual surplus value, constant capital, and variable capital. That is,

$$W = \sum_i w_i \tag{5a}$$

$$C = \sum_i c_i \tag{5b}$$

$$V = \sum_i v_i \tag{5c}$$

$$S = \sum_i s_i \tag{5d}$$

where the sum runs over all commodities.

Marx identifies R, the rate of profit on the total social capital with r, the general rate of profit as established by competition between capitals. *This identity is, for Marx, the link between production and circulation, and hence, between Volume I and Volume III.* He implements this algorithm by introducing 'prices of production', which are those prices that yield the general rate of profit on the capital advanced. Marx calls the value of this advanced capital its 'cost price'. Denoting the price of production of the ith commodity by $\bar{w}_i$, and its cost price by k_i, leads then to the following:

$$k_i = c_i, + v_i \tag{6}$$

$$\bar{w}_i = k_i(1 + R) \tag{7}$$

Furthermore, combining Eqs. (6), (7) and (5), the following identities hold:

$$\sum_i \bar{w}_i = \sum_i w_i \tag{8}$$

that is, total price of production is equal to total value;

$$R\sum_i k_i = \sum_i s_i \tag{9}$$

that is, total profit is equal to total surplus value;

$$R = \frac{\sum_i (s_i/k_i)k_i}{C + V} \tag{10}$$

that is, the general rate of profit is the average of the individual (untransformed) rates of profit, weighted by the value of the capital advanced; i.e., it is literally the average rate of profit.[30]

Yet another ambiguity in terminology (perhaps a reflection of an ambiguity in Marx's conceptual apparatus) must be clarified here. Marx calls the $\bar{w}_i$ *prices* of production and the k_i cost *prices*. However, it is easily seen that they are not prices at all but values. Marx seems to be ignoring the distinction, so carefully made in Volume I, between values and prices when he discusses the transformation problem in Volume III. (Of course it must not be forgotton that Volume III is culled from Marx's notebooks and is not a finished work.) The point is that it is incorrect to think of the transformation as being from value to price, as is so often done (and as we are encouraged to do by Marx's terminology). It is true that the category of price is much more concrete in Volume III than in Volume I, because Volume III deals explicitly with circulation. Nevertheless, value and price are distinct categories, present in *both* volumes. *The transformation from Volume I to Volume III is not a transformation from value to price, but from value and price considered purely from the point of view of production to value and price as modified by circulation and capitalist competition.* The relationship between value and price must be specified at both ends of this chain.[31] This is the only way to make sense of identities such as Eq. (8). The w_i are values and so the $\bar{w}_i$ must have the dimensions of abstract labor time. Prices however are 'the money name of the labor realized in a commodity,' (Marx, n.d.: 103) and as such cannot be simply equated to value.

Thus prices of production and cost prices are not prices at all but are values (or, at least, exchange values). It is extremely difficult to devise a terminology that (1) reflects these distinctions, (2) does not require long, awkward constructions, and (3) retains some contact with Marx's usages. Shaikh (1974) and Yaffe (1974) have tried to do this, not with complete success. Yaffe suggests calling the prices that correspond to values at the level of Volume I 'simple prices', reserving 'price of production' for the prices that correspond to the $\bar{w}_i$. Shaikh uses the adjective 'real' to refer to exchange value. Thus the left hand side of Eq. (9) would be called total real profit. Profit refers to the money expression of real profit. This terminology is adapted to Shaikh's notion that it is exchange value rather than value that is 'transformed'. In addition to these suggestions, which I shall follow, I shall refer to the $\bar{w}_i$ as modified values and the k_i as modified cost values, reflecting the view that although the meaning of value is modified when circulation is brought into the picture, it nevertheless remains Marx's central category. Since profit does not exist at the level of Volume I, Shaikh is correct in holding that it can refer only to circulation categories, that is, to exchange value and price.

iii Class interest and the State

It is helpful to look at the way in which Marx's transformation procedure resolves the intuitive objection to the simple theory of value, that capitalists do not act as if profit derived exclusively from living labor. In fact, it is now clear that this perception is correct for the individual capitalist. Each capitalist receives a share of the total social surplus value that is proportional to his own capital, both constant and variable. In particular, the number of workers he employs makes no difference. A capitalist whose own workers do not produce 'enough' surplus value relative to his constant capital to yield the average rate of profit 'receives' surplus value from those capitalists who are in a relative surplus position. Eq. (9) insures that this will work out correctly. (The quotation marks indicate that the description is metaphorical: production and circulation are not separate phenomena.) Thus, from the point of view of his share of the total surplus value, it does not matter to the individual capitalist whether he hires labor or buys machinery. Indeed, machines are less recalcitrant than workers and do not participate actively in the class struggle.

On the other hand, what is true for the individual capitalist is not true for the capitalist class as a whole. According to Eq. (9), total real profit is equal to total real surplus value, and total surplus value springs solely from surplus labor. The effect of competition forces the capitalist to cheapen his product, which he does by expelling living labor. However, while the individual capitalist happily fires workers and replaces them with machinery, this policy would be suicidal if practiced by the capitalist class as a whole. *The class interest of the capitalist class is not the sum of the interests of the capitalists who make up the class.* Thus the necessity and the nature of transformation have important consequences at the political level. Class interest appears only at the level of the class as a whole, and not at the level of individual members of the class. Thus the formation of the bourgeoisie into a class is not at all a simple matter. The articulation of bourgeois class interest is always problematic since, in any particular case, it may conflict with the interest of all of the members of the class. This is a fundamental problem for the capitalist mode of production at the level of the political superstructure. As Marx put it at the end of a discussion of these points:

> Here, then, we have a mathematically precise proof why capitalists form a veritable freemason society vis-à-vis the whole working class, while there is little love lost between them in competition among themselves. (Marx, 1971: 198)

A concrete example of the process of the formation of bourgeois class interest is given in Chapter X of Volume I, 'The Working Day'. Marx first notes that the struggle to define the 'normal' working day is a class struggle between 'collective capital, i.e., the class of capitalists, and collective labor, i.e. the working class'. He examines the brutal effects of the 14 or 16 hour day of the early industrial revolution on the most exploited sectors of the working class, from which it is clear that the working class would struggle and organize itself in favor of a shorter working day. But the degeneration of the working class was not in the interest of the capitalist class either, since capital requires a working class. 'It would seem therefore that the interest of capital itself points in the direction of a normal working day.' However, even in the event that an individual recognized this class interest it would be impossible for him to act upon it. 'But looking at things as a whole, all this does not, indeed, depend on the good or ill will of the individual capitalist. Free competition brings out the inherent laws of capitalist production, in the shape of external coercive laws having power over every individual capitalist.' *The problem is resolved by the state in the form of the Factory Acts.* (Marx, n.d.: 225, 253, 257)

Marx gave two examples of this process. In the first he cited an

1863 petition of 26 Staffordshire potteries (including Wedgwood, a major manufacturer) for 'some legislative enactment' to limit working hours. Marx's analysis: 'Competition with other capitalists permits them no voluntary limitation of working time for children, etc.' He found the second example 'much more striking'. It concerned smaller manufacturers who encouraged their own workers to agitate for legislative enactment of the nine hour system in order to rationalize their own competition with the larger manufacturers. (Marx, n.d.: 275n)

The upshot of this analysis and these examples is that the interests of the capitalist class are not merely expressed through and by the state, rather, they are, to a certain extent, formed by the state; not, of course, out of nothing according to the omnipotent whim of the state, but out of the material basis of those interests located in the process of capitalist production as a whole. *The state is not the tool of the united bourgeoisie, but is the institution that is crucial in creating that unity.*[32]

Thus the 'mathematically precise proof' that the class interests of the bourgeoisie are not formed as an aggregate of individual interests has far-reaching consequences. Political assertions about the nature of class, class interests, and the state grow out of this apparently obscure problem in the theory of value (itself frequently regarded as a scholastic question)—the transformation problem. Here is a powerful indication that Marx's concept of value and surplus value as the central categories of the capitalist mode of production is not misplaced. The importance of the transformation problem, in particular, is clear. The damage that an instrumental conception of the state has done to left strategy is incalculable. While it is certainly true that a non-instrumental view of the state does not need to be based on the transformation problem, it is hard to see how else the autonomous character of the bourgeois state can be linked to its determining material base.

iv The Bortkiewicz Critique

Marx's solution to the transformation problem has not lacked critics. Engels published Volume III in 1894. In 1898 Böhm-Bawerk, an Austrian economist, published his well-known attack. (Böhm-Bawerk, 1949) Exhibiting a total lack of understanding of Marx's project and method, he professed to find a great contradiction between Volume I and Volume III. This has, in fact, ever since been the position of vulgar economy. (See, for example, Samuelson, 1970, 1971) It needs no further refutation than has already been provided in Section I and Part ii of this section.[33] Böhm-Bawerk's critique was answered by Hilferding, whose analysis, however, is not satisfactory, which is hardly surprising in the light of the low level of Marxist understanding developed in the Second International.[34] Important to Böhm-Bawerk's 'discovery' of the 'great contradiction' is the assertion that Marx did not know, when he wrote Volume I, that prices could not be proportional to values in a capitalist system with a general rate of profit. This assertion is simply wrong. Internal evidence in Volume I, as well as an explicit solution to the transformation problem contained in a letter to Engels dated 1862, prove conclusively that Marx had developed his solution prior to the publication of Volume I. (Marx and Engels, 1965: 128–31)

Böhm-Bawerk's criticism was actually an attack on the whole of classical political economy from the viewpoint of vulgar economy. Much more interesting and penetrating is the critique (or rather critiques) of Bortkiewicz. (Bortkiewicz, 1949, 1952) Bortkiewicz's criticism turns upon a subtle point in Marx's 'mathematically precise' solution. However, as soon becomes clear, the criticism is really a full-fledged attack on Marx's entire theory in favor of a revival of Ricardo; that is, it removes all elements of the critical aspect of Marx's critique of political economy. The difficulty this raises is that the point made by Bortkiewicz is valid (although his conclusions from it are not) and must be confronted.

This is why Bortkiewicz's critique and alternate solution are at the heart of the contemporary debate between Marxism and neo-Ricardianism.

The technical point raised by Bortkiewicz is as follows. Marx's formula for modified value, Eq. (7), which can be rewritten in the following form,

$$\bar{w}_i = c_i + v_i + R(c_i + v_i) \tag{11}$$

does indeed yield a profit to each capital proportional to its size. But this size is calculated in values rather than in modified values. Bortkiewicz noted that capitalist competition, which is responsible for the equalization of the rate of profit, occurs completely at the level of prices of production, and not half at this level and half at the level of simple prices. The capital which figures into the capitalist's cost price (Marx's term), k_i, should really be valued at modified cost value, $\bar{k}_i$. In short, Marx transformed the value of the output of the production process but left the input unchanged. Consistency demands that they both be treated as modified values, to which correspond real cost prices, on the one hand, and real prices of production, on the other hand.

No more than in the case of the existence of the transformation problem itself can it be seriously argued that Marx was either unaware of, or rejected, the requirement of the transformation of inputs. Referring to the fact that in his solution the sum of modified value is equal to the sum of value, Eq. (8), Marx wrote:

> This statement seems to conflict with the fact that under capitalist production the elements of productive capital are, as a rule, bought on the market, and for this reason their prices include profit which has already been realized, hence, include the price of production of the respective branch of industry together with the profit contained in it, so that the profit of one branch of industry goes into the cost price of another. But if we place the sum of the cost prices of the commodities of an entire country on one side, and the sum of its surplus values, or profits, on the other, the calculation must evidently be right. (Marx, 1971a: 160)

We may reserve judgement on the validity of the final statement since it is open to mathematical investigation. The main point is that cost value is an input into the formation of cost value. Marx makes an almost identical argument slightly farther on:

> We had originally assumed that the cost price of a commodity equalled the *value* of the commodities consumed in its production. But for the buyer the price of production of a specific commodity is its cost price, and may thus pass as cost price into the prices of other commodities. Since the price of production may differ from the value of a commodity, it follows that the cost price of a commodity containing this price of production of another commodity may also stand above or below that portion of its total value derived from the value of the means of production consumed by it. It is necessary to remember this modified significance of the cost price, and to bear in mind that there is always the possibility of an error if the cost price of a commodity in any particular sphere is identified with the value of the means of production consumed by it. (Marx, 1971a: 164–65; see also 161, 206–207)

Given Bortkiewicz's criticism and Marx's own unambiguous remarks, it is hard to maintain that Marx's solution to the transformation problem is correct as it stands in Volume III.[35] The main area of controversy centers around the proper construction and meaning of the correct solution, and its relationship to that of Marx. The major exception to this seems to be Yaffe, who maintains that,

> the average profit is calculated on the average social capital, and with the formation of prices of production the capitalist recovers money in proportion to the *value of the capital consumed* in production plus the average profit on the capital advanced. (Yaffe, 1974: 46)

In other words, Marx's solution is correct,

> total value of commodities must be equal to total price and total surplus value equal to total profit. Anything else makes nonsense of Marx's theory of value . . . The reason why inputs are not converted into prices of production in the transformation of values into prices is that it is the *value* of the *capital* consumed in production that is decisive. (Yaffe, 1973: 43,44)

The logic of Yaffe's argument is (at best) obscure. Indeed, at the crucial points he produces no argument at all, simply asserting that his position is the only correct one. His major substantive point is that capitals obtain a 'share of profit in proportion to their share of capital invested as a part of the total social capital.' (Yaffe, 1974: 48) However, he gives no argument to justify evaluating this share in value rather than modified value terms. Thus the argument that capitals must be thought of as fractions of the total capital, while important and correct, is not an argument for or against transforming inputs. I have argued that the fraction must be computed in modified value terms. The reason is that individual capitals are distinguished in circulation, so their description necessarily involves circulation categories.

Yaffe criticizes any attempt to develop a Marxist solution to the transformation problem as a concession to empiricism. The problem with this approach, as was pointed out by Hodgson, is that Yaffe reacts to the undoubted empiricism of vulgar economy by retreating into pure idealism. (Hodgson, 1973) On the ideological level, Yaffe's assertion that 'Anything else makes nonsense of Marx's theory of value' can lead people only to the conclusion that it is Marx's theory of value that is nonsense. The pernicious effect of Yaffe's position, which is, ultimately, simply a sophisticated version of vulgar Marxism with its fetishized attitude toward the primacy of production, is that it opens the way for neo-Ricardians such as Hodgson to preempt the field of discussion.

A word should be said about Bortkiewicz's 'solution'. It is the most well known discussion of the transformation problem because of its inclusion in Sweezy's popular text. (Sweezy, 1968: 109–30) Actually Bortkiewicz proposed two solutions, publishing both in 1907. One was a careful and rigorous discussion, using the (ideological) Ricardian technique of treating constant capital as dated labor. (Bortkiewicz, 1952) While this solution is Ricardian through and through, and so removes the critical component of Marx's conceptions, it can at least be discussed analytically and rigorously. Unfortunately, the same cannot be said of Bortkiewicz's second solution, the one Sweezy chose to publish in his text and translate for his Böhm-Bawerk collection. (Bortkiewicz, 1949) This solution introduced the three-department model, which may be a useful approximation under certain circumstances but is not fundamental to the problem. It furthermore used Marx's scheme of simple reproduction, although it is totally irrelevant to the problem.

Thus, on the one hand, Sweezy was instrumental in bringing the existence of the transformation problem to a wide group of English-speaking Marxists. On the other hand, he was silent as to the implications of Bortkiewicz's neo-Ricardian position. Even worse, the solution he presented was confused and intertwined with extraneous and irrelevant factors. The overall combination could not help but discourage people from pursuing the problem further. The effect was thus to make serious discussions of the theory of value quite difficult, a result which is not inconsistent with Sweezy's later work which avoided the concepts of value and surplus value altogether, in favor of the ill-defined notion of the 'economic surplus'. (See, for example, Baran and Sweezy, 1966)

v The contemporary Neo-Ricardian critique

It was soon realized that the Bortkiewicz solution popularized by Sweezy was inadequate. The first to point this out was Winternitz, who showed that the schemes of simple reproduction had nothing to do with the transformation problem, even while he remained within the three-department approximation. (Winternitz, 1948) Winternitz's approach, which is closely related to input-output techniques rather than dated-labor techniques (the two are equivalent in the neo-Ricardian problematic) was generalized in a neglected paper by May, and by Seton, which removed the restrictiveness of the three-department model. (May, 1949; Seton, 1957)

At this point the nature and parameters of the problem had been almost completely specified. Unfortunately, the discussion took place in academic journals that are not very accessible to most Marxists, particularly in comparison to the popularizations of Sweezy and Mandel which ignored these advances. (Sweezy, 1968; Mandel, 1968) Furthermore, both May and Seton viewed the problem, in good neo-Ricardian style, as essentially a technical problem of mathematical economics. The role of value as the central category with which to understand the economic law of motion of the capitalist mode of production is a closed book to this school.

Following the publication of Seton's paper, which conclusively ended the debate about the mathematical factors involved, the discussion has proceeded in a couple of related directions. On the one hand, there have been attempts to find the most general mathematical statements that can be made about the value and price systems. (See, for example, Morishima, 1973, 1974; Okishio, 1963)

On the other hand, the contemporary neo-Ricardian attack has forced Marxists to clarify the fundamental aspects of the problem. (For the neo-Ricardian attack on Marxism, see, Steedman, 1972, 1973, 1975a, 1975b; Hodgson and Steedman, 1975; Hodgson 1973, 1975; for Marxist responses see Laibman, 1974; Yaffe, 1974, Shaikh, 1974) I shall enter this debate after a brief discussion of the Winternitz-Seton solution.

Seton's generalization of Winternitz's 1948 solution begins with Eq. (1), generalized to the case of N commodities,

$$w_i = c_i + v_i + s_i \tag{12}$$

Using the definition of 'cost price', k_i, given in Eq. (6) this can be written,

$$w_i = k_i + s_i \tag{13}$$

Now Seton noted that the value of the constant capital, c_i, is composed of the sum of the values of all of the means of production used in producing commodity i. Let c_{ij} be the value of commodity j transferred to commodity i in the course of production of one unit of the latter. Then,

$$c_i = \sum_j c_{ij} \tag{14}$$

Similarly, the value of labour power is the sum of the values of all of the commodities, including services, socially necessary to reproduce it.[36] Thus, letting v_{ij} be the value of commodity j necessary to produce the labor power needed to produce one unit of commodity i, we have,

$$v_i = \sum_j v_{ij} \tag{15}$$

and

$$k_i = \sum_j (c_{ij} + v_{ij}) = \sum_j k_{ij} \tag{16}$$

$$w_i = \sum_j k_{ij} + s_i \tag{17}$$

Now define x_i to be the transformation factor that modifies the value of commodity i. That is,

$$\bar{w}_i = x_i w_i \tag{18}$$

$$\bar{k}_i = \sum_j k_{ij} x_j \tag{19}$$

Seton's equation for the transformation from values to modified values is then,

$$x_i w_i = (1 + r) \sum_j k_{ij} x_j \tag{20}$$

That is, the modified value $\bar{w}_i$ exceeds the modified cost value $\bar{k}_i$ by an amount given by the rate of profit times the modified cost value.

Thus both inputs and outputs have been modified in a consistent manner. If we restrict ourselves to a world in which only three commodities are produced, and further specify that they are means of production, articles of consumption and luxury goods, corresponding to the decomposition of value into constant capital, variable capital and surplus value (in the model of simple reproduction) respectively, then Eq. (20) becomes Winternitz's model.

Eq. (20) has the following features. The unknowns in them are the n transformation coefficients x_i, one for each commodity, and the general rate of profit r. However, there are only n equations, one for each commodity. Thus, it appears at first sight that, with one less equation than the number of unknowns, Eq. (20) can be solved only to the extent of providing a single relationship between these unknowns. However, Eq. (20) is linear and homogeneous in the x's. That is, in every term one (and only one) x appears raised to the first power. This means that if we find a solution, say, X_1, X_2, . . X_N then aX_1, aX_2, . . . aX_N is also a solution where a is any constant, because the a's simple cancel out of all terms in Eqs. (20). Furthermore, it is a property of Eqs. (20) that they can be solved (in principle) for the rate of profit r, independent of the ambiguity in the normalization of the x's. There are, in general, n solutions for r. Presumably the largest is the one that corresponds to the actual rate of profit.

The upshot is that the entire ambiguity in Eqs. (20) concerns an overall normalization factor for the x's. This ambiguity can be resolved only by adding an independent normalization condition to Eqs. (20). *This normalization condition has nothing to do with the mathematics of the transformation procedure.* This, then, is a complete solution as far as the formal structure of the problem is concerned.

Seton's equations are not, in fact, the way that neo-Ricardians prefer to formulate the problem, even when they use the input-output type of approach.[37] Rather than using the value input-output coefficients, k_{ij}, that is, the *value* of commodity j needed to produce one unit of commodity i, the neo-Ricardians starts from physical (technical) input-output coefficients, a_{ij}, which are the *amount* (in appropriate physical units) of commodity j needed to produce one unit of commodity i. These technical coefficients are completed by specifying the amount of direct labor, 1_i, needed to combine the inputs a_{ij} and transform them into the output unit of i. From these coefficients two systems can be derived (see, for example, Morishima, 1973, for the most detailed exposition).

Value System

The value, w_i, of one unit of commodity i is the solution of,

$$w_i = \sum_j a_{ij} w_j + l_i \tag{21}$$

Price System

To derive the equations of the price system a couple of auxiliary concepts relating to wages must be introduced. Let b_i be the amount of commodity i necessary to produce one day's labor power, and let T be the length of the working day. Then if the price of one unit of commodity i is denoted by p_i the p_i's will be the solution of,

$$p_i = (1 + r) \sum_j (a_{ij} p_j + \frac{l_i b_j p_j}{T}) \tag{22}$$

where the first term on the right hand side represents the cost price of the means of production and the second term the wage cost.

Eq. (21) states simply that the value of any commodity consists of the sum of the transferred value of the means of production and the new labor l_i. Eq. (22) is the analogue of Eq. (20). The neo-Ricardians usually do not include the second term on the right hand side because they view workers and capitalists as 'sharing' the net physical product. Thus they do not calculate profits on the capitalist's total outlay, but only on the outlay for constant capital. (See, for example, Sraffa, 1960) The ideological bias of neo-Ricardianism is clear here, as has been pointed out by Lebowitz (1974). However, even if this fundamental error is corrected, as has been done in constructing Eq. (22), the neo-Ricardian scheme remains inadequate, as will be seen. The point is important because this is precisely the correction made by Emmanuel in his discussion of Sraffa. (Emmanuel, 1972: Appendix V; see also Medio, 1972) Thus Emmanuel's criticism of Sraffa (and Ricardo) remains within the classical framework. It does not cross the critical boundary to Marxism, although it is doubtless a more sensible formulation than that of Sraffa.

Note that Eqs. (21) can be solved for the N values w_i since there are N equations and only N unknowns. Eqs. (22) have the structure of Eqs. (20). They can be solved for the rate of profit, r, and for the N prices, p_i, up to an overall normalization factor.

The neo-Ricardian critique of the Marxist solution can now be specified by relating Seton's Eq. (20) to Eq. (21). This has already been partially done by noting that the term $\sum_j a_{ij} w_j$ in Eq. (21) is the value of the constant capital transferred to the final product. Thus,

$$c_{ij} = a_{ij} w_j \tag{23}$$

The term, l_i is taken to be the newly created value. It can be broken down into the value of labor power and surplus value as follows. Since b_i is the set of commodities necessary to produce one day's labor power, $\sum_j b_j w_j$ is the value of that day's labor power. The working day T, then, decomposes into two parts:

(1) $\sum_j b_j w_j$, the value of labor power;
(2) $T - \sum_j b_j w_j$, surplus value.

So if l_i is written

$$l_i = l_i \left(\frac{\sum_j w_j b_j + T - \sum_j w_j b_j}{T}\right) \tag{24}$$

it has been divided into parts proportional to the value of labor power and surplus value. That is,

$$v_i = \frac{l_i \sum_j w_j b_j}{T} \tag{25}$$

$$v_{ij} = \frac{l_i w_j b_j}{T} \tag{26}$$

$$s_i = l_i \left(\frac{T - \sum_j w_j b_j}{T}\right) \tag{27}$$

Thus, Eq. (21) can be rewritten, using Eqs. (23), (26), and (27) as,

$$w_i = \sum_j c_{ij} + \sum_j v_{ij} + s_i \tag{28}$$

which is the form of Seton's equation. In other words, Seton's equation looks like a rewriting of the input-output equation for value.

However, and this is the crucial point, the neo-Ricardians claim that Eqs. (21) and (22) are primary. In fact, they say, why even bother to solve Eq. (21) for values when the transformation, as given by Eq. (22) is, in actuality, from physical inputs to prices? Even more, they argue, Seton's Eq. (20) is not a suitable starting point for carrying out the transformation procedure because his coefficients k_{ij} contain the values w_i, which themselves can only be computed from Eq. (21), that is, from the a_{ij}'s. Thus it is not a choice between two equally good starting points, the k_{ij} or the a_{ij}. Only the a_{ij}, say the neo-Ricardians, provide an adequate starting point.

In mathematical terms the argument runs as follows. Seton's Eq. (20) is useless, say the neo-Ricardians, unless we use Eqs. (23) and (26) to write,

$$k_{ij} = a_{ij}w_j + \frac{l_i b_j w_j}{T} \tag{29}$$

which, when substituted into Eq. (20) yields,

$$x_i w_i = (1 + r) \sum_j (a_{ij}w_j + \frac{l_i b_j w_j}{T}) x_j \tag{30}$$

But this is exactly the neo-Ricardian transformation Eq. (22) if we identify

$$p_i = w_i x_i \tag{31}$$

Thus, the neo-Ricardians argue, either Eq. (20) is meaningless, or it must be supplemented with additional information, namely the a_{ij} and the l_i. But then why bother to go through these steps, since this supplemental information only turns Eq. (20) into Eq. (22), which could have been derived directly from the a_{ij} and the l_i in the first place? The argument, in short, is that the transformation is really from physical inputs to prices. The transformation from values to modified values is an intermediate step in this process and can equally well be omitted. The linking equation is Eq. (31), which links prices to modified values, and hence to values.

This argument is implicit in all discussion of neo-Ricardian solutions. It has been made explicitly most recently by Steedman (1975a: 78–9, esp. Fig. 1). Joan Robinson too is quite straightforward about it, '. . . the *values* which have to be "transformed into prices" are arrived at in the first place by transforming prices into *values*.' (Robinson, 1950: 363) Curiously, Yaffe accepts this logic:

> Only an empiricist methodology saves the other critics of Marx from Bortkiewicz's eventual conclusion 'we are thus driven to reject Marx's derivation of price and profit from value and surplus value'. (Yaffe, 1974: 32n)

It is important to clarify exactly what is wrong with this argument. Not to do so would be either to leave oneself open to neo-Ricardianism or to put oneself into Yaffe's position. I have complicated Eq. (22) by adding the second term on the right hand side in order to be able to locate the flaw precisely. It is not Sraffa's ideological position that capitalists do not make profit on variable capital that is essential. As mentioned above, Emmanuel's model corrects this point yet still leads to the neo-Ricardian conclusions concerning the relationship of price and value, as Emmanuel himself knows quite well,

> It is, I think, this contrast between absolute value and relative value that is the crux of my disagreement with Charles Bettelheim. I do not believe in absolute value. (Emmanuel, 1972: 326)

The problem with the neo-Ricardian critique lies in their misunderstanding of the nature of the commodity as discussed in the very first pages of *Capital* (see Section II, above). For Marx, a commodity is the unity of two contradictory aspects—use value and value. The neo-Ricardian insistence on the primacy of the a_{ij} and the subordinate and derived status of the w_i denies this unity. *They reduce commodities to their use value alone, and derive values (which naturally then have very little meaning or use) from the physical relationships of these use values.*

Recall that the dual nature of the commodity rested upon a more fundamental duality, that of labor. *Abstract labor, as such, nowhere appears in the neo-Ricardian formulation.* The quantities l_i represent concrete labor. But the substance of value is abstract labor. I have argued that these two aspects of labor are irreducible. Marx's theory of value is not a theory of price. Thus it is Eq. (21) that is wrong. Involving only technical coefficients, as it does, this equation denies the historical nature of commodity production.

Perhaps the best comparison between the neo-Ricardian approach to the transformation problem and the Marxist approach comes from contrasting Eqs. (18) and (31). The difference appears quite sharply. The Marxist approach transforms values into modified values. Value is the fundamental category on both ends of the transformation. The neo-Ricardian approach transforms values into prices. Thus the independent existence of value is denied because it does not survive the process of transformation. In fact, since the input values are simply calculated from technical coefficients, value is cut out as a category althogether. Thus the technical basis on which to maintain a Marxist approach in the face of the neo-Ricardian challenge is found in insisting on the fundamental nature of value, and, more fundamentally, between two levels of theoretical construction.[38]

In short, not surprisingly the neo-Ricardians exhibit exactly the limitations that Marx criticized in Ricardo. They do not distinguish between concrete labor and abstract labor, and so cannot ask 'why labor is represented by the value of its product . . .' For them, production is a matter only of technique. Production relations are conceived of as technical relations, while distribution relations, understood as the respective shares of capital and labor in the net product, are social relationships. Seton's Eq. (20) is correct from the Marxist point of view for the precise reason it is unsatisfactory to the neo-Ricardians. It involves both technical coefficients, the a_{ij} and the l_i, and abstract labor w_i. This is no disadvantage but expresses the two-fold nature of the commodity and is a reminder that Marx's theory of value is not a theory of price in the strong sense. The neo-Ricardians, holding opposite views on all of these matters, wind up by completely liquidating the category of value from their considerations.

vi The problem of normalization

The question of normalization can now be discussed. As with so many of the issues raised by the transformation problem it has been the subject of a seemingly endless debate. Seton was the first to show systematically that the difference between various solutions lay in their choice of normalization. Marx himself initiated the discussion by the emphasis he placed upon the fact that in his solution total value equals total price and total surplus value equals total profit. Subsequently, when it was discovered that these conditions could not be maintained simultaneously when both inputs and outputs are transformed (essentially because there is only one degree of freedom to the solution) several candidates were put forward in the form of quantities whose magnitude would remain invariant under the transformation.[39]

It is sometimes denied that a normalization condition can be at all meaningful. Thus, Seton, who maintains the correctness of and necessity for transforming values, claims that there can be no basis for choosing a normalization,

> The point which concerns us here is that *the principle of equal profitability in conjunction with any one invariance postulate will completely determine all prices* and thereby solve the transformation problem. However, there does not seem to be an objective basis for choosing any particular invariance postulate in preference to all the others, *and to that extent the transformation problem may be said to fall short of complete determinacy.* (Seton, 1957: 153)

By 'objective basis' Seton means, of course, mathematical necessity following from the equalization of the rate of profit. This is where Seton's commitment to classical political economy is made manifest. The denial of the 'non-economic' nature of the criteria leading to a choice of normalization, and of the necessity to make a correct choice, is the final refuge for those who attempt to use the transformation problem as the basis for an attack on the theory of value. In fact, the problem of correct normalization cannot be solved by formal mathematics.

The necessity for choosing a normalization lies in the concept of value itself, together with the approach taken here which holds that it is value that appears at both ends of the transformation. Normalization converts the transformation from one yielding only relative modified values to one yielding absolute modified values. Now, in fact, the question of absolute as opposed to relative value does not first arise in the transformation problem. It appears at the level of Volume I, when Marx moves from the phenomenal existence of exchange value, a relative concept, to the existence of value itself, an absolute concept. He does not give an argument for the existence of value but makes an assertion: 'The properties of a thing are not the result of its relations to other things but only manifest themselves in such relations . . .' (Marx, n.d.: 63) This assertion is a crucial element of Marx's value theory[40] The existence of value, the link between production and circulation, is intimately connected with its existence as an absolute, and not merely a relative, concept.

Far from being a subordinate, side aspect of the transformation problem, something in the nature of a loose end, *normalization is, in fact, the central aspect.*[41] Indeed, it is the mathematics embodied in Eqs. (20) that is the subordinate aspect. The derivation of Eqs. (20) required no great insight. They are simply the mathematical expression for the equality of profit rates. This is easily understandable since they refer to a problem that has its roots in circulation, the nondominant aspect of the economic region. Solving these equations exactly is beyond our capability, but it entails no conceptual problems outside of those located in the fact that Marx's value theory is, in the first place, not a quantitive theory of price but of price changes. Viewing the transformation problem as a transformation from production in itself to the unity of production and circulation linked by value, however, we see that it is precisely the normalization that provides the link. Without normalization, only a transformation to relative modified value exists, which is not surprising since only the requirement of equal profitability has been imposed. It is normalization that insures that the linkage between production and circulation has been constructed properly.

In this light, the choice of normalization is fairly obvious. For total value is the link between production and circulation, and so it must remain invariant. Thus, in addition to Eqs. (20) a final equation specifies the transformation problem completely. It is,

$$\sum_i w_i = \sum_i w_i x_i \qquad (32)$$

Only this choice insures that value, a social property of commodities, continues to be the same property after transformation as before, although its significance has changed. It is no problem that this is insured only at the level of total value, for value is, in the first place, a social quantitiy, the value of individual commodities existing only as fractions of the total social value. *Thus the transformation problem is not a transformation of value into something else, but a modification of the specific weights carried by commodities as parts of the invariant total value.*

Recently it has been shown that Marx's own solution is the first step of an iterative solution to the correct Eq. (20). (Shaikh, 1974; see also Morishima, 1973, 1975) Shaikh asserts that the iterative solution is somehow truer to Marx's intentions than an algebraic solution would be. (Actually, it is impossible to solve Eqs. (20) in the general case without some method of approximation.) This assertion is hardly tenable. A method of calculation is only that—a method. If, starting from the same input, two methods of calculation yield the same result, then they are equivalent. One or the other may be more transparent, or illuminate different aspects of the problem, but it cannot be asserted that one is 'right' and the other 'wrong'. Shaikh sees method of calculation rather than normalization as the choice. For him, the problem of normalization only arises from 'a confusion between value and exchange value.' (Shaikh, 1974: 25) However, Shaikh too has to choose a normalization condition in order to carry out the iteration procedure, which, in fact, will only be a solution if the same normalization is chosen at each iteration. He chooses total value invariance. Of course, starting from Marx's own solution one could equally well choose surplus value invariance and arrive at a 'correct' solution. Thus the method of calculation can in no way avoid the crucial problem of choosing a normalization. Shaikh's demonstration provides a valuable clarification of the transformation problem. However, he goes too far in asserting that an algebraic solution 'severs' the link between value and exchange value and 'forces' one to 'reject' Marx's solution. The link is severed only if the normalization is incorrectly chosen, and this choice is independent of the equations that express equal profitability.

With this solution to the transformation problem it will in general not be the case that total real surplus value is equal to total real profit. It is true that Marx emphasized this condition as much as, or even more than, that of total value invariance. From this it is sometimes maintained that the impossibility of the simultaneous validity of these two invariance conditions is a proof of the inconsistency of the transformation procedure or even of the theory of value itself.

In fact, the argument for total surplus value invariance is not a strong one. Recall that total value invariance is fundamental. It insures that value, as a social category, is present on both sides of the transformation. However, while surplus value is present at the level of production in itself, profit is not. Profit is a category that develops only at the level of the unity of production and circulation, since it is a category that develops out of capitalist competition. Thus profit is not a value form, but enters with exchange value and price.[42] Because profit is not a value form there are no fundamental arguments that demand its invariance. Indeed, as an exchange-value and price form profit shares the property of all such forms that they can differ from the value that underlies them.[43]

The possibility of a divergence between real surplus value and real profit is sometimes denied on the ground that it is essential to Marx's theory of exploitation that profit be a converted form of surplus value. Two responses can be made. The first is that, as discussed above, the theory of surplus value is not primarily a proof of exploitation but an element in understanding the development of the capitalist mode of production. If in this case real profit is not equal to real surplus value, then so be it. We will presumably learn something about the economic laws of motion that was not previously known. In the second place, it has been shown that real profit is nonzero if and only if real surplus value is nonzero (see, for example, Morishima, 1974)[44] Thus the deviation between the two is just that, a deviation. There is always a nonzero core of real profit that is equal to real surplus value (even if the deviation is negative).

The technical reason that real profit and real surplus value may deviate from one another is simple. Total value is invariant. However, its parts need not be, and in general will not be, invariant as well. In particular, the total value of labor power and the total value of constant capital may lie above or below their respective modified values. Thus the difference between profit and real surplus value is rooted in the difference between cost value and modified cost value. The discrepancy opens up an interesting possibility. Discussions of the falling rate of profit, one of Marx's economic laws of development, usually take place using an incorrect expression for the rate of profit, namely, that given by Marx's incorrect solution to the transformation problem, Eq. (4). Even so there is some question whether this quantity shows a tendency to fall. However, profit can and generally does deviate from surplus value, and this corresponds to an opposite deviation of cost price. If the deviation is in the direction of increasing profit over surplus value, then an entirely new mechanism countering the fall in the rate of profit is exhibited. Further investigation is required to determine the conditions under which this mechanism could be effective, and to correlate it with actual conditions. It remains the case, however, that there is not much point in discussing something as complicated as the falling rate of profit, while using the wrong expression for this rate.[45]

IV Summary

As a technical problem in mathematical economics the transformation problem is not difficult. The real difficulties arise in understanding between what objects the transformation operates. The position argued in this paper is that the transformation is between two theoretical levels, the first of which constructs the dominant instance of the economic level, namely production, while the second constructs the economic level as the complex unity of production and circulation. These theoretical steps are necessary not because they represent successive approximations to reality, that is, as models, but because this is the only way to clarify the articulation of a complex structure. In this sense the transformation problem we have been considering is only one of a set of such transformations, which arise whenever theoretical investigation increases the complexity of the level structure of a complex object. In the present case of the economic level of the capitalist mode of production the problem is complicated by the fact that the nondominant aspect, circulation, is nevertheless the place in which social links are created. It is this complication that leads to so many of the confusions that surround the transformation problems.

The analysis of value, the articulation of production and circulation, and the discussion of the transformation problem presented in this paper substantiate the view that Marx's work is not simply a superior version of bourgeois economic theory–replacing 'economics' with 'political economy,' or 'political economy' with 'radical political economy,' or even 'Marxist political economy.' Marx's scientific discovery is not a new version of a preexistent science, economics, but a new science, historical materialism. Of course, as much as the transformation problem is central in obtaining a correct understanding of the capitalist mode of production, it is still only preliminary. For the goal is to ground strategies and not simply to understand Marx's method. (Unfortunately, much of the debate between the neo-Ricardians and Marxists has been conducted as if this were what was at stake.) It is not so much a matter of crudely applying the transformation problem to concrete phenomena as of drawing appropriate conclusions at each level. An important area has been indicated in the discussion of the bourgeois class and the state in Section III. The positions grounded there in Marx's solution are even more secure in the light of the correct transformation. Thus the structure of the political level is articulated with the structure of the economic level in a concrete fashion. At the economic level itself a possible conclusion is contained in the suggestions made concerning the relationship of the falling rate of profit to the correct solution to the transformation problem.

In general, any discussion that would be grounded in the production relationships of the capitalist mode of production must take place in the light of the correct approach to and understanding of the transforamtion problem. And more than this, the kinds of transformation that are relevant to the transition from the competitive to the monopoly stage of capitalism must be investigated. Finally, the concept of the capitalist mode of production must be fully constructed and 'concrete analyses of concrete situations' produced. These are the kinds of analyses that have to be made, and the work has barely begun, in order to move debates about Marx's method.

Notes

1. A good survey of the neo-Ricardian critique of the neo-classical synthesis is that of Harcourt (1972); see also Hunt and Schwartz (1972), and Harcourt and Laing (1971). The classical statement is that of Sraffa (1960). Lebowitz (1974) suggests that the proponents of the two theories be identified with two sectors of the bourgeoisie, rentiers for the non-classical school (here Lebowitz follows Bukharin, 1972), and technocrats for the neo-Ricardians, and thus connects the theoretical struggle with a class struggle within the bourgeoisie.
.2 For the beginnings of such an assessment see Szymanski (1973), whose assessment, with which I concur, is that Baran and Sweezy misread contemporary capitalism because they 'generalize from the special conditions of the postwar era, to general laws of monopoly capitalism prematurely'. See also Mattick (1969).
3. Criticisms of the Second International are abundant. See for example, Colletti, 1972: 45-108; for the Third International see the important work by Bettelheim (1974).
4. 'Once for all I may here state, that by classical Political Economy, I understand that economy which, since the time of W. Petty, has investigated the real relationships in bourgeois society, in contradistinction to vulgar economy, which deals in appearances only, ruminates without ceasing on materials long since provided by scientific economy, and there seeks plausible explanations for the most obstrusive phenomena, for bourgeois daily use, but for the rest, confines itself to systematizing in a pedantic way, and proclaiming for everlasting truths, the trite ideal held by the self-complacent bourgeoisie with regard to their own world, to them the best of all possible worlds.' (Marx, n.d.: 85n) Keynes' definition of classical political economy eliminates the category of vulgar economy. (Keynes, 1964: 3n) The neo-classicists go him one better by calling Marx's classical school preclassical. They themselves are an outstanding example of what Marx meant by vulgar economy. The dogmatic which formed an important component of the Second and Third Internationals can be classified as vulgar Marxism according to Marx's own definition.
5. This was clarified by Gramsci in his prison writings 'When you don't have the initiative in the struggle and the struggle itself comes to be identified with a series of defeats, mechanical determinism becomes a tremendous force of moral resistance, of cohesion and of patient and obstinate perseverance. "I have been defeated for the moment, but the tide of history is working for me in the long term"' (Gramsci, 1971: 336)

6. Several attempts to draw this line have been made recently. See for example, Rowthorn (1974); Medio (1972); Lebowitz (1974); Roosevelt (1975).
7. Of necessity I have presented the barest outline of Althusser's structural theory. For details see Althusser and Balibar (1970), especially pp. 165 ff., 225–53. An extremely important but not widely read essay from the first edition of *Reading Capital* is once again in print. (Establet, 1973) In this essay Establet locates the articulations of *Capital* in much the same way that I do, although he does not focus on the importance of the transformation problem to concretize his 'articulation II.'
8. Balibar shares certain positions with vulgar Marxism in so far as he tends to consider the economic level in its productive aspect alone. Thus he does not consider the articulation between production and circulation which is such a crucial feature of *Capital.* This reductionist perspective goes hand in hand with his identification of the concept of 'mode of production' with the economic level alone, that has been criticized by Poulantzas (1973), p. 13.
9. 'For all the controversy generated by the "labor theory of value" it was tangential to classical value theory, and seldom was it even alleged that any substantive conclusion would be different without it.' (Sowell, 1974: 110)
10. These issues are still very much alive. Aspects of Smith's theory have been revived by Emmanuel in his theory of unequal exchange, although he presents it in an apparently Marxist framework. Emmanuel's work is an example of an attempted reconstruction of Marxism that winds up as a revival of classical polical economy. (Emmanuel, 1972)
11. 'All the implements necessary to kill the beaver and deer might belong to one class of men, and the labor employed in their destruction might be furnished by another class; still their comparative prices would be in proportion to the actual labor bestowed, both on the formation of the capital and on the destruction of the animals. Under different circumstances of plenty or scarcity of capital, as compared with labor, under different conditions of plenty or scarcity of the food and necessaries essential to the support of men, those who furnished an equal value of capital for either one employment or for the other might have a half, a fourth, or an eighth of the produce obtained, the remainder being paid as wages to those who furnished the labor; yet this division could not affect the relative value of the commodities. . .' (Ricardo, 1965: 13–14)
12. Underlying this paper is the view that there is no such thing as 'Marxist Political Economy.' Marx founded a new science, historical materialism, rather than improving an old one, whether it be called economics or political economy.
13. This has nothing to do with the question of market fluctuations. Ricardo's labor prices are the center of market price fluctuations just as are Marx's exchange values. The distinction between value and price is not to be found in the process of exchange but in the articulation of production and exchange.
14. This is one of Sweezy's errors. Indeed he refers to the 'qualitative value problem' and the 'quantitative value problem' as if they were somehow two separable things. (Sweezy, 1968: 23, 41)
15. The United States has maintained its lead in this questionable endeavor. Braverman (1974) shows how far we have come in making abstract labor a social reality.
16. An example of this ambiguous terminology, in an area of great importance, is found in the notion of *organic composition of capital.* In the first volume of *Capital* Marx writes, 'I call the value composition, in so far as it is determined by its technical composition *and mirrors changes of the latter* [my emphasis] the *organic composition* of capital.' (Marx, n.d.: 574) On the other hand, in Volume

III we find, 'The value-composition of capital, in as much as it is determined by, and reflects, its technical composition is called the *organic* composition of capital.' (Marx, 1971: 145–46) The Volume I definition makes organic composition a more inherently dynamic quantity than does the Volume III definition. In any event, it is fairly safe to say that almost no one treats organic composition as dynamic. Thus, when organic composition is used it is really value composition that is meant. The exception to this is Morishima, who discusses just this point. He misses, however, the fact that even value composition must be thought of as a dynamic quantity. (Morishima, 1973: 34–35)

17. It is perhaps worth noting that the major alternative to making the transformation problem the site of the unity between production and circulation is to locate this unity in the reproduction schemes. This was Luxemburg's choice. Thus we can say that while Luxemburg recognized the necessity to construct a complex unity of production and circulation, her choice of solution condemned her to a simple unity emphasizing circulation. In this regard see the comments of Palloix (1975: Vol. II, 41). See also Establet (1973).

18. For an extended statement see Steedman (1973: 40–41) and Bose (1975). General proofs of the theorem, using elegant mathematical techniques, are given by Okisio (1963) and Morishima (1973, 1974). Hodgson (1975) argues that neo-Ricardian results are simply statements of formal logic that can be given either Ricardian or Marxist content, a point of view with which I disagree.

19. See Marx's critique of Ravenstone, Hodgskin, and Bray. (Marx, 1971b: 238–325)

20. This passage appears in a discussion of the genesis of capitalist ground rent, that is, in a discussion of the transition between two modes of production characterized by different mechanisms of surplus extraction: feudalism by rent, and capitalism by surplus value.

21. Some thorny problems of interpretation crop up when we try to maintain a correct understanding of value and still follow Marx's own arguments. I have argued that Marx's theory is, in principle, not a theory of price, but at best of price changes. Yet it seems to be necessary to refer to commodities exchanging at their values. Probably a better language is needed, perhaps more mathematical. In the absence of this development the special and restricted meaning of statements such as that in the text above must be kept in mind. Part of the problem cannot be overcome since it lies in Marx's method. Volume I refers to a (nonexistent) world of production considered abstractly. This is not a model, that is, an approximation to reality which will later be corrected. Volume I deals with production because it is the dominant structure. Nevertheless, the categories used refer to circulation, and, moreover, will change meaning when circulation is introduced explicitly.

22. This is obviously a very complex idea, for labor power is not like other commodities but is unique. Some of the questions this raises are the significance to be attributed to the 'moral and historical' element in the value of labor power, and the way in which the domestic work of production and reproduction of labor power interconnects with capitalist commodity production.

23. Questions can be entertained about the validity of this statement. In the first place, there is the matter of skills and skilled workers, the value of whose labor power is greater than that of unskilled workers. This difficulty can, perhaps, be handled within Marx's framework. A more serious problem is the existence of structured labor markets as an apparently fundamental feature of the current stage of the capitalist mode of production. Marx predicted a trend toward the homogeneity of labor, instead the trend may be toward duality.

Finally there is the question of how these difficulties relate to the notion of the labor aristocracy, itself a problematic conception. See Braverman (1974) for a recent statement of some of these problems.
24. For a discussion of the use of the concept 'tendency' in classical political economy see Sowell (1974: 132-35).
25. Just as with labor market structure there is the problem of capital structure. In fact, the two are related. Capital is not perfectly free to move at will. Monopoly, one of the many tendencies of the development of the capitalist mode of production, limits this motion. The question that must be faced is to what extent these features are sufficiently basic to modify the concept of value in a fundamental way. See, for example, O'Connor (1973)
26. I have assumed that there is no fixed capital. This in no way affects the argument.
27. I have avoided using the concept of organic composition for the reasons outlined above in note 16. As written, c/v is actually the value composition of capital. Organic composition refers to particular kinds of value changes, either over time or between industries.
28. This argument is only an indication since it does not take into account the capitalist's motive for introducing new machinery—cheapening the unit cost of production. Nevertheless, no capitalist acts as if his profit comes from his workers alone. This is, as we shall see, a correct perception.
29. As shall be seen, this is where Marx goes partially astray. Eq. (1) structures the total social capital and the pieces of this structure are affected by the introduction of circulation.
30. Marx explained this transformation algorithm using numerical examples. The algebraic discussion in the text is completely equivalent to Marx's tables (Marx, 1971a: 154-57). Algebraically it is immaterial which of Eqs. (4) or (10) is taken to be the definition of R and which is regarded as derived. It is more consistent with the structure of Marx's argument to take Eq. (4) to be more fundamental.
31. This point has been made before. It is emphasized by May (1948, 1949), Yaffe (1974) and Shaikh (1974). Shaikh, however, maintains that w_i and $\bar{w}_i$ are exchange values rather than values.
32. This position is discussed at length, although from a slightly different point of view, by Poulantzas (1973).

Very suggestive is Balibar's demonstration that the connection between the legal and economic structures of the capitalist mode of production is located in the connection between production and circulation. (Althusser and Balibar, 1970: 231)
33. In this regard see Mattick (1972) for a similar point of view developed in the context of a critique of Samuelson's position.
34. For Hilferding's reply see Sweezy (1949).
35. There have been attempts to speculate why Marx did not proceed further to transform inputs. Hodgson blames it on Marx's poor knowledge of mathematical technique (Hodgson, 1973: 51), while Mattick guessed that Marx felt it to be unnecessary because a correct solution would have been no more illuminating than the one he used. (Mattick, 1972: 271)
36. This has been the subject of a broad discussion recently. The problem is the contribution that unpaid domestic work makes to the value of labor power. The statement in the text assumes that this labor does not contribute to the value of labor power. This is argued for in Gerstein (1973).
37. I shall not consider the technique that treats capital simply as dated labor inputs. I have already commented, in section II above, on the ideological implication of ignoring the qualitative difference between labor power and

constant capital located in the fact that they are owned by two different classes.
38. The second Bortkiewicz solution, as transmitted by Sweezy (1949, 1968), makes this error in a particularly confusing manner. Bortkiewicz's solution, as with all solutions in unique up to an overall normalization. Bortkiewicz specified the normalization by setting x_3, the transformation coefficient in the luxury goods sector, equal to unity. He then identified this sector with the production of the money commodity. Thus Bortkiewicz made the transformation one from value to price through the back door, so to speak, introducing the price of money (a meaningless concept) through the normalization condition.
39. A clear discussion of the various choices is given by Seton (1957) and Laibman (1974).
40. Marx expands on his insistence on absolute value in his comments on Bailey, who attacked Ricardo by asserting that value was only meaningful as a relative concept. (Marx, 1971b: 124–68) Playing down the importance of normalization falls into precisely this error.
41. This position is taken by Laibman (1974) also, although for different reasons.
42. It is this correct understanding of profit that leads Shaikh astray. He holds that '*Value* stems from production,' while '*price* and *exchange value,* on the other hand, stem from circulation.' From this he concludes that the transformation does not operate at the level of value but is a 'transformation from real price equal to values to real price of production.' (Shaikh, 1974: 20, 21) The premise is wrong. Exchange value does not stem from circulation, it stems from production and appears in circulation. Shaikh attributes the special property of profit, that it is a category that first appears at the level of the unity of production and circulation, and so appears only as exchange value, to exchange value itself.
43. 'The possibility, therefore of quantitative incongruity between price and magnitude of value, or the deviation of the former from the latter, is inherent in the price-form itself. This is no defect, but, on the contrary, admirably adapts the price-form to a mode of production whose inherent laws impose themselves only as the mean of apparently lawless irregularities that compensate one another.' (Marx, n.d.: 104)
44. Steedman (1975a) has 'constructed' a counterexample to this theorem in the case of joint production, while Hodgson and Steedman (1975) argue that fixed capital must be thought of as joint production. Thus, they challenge Morishima's result in the presence of fixed capital. However, their proof is carried out within the neo-Ricardian framework of the identity of concrete labor and abstract labor, and so, despite their intent, does not 'disprove' Marx's value theory.
45. Again the Marxist solution to the transformation problem leads to a different point of view than the neo-Ricardian solution. See, for example, Steedman's (1975) remarks on the falling rate of profit.

References

Althusser, L. and Balibar, E. (1970). *Reading Capital,* New Left Books, London.
Baran P. and Sweezy P. (1966). *Monopoly Capital,* Monthly Review Press, New York.
Bettelheim, C. (1974). *Les Luttes de Classes en URSS, lère përiode 1917–1923,* Maspéro/Seuil, Paris.
Böhm-Bawerk, E. von (1949). 'Karl Marx and the Close of His System,' in Sweezy P. (1949). (Original Version, 1898)
Bortkiewicz, L. von (1949). 'On the Correction of Marx's Fundamental Theoretical Construction in the Third Volume of *Capital,*' in Sweezy, P. (1949).

(Original Version, 1907)
— (1952). 'Value and Price in the Marxian System,' *International Economic Papers*, No. 2, 5–60. (Original Version, 1907).
Bose, A. (1975). *Marxian and Post-Marxian Political Economy*, Penguin Books, Baltimore.
Braverman, H. (1974). *Labor and Monopoly Capital*, Monthly Review Press, New York.
Bukharin, N. (1972). *The Economic Theory of the Leisure Class*, Monthly Review Press, New York.
Colletti, L. (1972). *From Rousseau to Lenin*, New Left Books, London.
Emmanuel, A. (1972). *Unequal Exchange*, Monthly Review Press, New York.
Establet, R. (1973). *Lire le Capital IV*, François Maspéro, Paris.
Gerstein, I (1973). 'Domestic Work and Capitalism,' *Radical America*, Vol. 7, July-October, 101–28.
Gramsci, A. (1971). *Selections from the Prison Notebooks*, International Publishers, New York.
Harcourt, G. (1972). *Some Cambridge Controversies in the Theory of Capital*. Cambridge University Press, Cambridge.
Harcourt, G. and Laing, N. (1971). *Capital and Growth*, Penguin Books, Baltimore.
Hodgson, G. (1973). 'Marxist Epistemology and the Transformation Problem,' *Bulletin of the Conference of Socialist Economists*, Autumn, 47–63.
— (1975), 'Communication,' *New Left Review*, No. 90, March-April, 110–12.
Hodgson, G and Steedman, I (1975). 'Fixed Capital and Value Analysis,' *Bulletin of the Conference of Socialist Economists*, June, unpaginated.
Hunt, E. and Schwartz, J. (1972). *A Critique of Economic Theory*, Penguin Books, Baltimore.
Keynes, J. (1964). *The General Theory of Employment, Interest, and Money* Harcourt, Brace, and World, New York.
Laibman, D. (1974). 'Values and Prices of Production,' *Science and Society*, Vol. 37, Winter, 404–36.
Lebowitz, M. (1974). The Current Crises of Economic Theory,' *Science and Society*, vol. 37, Winter, 385–403.
Mandel, E. (1968). *Marxist Economic Theory*, Monthly Review Press, London.
Marx, K. *Capital*, Vol. I (n.d.); Vol. II (1967); Vol. III (1971a), Progress Publishers, Moscow. (Original Version, Vol I, 1867; Vol. II, 1885; Vol. III, 1894).
— (1971b). *Theories of Surplus Value* Vol. III, Progress Publishers, Moscow.
— (1972). *A Contribution to the Critique of Political Economy*, International Publishers, New York.
Marx, K and Engels, F (1965). *Selected Correspondence*, Progress Publishers, Moscow.
— (1968). *Selected Works in One Volume*, International Publishers, New York.
Mattick, P. (1972). 'Samuelson's 'Transformation' of Marxism into Bourgeois Economics,' *Science and Society*, Vol. 36, Fall, 258–73.
— (1975). 'Marxism and *Monopoly Capital*,' Root and Branch. (Original Version, 1969).
May, K. (1948). 'Value and Price of Production: A Note on Winternitz's Solution.' *Economic Journal*, December, 596–99.
— (1959). 'The Structure of Classical Value Theories,' *Review of Economic Studies*, Vol. 17, 60–69.
Medio, A. (1972). 'Profit and Surplus-Value: Appearance and Reality in Capitalist Production,' in Hunt and Schwartz (1972), 312–46.
Morishima, M. (1973). *Marx's Economics*, Cambridge University Press, Cambridge.
— (1974). 'Marx in the Light of Modern Economic Theory,' *Econometrica*, Vol. 42, July, 611–32.
O'Connor, J. (1973). *The Fiscal Crisis of the State*, St. Martins Press, New York.
Okisio, N. (1963). 'A Mathematical Note on Marxian Theorems,' *Weltwirtschaftliches Arkiv*, Vol. 91, 287–99.
Palloix, C. (1975). *L'économie mondiale capitaliste et les firmes multinationales*, François Maspéro, Paris.
Poulantzas, N. (1973). *Political Power and Social Classes*, New Left Books, London.
Ricardo, D. (1965). *The Principles of Political Economy and Taxation*, Everyman's Library, London. (Original Version, 1821, 3rd ed.)
Robinson, J. (1950). 'Karl Marx and the Close of His System (Review),' *Economic Journal*, Vol. 60, June, 358–63.
Rowthorn, B. (1974). 'Neo-Classicism, Neo-Ricardianism, and Marxism,' *New Left Review*, No. 86, July-August, 63–87.
Roosevelt, F. (1975). 'Cambridge Economics as Commodity Fetishism', *Review of Radical Political Economics*, Vol. 7, Winter, 1–32.
Samuelson, P. (1969). 'The Transformation from Marxian "Values" to Competitive "Prices": A Process of Rejection and Replacement.' *Proceedings of the National Academy of Sciences*, Vol. 67, September, 423–25.
— (1971). 'Understanding the Marxian Notion of Exploitation: A Summary of the So-Called Transformation Problem between Marxian Values and Competitive Prices.' *Journal of Economic Literature*, Vol. 9, June, 399–431.
Seton, F. (1957). 'The "Transformation Problem" ', *Review of Economic Studies*, Vol. 24, June, 149–60.
Shaikh, A. (1974). 'Marx's Theory of Value and the So-Called "Transformation Problem" ', New School for Social Research (mimeograph), September.

Smith, A. (1965). *An Inquiry into the Nature and Causes of the Wealth of Nations*, Modern Library, New York. (Original Version, 1776).

Sowell, T. (1974). *Classical Economics Reconsidered*, Princeton University Press, Princeton.

Sraffa, P. (1960). *The Production of Commodities by Means of Commodities*, Cambridge University Press, Cambridge.

Steedman, I. (1972). 'Marx on the Rate of Profit,' *Bulletin of the Conference of Socialist Economists*, Winter, 104–109.

– (1973). 'The Transformation Problem Again,' *Bulletin of the Conference of Socialist Economists*, Autumn, 37–41.

– (1975a). 'Value, Price, and Profit.' *New Left Review*, No. 90, March-April, 71–80.

Steedman, I. (1975b). 'Positive Profits with Negative Surplus Value,' *Economic Journal*, Vol. 85, March, 114–23.

Sweezy, P. (1949). *Karl Marx and the Close of His System*, Augustus M. Kelly, New York.

– (1968). *The Theory of Capitalist Development*, Monthly Review Press, New York.

Szymanski, A. (1973). 'Military Spending and Economic Stagnation,' *American Journal of Sociology*, Vol. 79, July, 1–14.

– (1974). 'Reply to Critics,' *American Journal of Sociology*, Vol. 79, May, 1462–1477.

Winternitz, J. (1948). 'Values and Prices: A Solution of the So-Called Transformation Problem,' *Economic Journal*, Vol. 58, June, 276–80.

Yaffe, D. (1973). 'Value, Price and the Neo-Ricardians: An Introductory Note,' *Bulletin of the Conference of Socialist Economists*, Autumn, 42–46.

– (1974). 'Fundamental Questions of Marxist Theory,' *Revolutionary Communist*, No. 1, 31–49.

CHAPTER 4

Transformations of physical conditions of production: Steedman's economic metaphysics*

Heiner Ganssmann

Abstract

Steedman's rejection of Marx's theory of value rests on the proposition that one can derive both values and prices from physical conditions of production, the real wage and the capitalist drive to accumulate. This proposition is examined with respect to the kind of relations assumed to rule among both economic agents and economic objects in order to accomplish the transformations of physical data into values and prices. It is argued that the transformations not only rest on the adoption of an equilibrium framework, but that they also are rooted in metaphysical notions endowing physical conditions of production with the properties requisite to derive from them economic determinations. It follows that there is no need to accept the 'Sraffa-based critique of Marx', whatever problems one may have with Marx.

In his *Marx after Sraffa,*[1] Steedman arrives at the conclusion that 'Marx's value reasoning . . . must . . . be abandoned, in the interest of developing a coherent materialist theory of capitalism' (p. 207). This conclusion rests on the following basic arguments:

(A1) the demonstration that Marx did not solve the problem of transforming values into prices of production and arrived at false propositions as to the nature of their connection;

(A2) the demonstration that correct determinations of prices of production, the rate of profit, and accumulation are derivable from physical conditions of production, the real wage, and the capitalist drive to accumulate;

(A3) the demonstration that values are equally derivable from these data but remain without relevance for the determinations of prices and profits.

If these three arguments are sound, Steedman's conclusion as to the obsolescence of Marx's theory of value is justified.

Enough has been written on argument (A1). I will discuss arguments (A2) and (A3), without bothering to deal with the more complex issues of accumulation. The discussion centres on the issue of the functions of a theory of value. What those functions are will, hopefully, become evident in what follows.

To a reader of Marx and Steedman who is unfamiliar with the usual 'arithmomorphism'[2] of mathematical economics, the arguments (A2) and (A3) are surprising mainly because of the proposition that one can derive values as well as prices from physical conditions of production, the real wage, and capitalist propensities. This should not be surprising. As it turns out, both values and prices are, for Steedman, nothing but 'transformed' physical data. I will illustrate the nature of these 'transformations' using Steedman's examples. Then, I will discuss their explanatory value.

1 Values

Under the usual assumptions for simple linear models, Steedman starts from the following description of an economy in physical terms (p. 38):

(Q)	i	L		i	g	c
industry i:	28	56	→	56	–	–
industry g:	16	16	→	–	48	–
industry c:	12	8	→	–	–	8
Total	56	80	→	56	48	8

(where i, g, c, L are iron, gold, corn, labour measured in physical units). From (Q), Steedman proceeds to determine values by recapitulating what Marx meant: 'By the value of a commodity, Marx meant the quantity of labour socially necessary for the production of that commodity' (pp. 39f.). Then, Steedman introduces a notation: 'Let the values of a unit of iron, a unit of gold and a unit of corn be denoted by l_i, l_g and l_c, respectively' (p. 40). Now, the crucial step is taken. It consists of transforming the descriptions in (Q) into equations:[3]

(V)

$$\begin{aligned} i:&\quad 28l_i + 56 = 56l_i \\ g:&\quad 16l_i + 16 = 48l_g \\ c:&\quad 12l_i + 8 = 8l_c \end{aligned}$$

Using equations (V), numbers for l_i, l_g and l_c are easily calculated. Steedman claims that these numbers are 'the values of the commodities (l_i= 2, l_g= 1, l_c= 4)' and that they 'have been determined solely from the physical data given' (p. 40).

Of course, physical data do not arrange themselves in the form of equations. In order to evaluate Steedman's claims we have to examine the presuppositions which allow for the transformation of (Q) into (V). Taking as an example the first row in (Q)

$$(28i, 56L) \rightarrow 56i$$

and in (V)

$$28l_i + 56 = 56l_i$$

we may simply note three differences: (a) the equational form, with an operation of addition and a relation of equality; (b) the disappearance of L; and (c) the substitution of entries l_i for entries i.

As to (a), the equational form seems to be quite unjustified unless we know more about the nature of processes of production (which seem to hide behind the connection '→'). While there may not be much of a problem with the entries for physical goods as inputs and outputs, the entries for labour ('naturally measured in time-units', p. 39) are something quite weird, because they depict a process – in contrast to the palpable, peaceful nature of physical goods. An operation of addition seems to be completely impossible in (Q), because one cannot add red beets to brown boots, just as one cannot add red beets and the process of growing red beets, to arrive at numbers of red beets. Finally, a relation of equality could hold in (Q), at best, among entries for identical physical goods as inputs and outputs, if we neglect the fact that they must appear at different points in time.

As to (b), the transformation of the entry 56L in (Q) into the entry 56 in (V) is explained by the desire to map the heterogeneous elements of production processes and their results into the one dimension of homogeneous labour. Thus, all entries in (V) are entries in terms of labour-time, so that the first row reads

$$28l_iL + 56L = 56l_iL$$

where L can be eliminated, of course.

As to (c), we can now account for this and the other differences between (Q) and (V) by specifying a general *rule of transformation* of physical data into values which Steedman seems to apply:

(1) $l_iL = i$ (i = 1, . . . , n; a list of all goods).

Whether one can derive values from physical data depends on possible justifications of this, or some similar, rule.

1.1 *Production and reproduction*

Before discussing the rule of transformation, a possible misunderstanding of Steedman's frame of reference has to be cleared away. One may be tempted to accept too literally Steedman's repeated claim that physical conditions of production, the real wage and the capitalist drive to accumulate are sufficient to derive either values or prices. Too literally, in the sense of a supposition that Steedman's derivation would be placed strictly in the context of production in physical terms.

Indeed, this is not the case. A look at (V) shows that specific relations between labour and goods have to be assumed to accomplish the derivation of values. These relations have certain properties, as the one of equality assumed in the rule of transformation. If it is required for the derivation of values to assume the relations between labour and goods to be, e.g. reflexive, symmetrical, and transitive, then reference to the context of production in physical terms is insufficient. Within this context, there is no logically consistent way to endow the relations between labour and goods with these properties. This can be seen by considering the time aspect of production.

In (Q), it is evident that physical inputs along with labour are used to produce physical output. The process of production takes time. The time dimension is also presupposed to be able to measure labour. Time is usually thought to be irreversible, so if we want to even start thinking about, say, symmetry in the relation between goods and quantities of living labour appearing at different points in time, we have to adopt some device to 'neutralize' time. The device is to refer to a system in a steady-state, capable of reproducing itself without change in an endless time horizon. Thus, the context of reference necessarily is one of *re*production, not simply one of production in physical terms.

There are several other ways to demonstrate that it is necessary to refer to the context of *re*production in order to derive either values or prices from physical conditions of production, the real wage, and the capitalist drive to accumulate. Such a demonstration is unnecessary, because Steedman is quite explicit on this point, listing among his assumptions, taken as read: 'The capitalist economies considered are always in a self-reproducing state, . . . so that production, exchange and distribution are always considered as a unity' (pp. 18f.) It is arguable that a repetition of this assumption in connection with the repeated claim of a derivability of values and prices from physical conditions of production, etc., would have an enlightening effect on Steedman's readers. But be that as it may, it is more interesting to examine the implications of this assumption.

In considering 'production, exchange and distribution . . . as a unity', unity can mean two things. It may mean the simple proposition that the distinguishable parts of the process of reproduction belong together. It may also mean that the exchange and distribution relations corresponding to and complementing a system of production are assumed to be in a state of equilibrium. I will argue that it is necessary for Steedman to assume such an equilibrium in order to accomplish his derivation of values and prices, the difference between the two derivations being that values are derived with the use of an equilibrium rule of exchange only, while the determination of the rate of profit and prices of production involves the additional adoption of an equilibrium rule of distribution among capitalists. The argument may not be surprising. After all, Sraffians work on the assumption that the market has done its job, whatever that job may be. But it may be of interest to clarify the extent to which this assumption equilibrates away traditional problems of economic theory, Marxist or not.

1.2 *The rule of transformation*

Formally, the rule of transformation (1) amounts to assuming relations between physical goods and labour, such that with each unit of a good appearing in (Q) we can associate a quantity of (homogeneous) labour. We call the number of hours of labour associated with each good its value. What are the relations which allow for the mapping of heterogeneous goods into the labour space (one-dimensional by assumption)?

Whatever else may be required, a precondition for the determination of values is the idea of a binary relation between goods and labour; to each unit of a physical good is to correspond a definite quantity of labour. For simple linear models, there usually are some assumptions which help ensure such a correspondence. Granted those, there is still a difficulty. In (Q), labour is not only associated with physical output (to the right of the '$\rightarrow$' symbolizing production), but also with physical inputs (to the left of '$\rightarrow$'). To establish a binary relation between goods and labour, one has to get rid of the (usually, heterogeneous) inputs. The first step in the determination of values could be taken by eliminating physical inputs in the form of a calculation of net output. The net output of each process is then associated with the living labour expended in this process in terms of a binary *relation of embodiment,* which may be presented in the following way

(2) $l_i L \dashrightarrow i$

(where '$\dashrightarrow$' stands for the relation 'is embodied in'). Before discussing the characteristics of this relation, the difficulty of arriving at it should be pointed out. With the exception of extremely simplified cases, it is not possible to calculate net output unless one has previously transformed physical inputs into values. For example, in row 2 of (Q), the iron inputs cannot simply be subtracted from the gross output of gold in order to single out the relation of embodiment between labour (expended in period t) and net output of gold (appearing in period t+1). On the one hand, physical inputs and outputs have to be transformed into values in order to establish the required binary relation between labour and physical goods. On the other hand, this binary relation is a presupposition of the transformation. To escape the circularity lurking here, there seems to be none other than the resort to the customary device of simultaneous determination.

Using this device involves some opportunity costs. What started out as an attempt to pinpoint the relation constitutive for the association of values and physical goods (at the locus of production, where living labour results in net output), turns into a general assumption that all goods are to be considered as nothing but embodied labour on the same terms, regardless of the period of production in which they were produced, regardless of their place and function in the system. The distinction between living labour and labour already embodied in inputs is lost on the way, because in calculating values, we first have to establish a correspondence between gross output and total amounts of labour, embodied and living, before we can impute the existence of net output to the expenditure of living labour in each branch of production, thus singling out the relation of embodiment *in actu*. This relation (and the idea of value creation traditionally associated with it) turns out to be a construct, inconsistently derived and, certainly, not in any way observable.

That the correspondence between physical goods and labour established with the idea of embodied labour is one between gross output and total amounts of labour, living and embodied, can be illustrated with figure 1.

Using Steedman's example, we can depict the production activities in (Q) as combinations of iron (i) and labour (L), where q_i, q_g, and q_c are the iron, gold and corn producing activities. From (Q), we know the outputs produced in each industry. As it turns out, we only need to know the iron output (given by OA) to determine the aggregate values produced in all three industries (of course, this is due to the nature of the example used). Drawing a line from A through q_i to where it intercepts the L-axis (at point B), the distance OB will give the value of iron-output. The parallels to AB through q_g and q_c intercept the L-axis at points

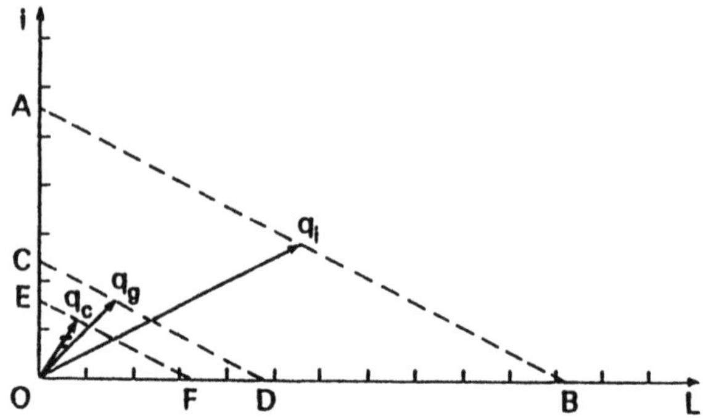

D and F, respectively, so that the values of gold and corn outputs are given by OD and OF, respectively. To determine unit values, we divide the values of outputs by the numbers of units produced.

From the figure, we can see that the idea of a genetic relation between labour and goods which is associated with the concept of embodied labour and which seems to provide for the underpinnings of a rule of transformation is metaphysical. Take the line AB to be the locus of all combinations (i,L) which yield output OA. The value of this output is defined by the one combination (0,112), where it is produced by labour alone. In general, physical output is viewed as the result of one of a definable manifold of possible combinations of physical inputs and labour. Values are determined by the one combination where all physical input quantities are zero and output is produced by labour alone.

This definition of values is based on the implicit notion that it is possible to theoretically treat conditions of production *as if* they were malleable. The notion is metaphysical – and it is also inconsistent with the initial argument according to which physical conditions of production are given as 'objective data', as the firm basis of all theoretical reasoning.

Reliance on the relation of embodiment alone does not justify the use of a rule of transformation à la Steedman. Understanding values as quantities of embodied labour does not open a way to derive values from physical conditions of production, the real wage and capitalist propensities. Maybe there are other ways to accomplish this derivation, but unless these are presented explicitly, there are no reasons for accepting Steedman's claim (A3).

Steedman's framework leaves enough room for speculation, however. Maybe reliance on the idea of reproduction as a unity of production, exchange and distribution can help in the derivation of values? Quite clearly, one of the shortcomings of the relation of embodiment is that it may give us an idea how labour is transformed into goods, but it does not give us an idea why goods should be transformed into labour (or be presented as so many quantities of labour). Maybe relations of exchange are constitutive of the association of values and goods, as Marx and the classical political economists would have it?

Contrary to the impression created by Steedman, assumptions on the nature of exchange relations are crucial for his derivation of values, too. They are not made explicit, since they are part of a general reference to economies in equilibrium.

1.3 *Exchange*

The briefest way to indicate the role of exchange analysis is taken if we reconsider the issue of the evaluation of physical inputs. How can it be accomplished in an economically meaningful way while maintaining a central role for the concept of embodied labour?

A simple procedure would be the following: first, we introduce an assumption that all physical inputs (and labour, for that matter) are acquired by exchange. Thus, exchange values are already associated with inputs when they "enter" production. Then, we stipulate a *rule of exchange* to determine exchange values quantitatively, say,

(3) $i \, \tau \frac{li}{lj} \, j \quad (i \neq j)$

(where 'τ' stands for the relation 'is exchanged with') stating that goods are exchanged according to the quantities of labour embodied in them.

The result is a *formally* complete argument which can provide for a dual foundation of a rule of transformation à la Steedman, if we neglect some additional complications for a moment. On the one hand, we have the relation of embodiment *in actu*, which can be interpreted as a *rule of value creation*. On the other hand, we have a *rule of exchange* which takes care of the evaluation of produced inputs by establishing an indirect link to the relation of embodiment.

Some of the additional complications are familiar. The most obvious one involves the neutralization of time and changes in time and it is usually accomplished by (implicit) reference to systems in a steady-state. A second complication involves the role of living labour as an input under an aspect quite different from the ones considered so far. How is the role of an input under the disposition of those agents who control production (capitalists) ascribed to those agents who perform living labour (workers)? A shorthand answer to this question is provided by introducing the concept of the real wage and treating quantities of living labour as equivalent to quantities of real wage goods which, in turn, are considered as quantities of embodied labour. This involves an asymmetry in the treatment of living labour. As a functioning input, it is counted simply in terms of hours. As an input to be acquired by *exchange,* it is counted to be equivalent to the (lesser amount of) labour embodied in the wage good bundle. Of course, there is the familiar idea of labour power as a commodity to avoid the apparent inconsistency implied in such a double role of living labour. But my point here is simply to stress again the need for exchange analysis as a prerequisite for the derivation of values. As soon as we make use of the concepts of capital, wages, surplus, etc., we do rely on some rule of exchange (as (3), and an appropriate modification of such a rule to cover those exchange transactions which involve the acquisition of living labour as an input).

Once this need for a rule of exchange is recognized, we have to analyse the nature of the exchange relations depicted by such a rule. Rule (3) does complement relations of embodiment between labour and goods in such a way that relations of equivalence between goods and goods in exchange are guaranteed. The existence of equivalence relations between goods in exchange implies a state of equilibrium of the exchange system complementing the system of production.

This can be seen by examining the implications of the transitivity of exchange relations posited with the assumption of equivalence.[4] Using Steedman's iron, gold and corn producing economy as an example again, transitivity of exchange relations implies that, if we observe

$$i \, \tau \, 2g$$

and

$$c \, \tau \, 4g$$

we are justified to conclude that

$$i \, \tau \, \tfrac{1}{2}c$$

without any further reference to observation, conditions of production, or whatever. Economically, this means that exchange transactions, although presumably subject to free contract among pairs of independent private agents, are completely interdependent and are so, moreover, in a way which will guarantee that no gains can be made by indirect trading. Obviously, assuming exchange relations to be transitive amounts to assuming away a whole rats' nest of traditional problems of exchange analysis concerned with explaining why agents should or could behave in ways which result in a state of equilibrium of the exchange system. But this is not all. A state of equilibrium of an exchange system defined in terms of equivalence relations between goods traded is one thing. The way in which such an exchange system is related to a system of production is another thing. However, with the use of a rule of exchange (3), the problem of compatibility between exchange and production is eliminated because the use of embodied labour-times as determinants of exchange ratios not only ensures the transitivity of exchange relations, but also their strict dependence on conditions of production.

Exchange relations are thus defined to be equilibrium relations not only with respect to the mutual consistency of exchange transactions themselves, but also with respect to their compatibility with conditions of production. Viewed in terms of an economy of thought, labour values are miraculous constructs because they help to solve these two problems in one stroke. A minimum number of propositions, namely, a rule of value creation, based on the idea of embodied labour, and a rule of exchange, is sufficient to portray the functioning of a self-reproducing economy (if we neglect issues of distribution). Viewed in terms of explaining the actual functioning of a capitalist economy, the miracle is a flop, of course. The white rabbit gets into the hat by assuming an interdependence between production and exchange defined in terms of an equilibrium state, with no questions asked on how such an equilibrium may be possible. For example, why would agents exchange according to labour-times embodied in their goods? How can they even know what those labour times are?

Questions of this nature are entirely absent from Steedman's discussion of the labour theory of value. What he finds to be deficient in that theory, as he presents it, is not its being deeply rooted in equilibrium conceptions. Rather, his concern is one in terms of economy of thought. Labour values may be sufficient to determine a 'unity' of production and exchange, but they are not powerful enough also to solve the one major problem of distribution, an equilibrium rule of equal rewards for capitalist exertions. Thus, to extend the miraculous achievement associated with labour values such that not only a production-and-exchange, but a production-exchange-and-distribution equilibrium may be determined in one stroke, Steedman proposes to substitute prices of production for labour values.

2 Prices of production

Turning to Steedman's argument (A2), the issue is whether the (uniform) rate of profit and prices of production can be derived from physical conditions of production, the real wage and the capitalist drive to accumulate. Before considering the transformation to (Q) into a price system (P), the issue of exploitation has to be taken up. The source of what is traditionally called the 'transformation problem' can thus be located. Again I will make use of Steedman's examples.

2.1 *Real wages and exploitation*

By assuming that real wages are lower than net output, Steedman posits in physical terms what is called exploitation in the value framework. If wages are equal for equal periods of work, a modified listing of inputs and outputs results from substituting real wage goods for entries of living labour:

(Q_e)

	i	c		i	g	c
i	28	3.5	→	56	–	–
g	16	1	→	–	48	–
c	12	.5	→	–	–	8
	56	5	→	56	48	8

There is a surplus product of 48g and 3c. Labour has disappeared, so there is no apparent reason why one should transform (Q_e) into a value system by mapping heterogeneous goods into the labour-'space'. In effect, there are good reasons against doing this, because the assumption of a real wage implies the need to modify the rule of exchange (3), which is constitutive of the value system (along with the rule of value creation). To assume a given real wage is nothing but an assumption on the nature of those exchange transactions which serve to acquire living labour to be realized in production.

While these transactions are of a quite complicated nature, because they usually involve an exchange of promises (to pay a specified amount of money on the part of the capitalist, to work a specified amount of hours on the part of the worker), the real wage assumption serves to reduce this complexity by positing that a given amount of living labour will be exchanged against a given amount of goods, specificable in kind. In the simple value framework suggested by Steedman, the assumption of a real wage would translate into a special rule of exchange for those transactions involving disposition over living labour, such that a unit of living labour (L′) would always exchange against less than a unit of embodied labour;

(3′) $L' \tau aL \quad (a<1)$

(In Steedman's example, a=1/4, while the additional restriction imposed by the real wage assumption, that living labour can be exchanged only against corn, cannot be portrayed in value terms, of course.)

The introduction of such a special rule raises some questions with respect to its consistency with the general rule of exchange (3) and, in turn, with the rule of transformation (1). Claiming equivalence relations between labour and goods (as embodied labour) is not easily compatible with rule (3′), where the explicit distinction between living and embodied labour and a differentiation with respect to their quantitative weight in exchange is used to make plausible the transformation of embodied labour (in the form of wage goods owned by capitalists) into living labour (as expended by workers in exchange for wage goods).

Leaving aside these issues, we simply take note of the point that the assumption of a real wage implies a special rule of exchange. At the same time, it settles one and, presumably, the most important part of the distributional problem by determining labour's share of the net product. There is an open question of how the surplus product is distributed among capitalists. But, again, there is no apparent reason for the expectation that the rules of value creation and exchange constitutive of the value system will imply a rule of distribution which is satisfactory for all agents involved.

(V_e)	C	V		W	S	S/C+V
i	56	14	→	112	42	.6
g	32	4	→	48	12	.33
c	24	2	→	32	6	.23
	112	20	→	192	60	.45

(C,V,W,S are constant, variable capital, value of output, surplus value; to avoid confusion, S/C+V is called the rate of valorization.)

2.2 *Distributional equilibrium*

(V_e) illuminates two points. First, rule (3′) for the exchange of living and embodied labour is not satisfactory for workers. Second, a rule of distribution based on the imputation of net output to the expenditure of living labour is not satisfactory for all those capitalists who use relatively small amounts of living labour compared to other inputs.

It is always tempting to speculate on the potential results of widespread social dissatisfaction. In our case, *workers* would insist on the abolition of rule (3′), demanding that there be only one general rule of exchange (3) involving no distinction between living and embodied labour. Certainly, workers would see no point in objecting to the imputation of net output to their labour. Alas, we know that workers are structurally disadvantaged in capitalist systems, so this is an empty speculation. Turning to *capitalists,* they would have no objections against rule (3′), but otherwise they are in an awkward position because they are in different positions. The iron producer would insist on continuing the game according to the rules played out in (V_e). But the gold and, more so, the corn producer would turn into believers in equity, take the iron producer to the side-line and threaten him with a mysterious weapon called *competition.* Without ever having to use that weapon, they succeed in convincing the iron producer that rules of value creation are arbitrary and rules of exchange are nonsense, exchanges being subject to free contract. The iron producer turns into an equally true believer in equity among capitalists. Together, they decide to forget about (V_e) and take a fresh look at (Q_e).

After some deliberations, they succeed in translating their moral beliefs into an assumption of '*equal difficulty of production*'[5] in all branches. The new rates of exchange are to be determined such that the surplus product is distributed as if it were a reward for overcoming this 'equal difficulty of production'. In this spirit, they rewrite (Q_e), fearlessly overcoming logical difficulties:

$$
(Q_p)\quad \begin{aligned} x(28i + 3.5c) &= 56i \\ x(16i + 1c) &= 48g \\ x(12i + 0.5c) &= 8c \end{aligned}
$$

Agreeing that all rates of exchange are to be fixed in unit terms of one of the goods traded, capitalists maintain that $L' \tau\, 0.0625c$ and find that

$$
\begin{aligned} &i\,\tau\, 0.3947c \\ &i\,\tau\, 1.7042g \\ &c\,\tau\, 4.2958g. \end{aligned}
$$

The effect of these terms of trade will be an equal rate of reward for all, $x{-}1 = 0.5208$. Happy with these results, capitalists decide to act accordingly and to consult regularly in the future whether changes in conditions of production or in workers' attitudes would require adjustments.

Returning from speculations to the real world of economic theory, we face the hard facts of the transformation problem.

2.3 *The real transformation*

Marx, to whom the dubious honour of having created the transformation problem is attributed, clearly recognized that (V_e) is in a state of disequilibrium as far as capitalists are concerned. Given their lower rates of valorization, the gold and corn producers would strive to become iron producers, too. If there was no mechanism to hold them in their respective branches of production, and if there was no way to change the rule of exchange (3), the most likely outcome of (V_e) would indeed be an economy of iron producers. Obviously, such an economy would not be feasible, so Marx was willing to concede that rule (3) was a softer spot in his argument than he had assumed before and that there would be some mechanism operative in exchanges which would satisfy capitalists to stay in their proper places. Unfortunately, Marx was willing to speculate about the new rules of exchange and distribution before ever specifying the mechanism which would bring them about.[6] So he became hopelessly entangled, mainly because he was not radical enough to sacrifice not only rule (3), but also the rule of value creation which imputes the increase in social wealth to the expenditure of living labour.

Steedman, as others before him, is sufficiently radical to take this step. His argument (A2) suggests that, right from the start, Marx should have based the theory of a capitalist economy on the recognition of a rule of distribution among capitalists. The rule is that the rate of profit is uniform in equilibrium. The underlying idea is that capitalists will demand equal rewards for equal efforts, where the efforts are measured by the respective outlays of capital. The Sraffian problem involved is that the measure itself cannot be independent of the rate of profit, because the only consistent measure of capital outlays is given by the exchange ratios among goods and labour functioning as inputs. These exchange ratios are not independent of the rate of profit, so they all have to be determined simultaneously. For Steedman, these considerations point to the need to return to the description of production conditions and wages in physical terms, as the empirical starting-point of economic reasoning.

(Q) is transformed into (pp. 45f.)

$$
\begin{aligned}
\text{(P)}\quad & \text{i:} && (1+r)(28p_i + 56w) = 56p_i \\
& \text{g:} && (1+r)(16p_i + 16w) = 48 \\
& \text{c:} && (1+r)(12p_i + 8w) = 8p_c \\
& \text{with} && \qquad\qquad\quad 80w = 5p_c;\ p_g = 1.
\end{aligned}
$$

The unknowns are the rate of profit, r, the money wage, w, and the iron and corn prices, p_i, p_c. They are easily determined, and Steedman draws the far-reaching conclusion that one can 'derive from the physical picture of the economy a coherent theory of profits and prices' (p. 48). In considering this claim, one should not be misled by the simplicity of the examples or by the normalization used here – with gold prices being somewhat out of fashion nowadays. Also, I do not want to discuss whether the term 'theory' is a somewhat inflated label for the demonstration that the adoption of an equilibrium rule of distribution for capitalists enables one to derive prices, etc., from physical conditions of production, etc.

However, I do want to take a second look at the transformation from (Q) to (P).

2.4 *Prices and exchange*

According to conventional wisdom embodied in economic theory, a price is a positive or zero number associated with each commodity. Steedman's solutions to (P) thus allow us to associate the numbers 1.7052 with iron, 4.2960 with corn, 0.2685 with labour, 1.0000 with gold (the last association being given by definition). Of course, from a theory of prices we expect to learn something about the economic significance and the rules of such association. Steedman, staying as close to Marx as he can, suggests that we follow Marx and 'treat gold as the money commodity, so that the price of a commodity is the quantity of gold with which it exchanges' (p. 45). The numbers calculated have the following significance:

$i \tau 1.7052g$
$c \tau 4.2960g$
$g \tau g$
$L' \tau 0.2685g.$

In general, we have exchange transactions described by

(4) $i \tau p_i M$ and
(5) $L' \tau w M$

(where M is money, leaving aside whether gold, paper currency or shells serve as money). Thus, (P) is a monetary picture of (Q). The transformation of (Q) into (P) rests on the assumption that relations (4) and (5) depict necessary and ubiquitous transactions. Steedman suggests this much: 'It is to be taken as read throughout that the exchange of commodities takes place via the medium of money' (p. 19). The goods and labour described in (Q) are presented in (P) according to their capacity to attract money in exchange. At the same time, the rate of increase in monetary wealth achieved by production is expressed by the rate of profit.

Introducing money seems to solve the problem of selecting a dimension into which heterogeneous goods and labour can be mapped. The selection seems to be less arbitrary than the one of labour, underlying (V), because it reflects characteristics of actual capitalist economies. However, the realism of assumptions is a bad substitute for theoretical argument. The argument which is lacking in Steedman is one on why goods should be exchanged against money and where money would originate. Whereas labour in (V) is an element of (Q), money in (P) has to be introduced exogenously, even if one of the goods from (Q) serves as money. Despite the assumption of ubiquitous buying and selling, money has no necessary function in (P), except to make plausible the accounting convention which serves the theoretician to calculate prices. Money does not serve as a medium of exchange, a means of payment or a store of value. Analytically, the monetary economy (P) is indistinguishable from the barter economy (Q_p).

Actually, this is not surprising. The determinability of the unknowns in (P) rests on assumptions which make money superfluous, except in its property as an accounting device. The reasoning underlying the transformation of (Q) into (P) is approximately the following: First, we have to bring the heterogeneous ensemble of goods and labour in (Q) into a form accessible to algebraic operations. This is accomplished by assuming that every good and every kind of labour have a price. To determine prices quantitatively, it is not sufficient to think of every entry in (Q) in terms of a price tag attached to it. One has to assume prices to be equilibrium prices, with the physical changes occurring in (Q) through production – the increase in material wealth – being captured by a uniform rate of profit. That the price system is taken to be in a state of equilibrium is evident, on the one hand, from the implicit assumption of uniform prices for uniform goods. On the other hand, the mode of calculation of prices demonstrates that exchange relations are assumed to be equivalence relations in the formal sense. Otherwise it would not be possible to determine, for example, the price of one good from the knowledge of the prices of other goods and the rate of profit.

The possibility to determine prices is tied to the assumption of an equilibrium of the price system which, in turn, reflects the mutual compatibility of production, exchange, and distribution conditions. Since processes of convergence towards equilibrium, in which money could play a role, are not considered, and money is not essential for defining the mutual compatibility of production, exchange, and distribution conditions, money is indeed superfluous for the determination of prices, which, as numbers, describe barter arrangements under an accounting convention.

Maybe I am overemphasizing a trivial point, but it should be clear that neither the theory of value nor the theory of prices and profits as presented by Steedman have anything to do with a theory of a monetary economy. Less trivially, it is even questionable whether conceptions of an economy so deeply rooted in equilibrium notions as both the value and the price-of-production systems can serve as a starting-point for such a theory. If one separates the theory of prices and profits as proposed by Steedman from all ill-founded connotations with a theory of a monetary economy, the results of the transformation of (Q) into (P) are very limited. The possibility is demonstrated of constructing, for any economy described in physical terms and given standard assumptions, an exchange system which will ensure a distribution according to the fiction of an 'equal difficulty of production'. Why one should do this is another question.[7]

3 Conclusion

I think Steedman's arguments (A2 and A3) are not sufficient to support his claim that Marx's value reasoning must be abandoned. Whatever may be right or wrong with Marx, the Sraffa-based critique can 'be met head on' (p. 25), because it rests on questionable and often implicit assumptions and, most importantly, on a redefinition of some traditional problems of economic theory. The redefinition occurs when it is assumed that descriptions of self-reproducing economies in physical terms can be used as the starting point of theoretical reasoning. Implicit assumptions abound when it is assumed that one can transform these descriptions into equational systems in either value or price terms. The transformations are tied to assumptions of equilibrium, as shown by the need to adopt a rule of exchange or a rule of distribution among capitalists. Relying on equilibrium assumptions leads Steedman along the well-trodden path of dichotomizing economic theory into one branch, where money is a veil and prices can be determined, and another branch, where money plays some role and everything else is quite uncertain.

To conclude, I think Steedman's arguments must be accepted on logical grounds only if the decisions underlying the modelling of capitalist economies are *not* a matter of logic. I would prefer to think that they are, at least, if there can be a consensus about the central features of the economy to be explained. Certainly, one of these features is the co-ordination of production decisions on markets through the exchange of commodities and money. A theory of prices and profits which has no place for money and assumes that production activities are co-ordinated provides for very fragile leverage against a theory of value whose, literally, first objective is to account for the necessity of money in commodity producing systems. Steedman is right to label Marxists 'obscurantist' and 'evasive'. But sometimes it is better to be wrong for the right reasons than to be right for the wrong reasons.

Appendix

A tax in kind on labour employed

The following example is intended to demonstrate that the problem of distribution (equal rates of return on capital outlays) solved by the derivation of prices of production by reference to the *deus ex machina* of competition can also be solved by reference to the *deus ex machina* of the state. The significance of this alternative solution lies in the fact that all exchanges conducted after state intervention can take place according to the values associated with each good. The uniform rate of return on capital outlays is equal to Marx's rate of profit.

Economically, this alternative solution is nonsense, but so is the familiar one, unless the processes leading to the equilibrium state of the prices of production regime can be specified. In other words, unless there is a theory of competition, the prices of production derived in linear models of production have as much explanatory value as the activity of counting unknowns and equations.

Using Steedman's example of a simple iron, gold, and corn producing economy and reducing it to its implicit status of a barter economy, the state would intervene in the following way:

Since the net output of each industry is imputed to the living labour employed, the tax rate is fixed with respect to these amounts of labour, such that total surplus value is absorbed in kind by the state. The surplus product is then redistributed according to each industry's share of total capital outlays (measured in values). The resulting rates of valorization (η) are equal for all capitals. Capitalists can then engage in the barter activities necessary to ensure the simple reproduction of the economy, using values to determine exchange ratios.

Given (Q) and (V) as above, the net output in each industry is imputed to the living labour employed. A tax rate of 75 per cent on the product imputed to each hour of living labour will absorb portions of gross output 21i, 12g, and 1.5c, such that the after-tax-before-redistribution state of the economy is as follows:

(Q′)	i	g	c	(V′)
i:	35	—	—	70
g:	—	36	—	36
c:	—	—	6.5	26
state:	21	12	1.5	60

After redistribution, the account for the state has disappeared again and the economy looks as follows:

(Q″)	i	g	c	(V″)
i:	46.13	6.36	0.8	101.82
g:	5.67	39.24	0.4	52.18
c:	4.2	2.4	6.8	38

In other words, the state has redistributed the surplus product according to each industry's share of total capital outlays (measured in values). Capitalists are considered as shareholders in a common enterprise. Dividends are paid out in kind, such that the rate of valorization is equal (η = 0.45). Considering the reproduction requirements, we can now tabulate deficits to determine the necessary barter transactions (c_L is the corn required for real wages):

Deficits:	i	c_L
i:	+18.13	−2.7
g:	−10.33	−0.6
c:	− 7.8	+6.3

Barter will lead to the following 'final' state of the economy:

(Q*)	i	c_L	c_K	g
i.	28	3.5	1	27.82
g:	16	1	1	12.18
c:	12	0.5	1	8

(where c_K is the corn consumed by capitalists). The corresponding values are

(V*)	C	V	S_d	$\eta(= S_d/C+V)$
i:	56	14	31.82	0.45
g:	32	4	16.18	0.45
c:	24	2	12	0.46

(where C, V, S_d are constant and variable capital and surplus value acquired through redistribution). Apparently, the tax authorities made a slight error through rounding, so that agriculture receives a little subsidy.

The example demonstrates that it is possible to construct a redistribution mechanism such that there is a distributional equilibrium and exchange transactions are governed by values. Of course, introducing the state and taxation bears all the marks of an *ad hoc* assumption. But precisely this is the point. As long as the assumption of (perfect, unlimited?) competition underlying the standard derivation of prices of production remains an *ad hoc* assumption, other assumptions of the same methodological status can be substituted for it. This will be true until a theory of competition is elaborated which supports the results derived in the comparative statics framework of linear models of production.

Notes

*Thanks to Ulrich Krause and Johannes Berger for comments and criticisms. Remaining errors are my own, of course.

1. NLB, London 1977. All page references in the paper refer to this text. To avoid misunderstanding I want to emphasize that the argument following is at no point intended to present Marx's theory of value. As to Steedman's arguments, I take them to be representative of a school of thought.
2. Cf. Georgescu-Roegen (1979) for a well-informed complaint on the 'prevailing arithmomania' in economics.
3. (V) does not appear in Steedman in this form, because he immediately introduces the distinction between variable capital and surplus value.
4. Cf. Krause (1979) for an analysis of the conditions of transitivity with regard to Marx's 'forms of value'.
5. Cf. Benetti/Cartelier (1980, p. 97).
6. To reverse the order of chs 9 and 10 in Marx (1972) may illustrate this point.
7. Cf. Appendix.

References

Benetti, C. and **Cartelier, J.** (1980) *Marchands, salariat et capitalistes*, Maspero, Paris.

Georgescu-Roegen, N. (1979) Methods in Economic Science, *Journal of Economic Issues*, vol. 13/2, pp. 317–28.

Krause, U. (1979) *Geld und abstrakte Arbeit*, Campus, Frankfurt.

Marx, K. (1972) *Capital*, vol. 3, Lawrence & Wishart, London.

Steedman, I. (1977) *Marx after Sraffa*, NLB, London.

CHAPTER 5

On Marx's theory of agricultural rent*

Ben Fine

Abstract

This paper shows that Marx's theory of agricultural rent is not an adjunct to his theory of capital at the level of distribution but is inseparably developed from it. The forms of differential and absolute rent are shown to correspond to the formation of market value and price of production in the agricultural sector respectively, these in turn depending upon the barriers posed by landed property to intensive and extensive cultivation. In appendices, Marx's critique of Ricardo's theory of rent, differential rent on the worst land, a critique of other interpretations of Marx, and the 'historical transformation problem' are each considered briefly.

Marx's own treatment of rent has been open to a variety of interpretations for a number of more or less well-recognised reasons. His first treatment of the subject at length comprises the majority of Part II of *Theories of Surplus Value* (TSV II).[1] *Theories of Surplus Value* was intended to comprise Volume IV of *Capital* and like Volumes II and III, it was never finally prepared for publication. In addition, it was written prior to the first three volumes of *Capital*, but on the basis that these had already been written and thereby absorbed by the reader. In fact, one could go even further in characterising the difficulty of the *Theories of Surplus Value* by seeing them at times as Marx's notes to himself on how to present a critique of classical political economy. The net result is that Marx's theory is obscured by two factors. On the one hand, his treatment of rent presupposes an understanding of *Capital* that was itself yet to be written and subject to revision. On the other hand, apart from the implicit and underdeveloped theoretical basis for the treatment of rent, Marx's views on the subject were not systematically presented to the reader nor, like the theory that underlay them, pursued to their logical conclusion. To some extent, these difficulties are moderated by Marx's lengthy discussion of rent in Volume III of *Capital*. However, exactly the same considerations apply here as for TSV II, because Volume III was written prior to the earlier volumes, never finally prepared for publication and subject to revision in the light of Marx's development of his analysis of capital as well as the specifics of rent.

Despite these problems, it is the intention of this paper to show that Marx developed a coherent and consistent theory of rent that is uniformly present in both TSV II and Volume III of *Capital.* To do this, it is necessary, however, to elaborate the meaning and significance of a number of Marx's concepts. As has already been stated, these are the basis on which rent is analysed by Marx. Indeed, his treatment of rent is often a running dialogue in consideration of the conditions which prevail in the agricultural sector in contrast to or in conformity with the conditions which prevail in industry. In other words, Marx's rent theory is concerned with the question of how the laws that apply to industrial capital in general are modified by the existence of landed property. It is, therefore, essential to have a solid grasp of Marx's understanding of capital in the absence of landed property. More generally, it can be observed that corresponding to a particular interpretation, conscious or otherwise, of Marx's political economy, there will be a particular interpretation of his rent theory whose validity will be circumscribed by the initial understanding taken of Marx's analysis of capital. As Marx's theory of capital is itself open to many conflicting and controversial interpretations, including downright rejection, the differences concerning rent theory must necessarily be magnified. In those instances where Marx's economic theory is rejected, the analysis by which it is displaced then becomes the basis for a particular understanding of the rent category. If the argument of this paper is correct – that Marx has a coherent theory of rent rooted in his analysis of capital – then those interpretations of Marx's rent theory that reject his analysis of capital must do so at a level other than that simply concerning rent alone. As it were, to reject Marx's theory of capital is to reject his theory of rent, and his theory of rent cannot be represented by appending an interpretation of it to an alternative theory of capital. We begin then with certain elements of Marx's analysis of capital.

The transformation problem

Marx's treatment of the transformation of values into prices of production and its relation to his value theory is not of direct concern to us. It does, however, have considerable bearing on the development of his rent theory. Unfortunately, the debate over the transformation problem has had the effect of obscuring some of the elements of Marx's theory at the expense of others. In general, it has been taken for granted that there exists a set of commodities each with a corresponding value, and the 'problem' concerns how those values become expressed as prices of production. Different contributions have emphasised the quantitative or the qualitative aspects of the problem, and in the course of doing so have generated and utilised different understandings of the concept of value. What is important for our purposes is the location of Marx's treatment of the transformation.

On the basis of commodities exchanging at prices which equal their given values, Marx argues that different rates of profit would prevail in different industries according to differing organic compositions of capital. The result is well-known and follows from the production of more surplus value per unit of capital advanced in those industries where the ratio of living labour to constant capital is higher. Accordingly, *competition between capitals in different sectors* would ensure a flow of capital into those with a low organic composition from those with a high organic composition, adjusting prices of production until rates of profit become equalised.

The simple mechanism described here for creating equalised rates of profit through competition is common to most economic theories. It has, however, a different significance according to the economic theory to which it is related. In Marx's theory, it is understood that the values are logically prior to the prices of production. What competition between sectors does is to redistribute value (and surplus value) in the formation of equalised rates of profits and prices of production: 'It is quite appropriate to regard the values of commodities as not only theoretically but also historically *prior* to the prices of production.' We shall return to the question of the historical priority later.[2] For the moment, it suffices to observe that in Marx's scheme, competition between capitals in the formation of a general (averaged) rate of profit occurs from a situation in which sectoral rates of profits are unequal and excess surplus value exists in some industries, a deficiency in others, according to the respective organic compositions of capital. It is worth emphasising that values are not taken as the point of departure for the transformation because of their historical, but because of their logical importance. Although Marx takes a system of simple commodity production as a starting point for some of his exposition (III, p. 175), he makes it clear that the formation of prices of production 'requires a higher development of capitalist production' (III, p. 180).

These remarks are borne out by consideration of the element of the transformation problem that has suffered neglect in the recent debates. It concerns the question of where the values that form the basis for the transformation come from in the first place. Marx argues that values are first formed *by the process of competition between capitals within a sector* and calls the process involved the formation of market values. In general, these sectoral values are formed out of the average labour time required to produce the commodities concerned. There will be a range of more or less efficient techniques in use, each with an individual value. In the formation of the market value, excess or surplus profits will accrue to those individual capitals whose individual value is below the market value. Significantly, Marx does not insist that the market value always equal the average value (III, p. 183). If either the most favourable or the least favourable technique is sufficiently weighty as compared with the average, then the technique concerned rather than the average regulates the market value.[3]

It follows that there is a two-stage process in Marx's transformation. First, competition within sectors establishes market values and thereby unequal rates of profit. Secondly, competition between sectors establishes prices of production from those market values on the basis of equalised rates of profit:[4]

> What competition within *the same* sphere of production brings about, is the determination of the *value of the commodity in a given sphere* by the average labour-time required in it, i.e., the creation of the *market-value*. What competition between the *different* spheres of production brings about is the *creation of the same general rate of profit* in the *different* spheres through the levelling out of the different market-values into market-prices, which are *cost-prices* that are different from the actual market values. (TSV II, p. 208).[5]

Accumulation, productivity increase and the organic composition of capital

In Volume I of *Capital*, Marx argues that accumulation can take place either through concentration or through centralisation. One involves the reinvestment of individual profits, the other depends upon the gathering together of many individual capitals and/or their profits. Nor are concentration and centralisation simply different methods of financing investment. They belong to distinct stages of capitalism, one predominant in its infancy and the other characteristic of a highly developed capitalism.[6]

Our interest lies in the centralisation of capital associated with developed capitalism. The coercive force that compels individual capitals to centralise is competition to establish high levels of productivity (lower individual values) through the introduction of large-scale production utilising machinery in the factory system. The result is to revolutionise the labour process by substituting machinery for the labourer, so that a given mass of raw materials is worked up into commodities through the use of less direct labour. Marx speaks of the relative expulsion of living labour from the production process and the rising technical composition of capital (TCC – ratio of physical means of production to direct labour). In these terms, Marx analyses the specific form of accumulation and productivity increase associated with the development of capitalism.

As well as defining the technical composition, Marx also distinguishes the organic and value compositions of capital (OCC and VCC). The VCC is the TCC expressed in value terms. It is simply $\frac{c}{v}$. The OCC is quantitatively equal to the VCC in so far as the latter expresses *changes* in the TCC. It is also measured by $\frac{c}{v}$ but clearly depends for its definition and for its separate identity from the VCC on the dynamics by which the TCC grows. What Marx has in mind is that accumulation leads to an increasing TCC in the production process and the OCC measures this in value terms. The increasing TCC is, however, necessarily also associated with a reduction in the values of commodities. When the TCC is measured at these new (reduced) values, the result is the VCC. Chronologically, the distinction between the OCC and VCC can be made by noting that they are calculated at old and new values, respectively. But the distinction is not one ordered by time as much as it is ordered by Marx's concept of the structural relations comprising production, distribution and exchange in the capitalist economy. Marx refers to the OCC rather than the VCC when discussing changes in the TCC from the perspective of use values rather than values. In addition, references to the OCC concern accumulation and productivity increase. It is the failure of many writers to distinguish the three compositions of capital, and particularly the OCC and VCC, that has led to errors of interpretation of Marx's theory of accumulation whether in the context of rent or not.

As mentioned earlier, the distinction between accumulation through the centralisation and concentration of capital does not simply concern the method of financing, it is related to definite stages of capitalist development. With concentration as the predominant form of accumulation, it will tend to take the form of reproduction on an extended scale, that is a simple reproduction (without accumulation) which is expanded, the composition of capital remaining the same. In contrast, for centralisation, organised through a developed credit system, accumulation takes the form of expanded reproduction in which the TCC (and OCC) rise. It is this that marks the stage of a developed capitalism.

Competition between capitals

In the first section, we examined competition between capitals at two different levels. In the formation of market values, competition within a sector establishes different individual rates of profits.[7] In the formation of prices of production competition between sectors established a general rate of profit. In the first case unequal rates of profit are established, in the second they are eroded. For both cases, the competition between capitals is located at the level of commodity exchange. It is governed for the competition between sectors by the free flow of capital.

The previous section considered competition between capitals of a different sort. It was located at the level of production for which productivity increase is the means of competition. As such, it concerns competition within a sector to establish individual values below the market value as a means of appropriating surplus profit. This competition explains the divergence of individual values from the market value. The net result of this competition is not to establish permanent surplus profits. All capitalists within a sector compete to obtain surplus profits but not all can establish an individual value below the market value for then the market value would itself be lower. Nevertheless, at any one time, there will be a range of techniques in use some of which yield surplus, others deficient, profits.

The matter cannot be left here, however, because it presents a static and one-sided picture. There is a tendency for the competition for surplus profits to lead to a divergence of individual from market values, but exactly the same competition tends to make general the most advanced techniques so that the market value is successively reduced. Nor must these tendencies be seen in isolation from the means by which productivity increases and surplus profits are created. While in the labour process a relative expulsion, increasing intensity and deskilling of labour is required, the precondition for these developments is the gathering together of the money-capital required to finance the increased expenses of fixed capital, raw materials and labour supply. Necessarily the competition between capitalists to establish surplus profits is conducted at the level of access to credit. As capitalism develops through centralisation, there is a continuous increase in the minimum level of capital required to maintain competitiveness, and consequently an increasing level of capital that is the average or normal. For these reasons, Marx emphasises that the accumulation in developed form depends upon the creation of a sophisticated credit system as the lever of centralisation, and that the primary basis of competition between capitals is the size of capital controlled by each. That these results represent Marx's view can be verified by reference to many quotations. We choose two:

> The reduction in cost-price and the surplus profit arising from it are here the result of the manner in which the functioning capital is invested. They result either from the fact that the capital is concentrated in the hands of one person in extraordinarily large quantities (a condition that is cancelled out as soon as equal magnitudes of capital are used on the average), or from the fact that a certain magnitude of capital functions in a particularly productive manner (a condition that disappears as soon as the exceptional method of production becomes general or is suppressed by a still more developed one). III, p. 644.

> The various investments may also employ unequal quantities of capital. Indeed, this is generally the case . . . This is the general prerequisite for the existence of surplus profit *in any sphere of capital investment* (III, p. 649, emphasis added).

In short, within a sector individual values diverge from market value creating excess profits more or less in line with the size distribution of individual capitals. Correspondingly, the market value is itself reduced as the normal size of an individual capital is increased. Referring back to our analysis of earlier sections, the developments summarised here can be seen to be associated with a rising OCC.

The basis for capitalist rent

Marx wrote to Engels that one of 'the (two) best points in my book (Volume I of *Capital*) (is) the treatment of *surplus value independently of its particular* forms as profit, interest, ground rent, etc.' It follows that when rent is introduced into the analysis as a form of surplus value, it must be done so with an adequate *logical* and *historical* basis.

The logical basis on which Marx analyses rent is that which takes it as a product of capitalism in its most developed form. His first sentence in Volume III of *Capital* on the question of rent is to limit himself precisely to these considerations. 'The analysis of landed property in its various historical forms is beyond the scope of this work.' He continues:

> We shall be concerned with it only in so far as a portion of the surplus value produced by capital falls to the share of the landowners. We assume, then that agriculture is dominated by the

> capitalist mode of production, just as manufacture is; in other words, that agriculture is carried on by capitalists who differ from other capitalists primarily in the manner in which their capital, and the wage-labour set in motion by this capital, are invested. So far as we are concerned, the farmer produces wheat, etc., in much the same way as the manufacturer produces yarn or machines. The assumption that the capitalist mode of production has encompassed agriculture implies that it rules over all spheres of production and bourgeois society, i.e., that its prerequisites, such as free competition among capitals, the possibility of transferring the latter from one production sphere to another, and a uniform level of the average profit, etc., are fully matured.

Marx's starting point then is the existence of landed property as a specific means by which surplus value can be appropriated in the form of rent. As such, it is immediately linked to the historical conditions of existence of landed property. Just as these conditions differ so the effects of landed property differ. There is therefore no general theory of rent, nor can the conclusions reached for one instance in which a rent relation exists be automatically applied to others.[8] In other words, rent cannot be analysed simply on the basis of its effects – such as the barrier to capitalist investment. Logically, rent would then arise wherever there was any obstacle to capitalist investment, that is in all but the most abstract existence of the capitalist mode. In contrast, rent must be examined in conjunction with specific historical conditions particularly as capitalism, as a mode of production, demonstrates a tendency to eliminate the conditions which obstruct its development, thereby rendering such obstacles theoretically redundant. It is in this context that the historical dimension of Marx's analysis comes to the fore. As he observes in the *Grundrisse* 'the dialectical method of presentation is only correct when it knows its limits', and these limits are themselves bounded by the historical concretisation of what are otherwise ideal logical possibilities to the obstruction of capital accumulation. In his opening remarks on rent in Volume III of *Capital*, continuing the long quotation from above, Marx writes that

> the form of landed property which we shall consider is a specifically historical one, a form *transformed* through the influence of capital and of the capitalist mode of production, either of feudal landownership, or of small-peasant agriculture as a means of livelihood, in which the *possession* of the land and the soil constitutes one of the prerequisites of production for the direct producer, and in which his *ownership* of land appears as

> the most advantageous condition for the prosperity of *his* mode of production (III, p. 614).

Thus, historically, capital transforms landed property from a situation in which it confronts individual possession and even ownership of the land. It creates landed property which 'is based on the monopoly by certain persons over definite portions of the globe, as exclusive spheres of their private will to the exclusion of all others' (III, p. 615). As a result the 'capitalist farmer pays the landowner, the owner of the land exploited by him, a sum of money at definite periods fixed by contract' (III, p. 618).

So much for the historical dimension in relation to the development of capitalist agriculture from precapitalist modes of production. In addition, we have to consider whether the development of capitalism itself destroys the effects inherited in the form of landed property, so that 'the investment of capital in the land can take place without payment of rent.' There

> we shall find that they are all based on a *de facto* abolition of landed property, if not also the legal abolition; this, however, can only take place under very specific circumstances which are by their very nature *accidental* . . . Such cases occur in practice, but only as *exceptions* . . . This abolition of landed property is *fortuitous. It may or may not occur* (III, p. 751, emphasis added).

In short, the historical basis for pursuing the effects of landed property on agriculture is well-established in Marx's view.

Differential rent

Marx's theory of differential rent (DR) for agriculture is more easily understood once it is seen to be based upon *competition within the agricultural sector.* In terms of our earlier analysis, this implies it concerns the formation of market values from differing individual values, these in turn yielding surplus profits. These processes are themselves prior to the competition between sectors which establishes market prices from market values. Now, the existence of surplus profits is not itself an explanation for the specific existence of agricultural rent. For, otherwise, such rents would exist in all industries, just as surplus profits do. Nor are natural conditions of differential productivity the source of rent or even surplus profits. They may be a condition for productivity differences, but they do not thereby create either the categories of surplus profit or rent. These depend upon the utilisation of natural conditions under capitalist relations of production and, respectively, with the intervention of landed property. Thus,

> the natural force is not the source of surplus profit, but only its natural basis... This surplus profit would also exist if landed property did not exist . . . Hence landed property does not create the portion of value which is transformed into surplus profit, but merely enables the landowner . . . to coax this surplus profit out of the pocket of the manufacturer and into his own. It is not the cause of the creation of such surplus profit, but is the cause of its transformation into the form of ground-rent. (III, p. 647)

Differential rents exist, not because surplus profits exist, but because these are appropriated by the landlord rather than by the capitalist.

However, it is not sufficient that surplus profits exist to be appropriated in the form of rent, it is essential that they be fixed. For if they were not permanent the rent as the form of surplus profit would itself be eroded. Marx's analysis of surplus profits for industrial capital leads to the conclusion that they are eroded since exceptional methods of production become general through competition between capitalists.

An immediate result is the explanation of differential rent of the first type (DRI), which is usually associated with Ricardo's extensive margin. The differences of fertility[9] between lands are the source of surplus profits which are consolidated in the form of rent. Capital cannot flow onto lands of equal fertility, since they do not exist. Moreover, those capitals that do flow onto the better lands meet the barrier of landed property and forego the surplus profit in the form of rent. The result is not simply the creation of rent but also a distortion in the formation of market-value. For DRI, the market value is not formed from the average or normal values, but by the worst *method* of production. This is not because the worst method is predominant, but because the intervention of landed property modifies the social formation of value in agriculture:

> This is determination by market-value as it asserts itself on the basis of capitalist production through competition; the latter creates a false social value. This arises from the law of market value, to which the products of the soil are subject. The determination of the market value of products, including therefore agricultural products, is a social act, albeit a socially unconscious and unintentional one. It is based necessarily upon the exchange value of the product, not upon the soil and the differences of its fertility (III, p. 661).

Marx's treatment has been quite wrongly seen by many to be

identical to Ricardo's theory of the extensive margin.[10] It is based upon the application of equal quantities of capital to unequal lands, rent being formed out of the differences in productivity between the better and the worst lands. Marx makes abundantly clear in many places that the case of DRI is to be distinguished from that of DRII by the latter's dependence upon unequal applications of capitals to lands.[11] Even in TSV, in which DRII does not appear, we find the distinction made for

> the existence of modern ground rent. *With a given capital investment*, the variation in the amount of rent is only to be explained by the varying fertility of the land. The variation in the amount of rent, *given equal fertility*, can only be explained by the *varying amount of capital invested* (TSVII, p. 43).

In Volume III of *Capital*, the distinction between DRI and DRII on the basis of differing lands as opposed to differing capitals is well-established and uncontroversial.

What cannot be accepted is that Marx's treatment of DRII is an extrapolation of his Ricardian DRI (which it is not) to the Ricardian intensive margin. For the Ricardian intensive margin, the determination of exchange value by the worst land in use is displaced by and generalised to the determination of exchange value by the worst unit of capital in use, which may or may not be applied to the worst land. Rent is now paid on every unit of capital that has higher productivity than the worst unit, and this includes the units of capital applied to the worst land. For 'perfect' competition, capital will flow intensively onto all lands until the margin is the same for each. There will be different rents according to the quantity and fertility of the capitals on each land that are superior to the uniform margin.

If this were Marx's theory of DRII, then it would require the abandonment of his value theory. For the argument applied for the intensive margin is not dependent upon the intervention of landed property. It implies that the surplus profits take the form of rent, but it has the implication that the exchange value of commodities should always be determined by the uniform intensive margin rather than by the market value (in general, the *average* of individual values).[12]

Marx does not, however, locate the source of (surplus) profits in the difference between average and marginal productivities. The significance for him of unequal capitals is their unequal size as a source of productivity increase and surplus-profits. It is a point that is emphasised again and again in the treatment of DRII. Nor does this source of surplus profits have its basis in the technical conditions of production, rather it is a product of the competition for finance that is characteristic of the accumulation of industrial capital: 'in the differential rent in form II, the differences in distribution of capital (and ability to obtain credit) among tenants are added to the differences in fertility.' (III, p. 677.) Just as in industry a normal minimum (and average) level of capital is established, on the basis of which surplus profits are earned by accumulating large capitals, so in agriculture the same applies, so much so that Marx makes an empirical estimate of the change in the average following the Repeal of the Corn Laws:

> a definite amount of capital is invested which, under the prevailing conditions of production is considered normal . . . it is evident that this average investment of capital, say, in England, of £8 per acre prior to 1848 and £12 subsequent to that year, will constitute the standard in concluding leases. For the farmer expending more than this, the surplus profit is not transformed into rent for the duration of the contract (III, p. 706).

What Marx has added in this final sentence is the difference that exists between agriculture and industry – the surplus profits resulting from large scale investment are only *temporarily* the prerogative of the capitalist farmer, but not because they are eroded by competition from other capitalists. Ultimately, like the surplus profits forming DRI, they accrue to the landowner in the form of rent, DRII.

The theory involved here is best exemplified by considering DRII in the pure form of unequal applications of capital to equal lands. In other words, the complexity of the co-existence of DRI and DRII is eliminated since there are no 'natural' differences in fertility. For an unlimited supply of land of equal quantity, the Ricardian theory would conclude that all land would bear no rent and that capital would be apportioned equally between lands. The result, particularly in its modern, neo-classical clothing, would depend upon the assumption of eventual decreasing returns to intensive investment. For increasing returns, there could be no competitive equilibrium and efficiency would require all capital to be invested intensively upon a single land.

In contrast, for Marx's theory, DRII would exist as capital investments larger than the normal were undertaken. These intensive cultivations would have to yield economies of scale in the use of capital, otherwise the capital would be divided and used on new no rent land. The result is to reduce the individual value below the market value, create surplus-profits, which are, however, appropriated in the form of rent. The outcome is the use of equal lands, in which unequal applications of capital result in rent on large scale producers and an equalised rate of profit for capitalists irrespective of their size of capital. The paradox is that there are equal lands some of which yield rent and some of which do not. The lands are, however, not equal since they have different sizes of capital invested upon them. Landlords can then benefit from the progress of society in organising large-scale production through the credit system because of the way in which society progresses, through the temporary creation of surplus-profits.

DRII is based on the *temporary* surplus profits derived from the magnitude of capital invested rather than from the more or less *permanent* natural differences in fertility that are the basis for DRI. There is a tendency for competition between landowners to establish equal rents for equal lands, but this in turn 'will depend upon the competition among farmers who are in a position to make the same extra capital advance' (III, p. 706). Clearly all the surplus-profits that form the potential basis of DRII may not accrue to the landlord. Eventually they are eroded as the abnormal size of the investments concerned becomes normal, but this process, parallel to the one for industry, is blunted by the appropriation of DRII. Within agriculture itself, the less the incentive to the farmer to invest intensively rather than extensively the higher DRII eats into surplus profits. Between industries, those capitalists who obtain access to large-scale credit will tend to seek sole appropriation of potential surplus profits outside the agricultural sector. Thus

> a certain minimum capital is required for every individual branch of industry in order that the commodities may be produced at their price of production. If this minimum is altered as a result of successive investments of capital associated with improvements on the same soil, it occurs *gradually* . . . But as soon as the new method of cultivation has become general enough to be the normal one, the price of production falls (and) the rent from the superior plots declines again (III, p. 706).

Thus, whilst agriculture may not resist absolutely the capitalist form of development it exhibits a slow pace of progress relative to industry. This is perhaps the most important conclusion to be drawn from Marx's theory of DRII, its preoccupation with obstacles to the development of capital accumulation rather than the static formulation of the distribution of surplus value in the form of rent. It is a general consideration that is at the forefront of all of Marx's rent theory:

> But as soon as the time stipulated by contract has expired . . . the improvements incorporated in the soil become the property of the landowner as an inseparable feature of the substance, the land . . . But this is at the same time one of the greatest obstacles to the rational development of agriculture, for the

> tenant farmer avoids all improvements and outlays for which he cannot expect complete returns during the term of his lease (III, p. 620),

and the basis for this obstacle is more general than improvements for:

> if there are, in agriculture, *any causes* . . . which raise the rate of profit (not temporarily but on an average as compared with industry) then the mere existence of the landlord would cause this extra profit to consolidate itself and accrue to the landlord rather than enter into the formation of the general rate of profit (TSVII, p. 21, emphasis added).

Marx's discussion of DRII in Volume III of *Capital* never undertakes an analysis of the type laid out here. DRII is not examined in the pure form of unequal applications of capital to equal lands. Marx always discusses DRII in the presence of DRI, that is of lands of unequal quality. His reason for doing so was to analyse the quantitative determination of DRII having laid down the qualitative basis for its existence. If DRI and DRII were independent of each other, the analysis of DR would now be complete. For then, DRI would have the effect of equalising lands so that DRII could be calculated from the profitability of surplus capital. Alternatively, DRII would have the effect of equalising the effects of different applications of capital so that DRI could be calculated from the differing fertilities between lands. In effect, DR is the simple addition of DRI and DRII.

This procedure is, however, invalid. DRI and DRII have each been calculated on the basis of certain abstractions concerning the distribution of capitals and fertilities. There is no presumption that the interaction of DRI and DRII is simply additive. A more complex analysis is necessarily involved concerning the co-existence of unequal lands and unequal capitals on those lands. For DRI, there is the problem of determining the worst land in the presence of unequal applications of capital (DRII). Some lands may be worst for one level of investment but not for others, for example. Second, for DRII, there is the problem of determining the normal level of investment in the presence of differing lands (DRI). Some capitals may be normal for some types of lands, other capitals normal for other lands. There is a further difficulty for DRII, since decreasing productivity of additional investments would not allow for surplus profits for abnormally large capitals unless the market value of the agriculture product rises. This raises the question of whether the market value should be determined by the individual value on some plot of land or whether it may be determined by some part of capital on that land. In other words, is the size of normal capital always the total capital applied to some land, or can it be some part of that capital? Even the term 'normal capital' becomes inappropriate for the capital's application to a particular land to determine market value is in no sense general.

These problems concern the simultaneous determination of worst land and normal capital in agriculture. The interaction of the two gives rise to market value from which differential rents can be calculated. For industrial capital, the determination of normal capital is synonymous with the determination of value. The problem does not arise. The same is true for each of DRI and DRII in the absence of the other. For DRI in its pure form (equal capitals), the determination of worst land is synonymous with the determination of value, whereas for DRII in its pure form (equal lands) it is the determination of normal capital that comes to the fore in the determination of value.

Marx turns to the quantitative determination of differential rent as a whole before adequately resolving these conundrums. He does so in an ingenious way, which in itself constitutes a solution to the difficulties that have been raised. What Marx does is to consider the level of DR under three different cases, according to whether the price of production of corn rises, remains constant or falls. He then calculates rents quite simply but more significantly discusses what changes in conditions of production may have brought about these price movements. Clearly, the predetermined movements in the price of production are equivalent to presuming a given market value. However, each discussion of the conditions of production which give rise to these values necessarily sheds light on the formation of worst land and normal capital in agriculture.

Before considering the implications of Marx's analysis, it will be instructive to see why these problems do not arise for the Ricardian treatment of rent, the theory with which Marx's DR is often incorrectly identified. The reason is that the Ricardian theory locates the margin according to the last unit of capital applied, or more precisely according to the least productive unit of capital. This in turn determines the exchange value of corn against which all other rents can be calculated. As there is no question of a normal size of capital and a surplus profit for larger capitals (which may be less productive on average than smaller ones), there is no difficulty in the Ricardian theory.

Marx recognises Ricardo's treatment of intensive cultivation as a *special* instance of DRII:

> this one case, in which decreasing productiveness of subsequent additional capitals invested in already cultivated soils may lead

> to an increase in price of production . . . has been labelled by Ricardo as the only case, the normal case – to which he reduces the entire formation of differential rent II (III, p. 681).

Nevertheless, there are differences between Marx's treatment of this special case of what is for Ricardo the general case. For, the Ricardian theory ultimately is reduced to the logic of taking the intensive margin to be based on infinitesimally small increments of capital, whereas Marx's theory is concerned with a normal size of capital. Nor is this simply a technical matter, the difference between a Ricardian infinitesimal margin and a Marxian 'lumpy' margin corresponding to the normal size of capital. Marx's theory requires a determination of the size of the normal capital. We now turn to this question directly.

The formation of the normal capital, like the formation of values, is a social process which has the specific characteristic in agriculture of modification according to the intervention of landed property. Thus, capitals cannot flow freely within the sector, but meet the barrier imposed by the need to pay rent. It follows that these rents modify the structure of capital accumulation on the land and the formation of the normal capital. It is not simply a case of an exogenously given structure of capital accumulation on the land from which a given market value drops out together with differential rents corresponding to the surplus profits associated with better lands or bigger capitals. The structure of rents itself intervenes in the formation of the structure of capital accumulation. This is not to reverse the argument and insist that whatever rents are charged will be paid, because capital is not compelled to move onto particular lands. It will only do so if the corresponding surplus profits can be produced and paid as rent given the market value formed. It follows that DR (co-existence of DRI and DRII) is not formed simply from the application of unequal capitals to unequal lands – and hence our earlier difficulties – but from these in conjunction with the structure of rents that are charged and hence formed.

As observed earlier, Marx discusses these processes on the basis of the prices of production to which they give rise. It is significant that he does so according to rising, falling or constant price of production rather than simply the *level* of price of production, for this emphasises the dynamic effects of capital accumulation rather than the static distributional formation of rents. Nevertheless, this method of procedure tends to conceal the relationships involved and is partially responsible for the common identification of Marx's with Ricardo's theory of DR. In addition, Marx's discussion of the role played by rent in the formation of market value tends to be focussed around the case of decreasing productivity, for then there are no 'natural' surplus profits to be appropriated in the form of rent. Thus, an increase in the normal size of capital on a better land may be limited if it would lead to a reduction in rent (surplus profit) as decreasing productivity pushes the individual price of production of the additional output above the general price of production for,

> under the law of landed property . . . the case in which the additional capital produces only at the general price of production, would have constituted the limit. Beyond this point, the additional investment of capital in the same land would have had to cease (III, p. 735).

Similarly, it is the landowners' intervention which influences both the formation of normal capital and market value (price of production).

> It would again depend to what extent a second investment of capital in the available soil . . . had become general, whether the price of production is equalised at the average price or whether the individual price of production of the second investment of capital becomes regulating. . . . The latter occcurs only when the landowner has sufficient time until demand is satisfied to fix as rent the surplus profit derived at the price (of production associated with the second investment) (III, p. 744).

However, whilst Marx's discussion of the role played by landed property on the formation of normal capital and market value is at its sharpest in the case of diminishing returns to capital, it is of wider applicability. Because the surplus profits of increasing returns from intensive cultivation can be appropriated in the form of rent, indeed an increased rent is the possible condition of the increased application of capital, the structure of capital accumulation will be influenced by as well as form the structure of rents in this instance also, since an increased rent may discourage a particular intensive cultivation.

> Thus although differential rent is but a formal transformation of surplus profit into rent, and property in land merely enables the owner in this case to transfer the surplus profit of the farmer to himself . . . in fact a more or less artificial barrier is reached as a consequence of the mere formal transformation of surplus profit into ground rent, which is the result of landed property (III, p. 737).

Marx argues that this barrier is reached 'more rapidly when the rate of productiveness of the capital decreases and the regulating price remains the same' so that a rise in price becomes necessary, one corresponding to the productivity of the additional rather than the total capital. The more rapid attainment of the barrier is not, however, chronological but by comparison with the hypothetical situation in which the normal capital is not determined by a fragmentation of the capital applied to a single land. It is by way of a contrast to the case of increasing productivity of capital, for which increased rents can be provided for out of the surplus profits of increased productivity (to the extent that these do not lead through an increase in the normal size of capital to a reduction in market value).[13]

Absolute rent

If the key to the formation of differential rent is the establishment of market value and surplus-profit through competition *within* the agricultural sector, the basis for the formation of absolute rent (AR) is to be found in the surplus profits that exist in the transformation from market values to prices of production. In these terms, AR can be seen to have DR as its point of departure. Both concern the obstacle to capital investment posed by landed property and the associated appropriation of surplus profit in the form of rent, but each is located at a different level of analysis and therefore has a different source of surplus. DR depends upon the divergence between individual and market values, AR on the divergence between market values and prices of production.

This basis for the formation of AR has been confused with a condition for its existence, the flow of capital onto new lands. The formation of prices of production depends upon the flow of capital between sectors. The flow into agriculture is obstructed by the existence of landed property. If this flow were, despite the barrier, to be located on existing lands in use then the principles of differential rent would apply. AR depends then upon the flow of capital *onto new lands*. But, if this use of new lands is taken to be the basis of AR, then its existence is independent of the formation of surplus profits. It is simply an extra payment for the use of new land, which must be added to the price of production of agricultural goods to form market *price*. As such, it corresponds to an appropriation of surplus value from the *social* 'pool' and does not have its origins in the production of surplus profit within agriculture. The resulting increase in market price is best categorised as a monopoly price.[14] If the monopoly price exists as a result of the intervention of landed property so that the surplus profits accrue in the form of rent, then a monopoly *rent* is formed. Thus, those who interpret Marx's theory of AR in these terms either deny the existence of AR because of competition between landowners, or locate it precisely as a monopoly rent for the use of the land.

It is true that Marx's discussion of AR in Volume III of *Capital* begins with the need to pay rent even on new land which would be worst in use. However, only after more than ten pages of such analysis is AR eventually defined – quite clearly as depending upon the production of ***additional*** surplus value in agriculture rather than upon the appropriation of surplus value in the form of monopoly rent:

> a capital of a certain size in agriculture produces more surplus value, or what amounts to the same, sets in motion and commands more surplus labour (and with it employs more living labour generally) than a capital of the same size of average social composition. This assumption, then, suffices for that form of rent which we are analysing here, and which can obtain only so long as this assumption holds good. Wherever this assumption no longer holds, the corresponding form of rent likewise no longer holds.

The first mention of AR in *Capital* then follows:

> a rent, in short, which is to be clearly distinguished in concept from differential rent and which we may therefore call ***absolute rent*** (III, p. 760).

Moreover, Marx's treatment here of AR is a continuation of that undertaken in the TSVII where the emphasis is forever upon the lower composition of capital in agriculture (as compared to industry), the production there of additional surplus value, and the appropriation of that surplus value as AR. The divergence of Marx's concept of AR from monopoly rent is complete, since for the latter the composition of capital in agriculture is irrelevant for the determination of rent (except in so far as it affects competition between landowners – a consideration never taken up). Those who subscribe to the theory of absolute as monopoly rent must and do therefore reject the totality of Marx's analysis of AR.

In purely technical terms, Marx's theory of AR is as follows. Because agriculture has a lower organic composition of capital than industry it produces additional surplus value because of the higher proportion of living labour employed. Consequently, in the absence of landed property, its price of production would be below value. However, landed property makes an intervention that prevents the formation of price of production in agriculture, and agricultural commodities sell at a price above price of production and in the limit at value, the difference from price of production making up AR. In addition, the conditions in which AR would disappear are (i) if the composition of capital in agriculture were equal to or higher than average, or (ii) if all land had been taken into cultivation i.e. AR depends upon the movement onto new lands; (iii) if the level of development of agriculture were equal to that of industry:

> if the average composition of agricultural capital were equal to, or higher than that of the average social capital, then absolute rent . . . would disappear (III, p. 765).
> if all the land suitable for agriculture in a certain country were leased . . . there would not be any land paying rent; but there might be some capitals, certain parts of capitals, invested in land, that might not yield any rent. For as soon as the land has been rented, landed property *ceases* to act as an *absolute* barrier against the investment of necessary capital (III, p. 764, emphasis added).
>
> But if conditions of production in intensive cultivation became the same as those prevailing on an average in industry . . . then rent for the least fertile land would disappear and for the most fertile it would be reduced merely to difference in land. *Absolute* rent would no longer exist (TSVII, p. 104).

If we restrict our interpretation of Marx's theory of AR to technical considerations alone, then it remains a *static* theory of surplus value distribution, and the notion of absolute rent as monopoly rent is certain to prevail. In addition, Marx's conditions for existence of AR become purely arbitrary. This is true of the dependence of AR on low OCC in agriculture, particularly when it is recognised that OCCs differ within industry without rent being formed. Leaving this objection aside, there would be no reason for AR to be limited to the difference between value and price of production. As a monopoly rent, the market price could rise above the value according to ability and willingness of industry to pay and landowners not to compete.

However, Marx's discussion of the conditions under which AR would disappear suggest that a static theory is not involved. It is the pace of development of agriculture relative to industry and the movement of capital onto new lands that is of importance. Of course these conditions can be interpreted statically (all land is leased, all sectors have equal levels of development), but if they are not then the other concepts utilised, in particular the OCC, must themselves be interpreted in a dynamic context relative to Marx's theory of accumulation. In understanding this task, it will be shown that Marx's theory of AR is correct in all essential respects and does not require modification or rejection to be consistent with his analysis of capital.

Just as for DRII in its pure form, the appropriate abstraction to be made is unlimited lands of equal quality (to focus on unequal applications of capital) so the same abstraction is appropriate for the treatment of AR. Further, the application of equal capitals *cannot* be presumed, for the flow of capital into agriculture can have two different effects. It will change the intensity of capital if it flows onto lands in use, whereas it need not do so if it is applied to new lands. This simple starting point is crucial in understanding AR. Recall that Marx is analysing developed capitalism for which accumulation typically takes the form of centralisation and intensification of production. There is expanded reproduction with a rising OCC, rather than extended reproduction with a constant OCC. Consequently, if capital flows onto new lands rather than being applied intensively upon existing lands in use, the sector tends to be characterised by extended rather than expanded reproduction, concentration rather than centralisation, and a slow pace of increase in the OCC. Here it is important to remember that the OCC is the VCC only in so far as it reflects changes in the TCC. It is concerned with productivity increase rather than the static formulation of the distribution of surplus value (based on differences in value compositions). Marx even goes to the trouble in the middle of the chapter on AR in Volume III of *Capital* 'to make a distinction here' because

> a capital of lower organic composition could assume the appearance of being in the same class with one of a higher organic composition, merely from a rise in the value of its constant portions, solely from the viewpoint of its value composition . . . The mere circumstance, then, that agricultural capital might be on the general level of value-composition, would not prove that the social productivity of labour is equally high-developed in it (III, p. 766).

Now it might well be that it is the natural conditions of diminishing productivity to capital increase that turns new capital onto new land. If so, the rent formed will be a differential rent, arising out of the need for an increase in price to solicit supply from new lands, and equivalent to a reduction in the normal size of capital. It can be observed in this case that the movement onto new land is not inefficient, and any disparity in the relative development of agriculture and industry has a purely technical basis comparable to differing OCCs within industry. AR does not apply.

Alternatively, the intensive cultivation of existing lands and the resulting rise in OCC may be obstructed by the intervention of DRII. As we shall see, it is this which determines the extent to which surplus value produced in agriculture can be retained in the sector as AR rather than entering the pool of social surplus value to be distributed equally according to individual capitals advanced. But the prior question is the production of surplus value within the agricultural sector. The result of extended reproduction, with no increase in the OCC to the extent that capital flows onto new lands, implies an increase of surplus value produced in the sector proportionate to this expansion of capital rather than a porportionate decline as in industry for which there is a relative expulsion of living labour as the OCC rises. So the agriculture sector produces additional surplus value as a result of the movement onto new land and its quantity corresponds precisely to the differences in OCC between agriculture and industry. This determination of the additional surplus value produced in a sector with low OCC is uncontroversial although its relevance has been challenged by the interpreters of absolute as monopoly rent. It is Marx's sole and frequent preoccupation in the discussion of the quantitative determination of AR. He asserts that the limit on absolute rent is simply the difference between value and price of production in that sector without specifying why in any other way than that the surplus value concerned is a surplus profit which remains confined to the agricultural sector as AR.

We have argued above, however, that Marx's analysis of capital in conjunction with his theory of rent should suggest that DRII is the basis for determining the extent to which the surplus value is retained in the agriculture sector. This follows since the creation of surplus profits that are the basis for AR come from the extension of capital onto new lands rather than the intensive cultivation of existing lands which would form the basis for surplus profits and DRII. AR cannot rise above the DRII associated with the surplus profits of intensive cultivation on existing lands, for otherwise the intensive cultivation would take place at the expense of the extensive. Moreover, because DRII measures the surplus profitability of intensive accumulation, that is of a rising OCC, the surplus value *produced* in agriculture through extensive cultivation corresponds precisely to the difference between value and price of production in that sector. In other words, Marx was correct to identify the maximum level of AR with the difference between value and price of production in agriculture. He simply bypassed the step of relating the low OCC in agriculture to the role played by DRII in obstructing intensive cultivation, a role already discovered in the separate treatment of DRII.

The results of the previous paragraph can be demonstrated more formally. Suppose initially that the OCC is equal across all industries and given by c relative to v, and that the OCC in industry and potentially in agriculture can be increased by a proportion $b > 1$ (so that given labour now converts bc constant capital into final goods rather than c). For agriculture: value minus price of production

$$= c + v + ev - (c + v)(1 + r)$$ where r is the rate of profit and e the rate of exploitation

$$= ev - (c + v)r$$

$$= ev - \frac{(c + v)ev}{bc + v} \quad \text{since } r = \frac{ev}{bc + v}$$

$$= \frac{ev}{bc + v}(bc + v - c - v)$$

$$= rc(b - 1).$$

But $rc(b - 1)$ is precisely the surplus profits arising out of the increasing OCC, since it is the rate of profit multiplied by the additional constant capital set in motion. These surplus profits correspond to the DRII which would be charged if the OCC were increased on existing lands in use. It follows that AR is limited by the difference between value and price of production in correspondence to the upper limit on the charge for extensive cultivation posed by the alternative application of capital to intensive cultivation (DRII).

In the light of this understanding of AR, it is possible to reinterpret the conditions in which it would disappear. Once the OCC in agriculture has developed to the same level as industry, the obstacle posed by DRII to intensive cultivation must have been eroded. This condition is equivalent to the equal development of agriculture and industry given a correct interpretation of the OCC. It is a sufficient but not necessary condition for the disappearance of AR, because it also requires the erosion of the effects of DRII as an obstacle to capital accumulation. On the other hand, if all land were leased, cultivation would have to progress intensively, but not necessarily efficiently, and the obstacle posed by landed property would be formed.

We have shown that the movement onto new land, the relative underdevelopment of agriculture, and a low OCC in agriculture are all conditions for the existence of AR. None are causes of its existence. Rather, all are the result of the obstacle to capital accumulation posed by landed property as capital moves between sectors of the economy, creating surplus profits in agriculture that are then appropriated as rent.

Conclusion

It has been shown that Marx's theory of rent is a coherent extension of his theory of capital to accumulation confronting the barrier of landed property. Differential rent has been seen to depend upon the existence of surplus profits formed through competition within the agricultural sector. DRI results from the divergence of individual values from market values due to 'natural' conditions, DRII from the divergence due to unequal applications of capital. AR is shown to arise from the existence of surplus profits on the basis of competition between capitals of different sectors. Each aspect of Marx's rent theory has been seen to have deep roots in his analysis of capital and its accumulation. Thus, the rejection of a correct interpretation of Marx's rent theory requires a rejection of Marx's theory of capital in the absence of rent, at least in some of his aspects. Whilst it is true that many revisers of Marx's rent theory also revise his theory of capital (whilst misinterpreting both), there are others who believe that Marx's theory of rent needs to be revised to be consistent with his theory of capital. I hope to have shown them to be wrong.

Appendix I

Marx's critique of Ricardo's theory of rent

It is well known that Marx's critique of Ricardo's value theory is based on the latter's failure to distinguish value from its form as exchange value.[15] What is less well-recognised is that this is also the pivot upon which is constructed Marx's own theory of rent and his critique of Ricardo's. As we have seen, Marx's theory of rent is intimately related to the quantitative determination of exchange value by value as well as the qualitative relationship between the two. Differential rent arises out of the divergence between individual values and market value, absolute rent out of the divergence between market value and price of production. Marx's rent theory concerns precisely the modifications in the formation of values and the formation of prices of production from these values that results from the intervention of landed property. As Ricardo identifies value with exchange value, quite apart from the existence of rent, his formation of values and exchange values must be erroneous. The errors thereby become compounded when carried over to rent theory and the inconsistencies of Ricardo's value theory become extended.

It is because the transformation problem is crucial to Marx's theory of rent, that his criticism of Ricardo's theory of rent is laced with repeated reference to and exposition of the criticism of Ricardo's theory of value. Ricardo initially bases his theory of exchange value, his value theory, on labour time, the scientific element of his theory according to Marx. As Ricardo realised that exchange value is modified according to unequal turnover times and compositions of capital, he modified his theory of (exchange) to include the effects of these. This constitutes the bourgeois and vulgar element of his theory, because profit becomes based on capital advanced before the source of profit in surplus value has been explained. Because value is identified with exchange value, surplus value as a category is *absent* from Ricardo and the competition between capitals to distribute (surplus) value according to capital advanced is inconsistent with the determination of (exchange) value itself.

In his theory of differential rent, Ricardo searches for the (exchange) value of corn. He selects the labour time of an individual production process, the one on the margin of cultivation. In doing so, he appears to be seductively close to Marx's theory of DRI. Formally there is a similarity, because Ricardo chooses what for Marx is the distorted formation of market value in the agricultural sector. But for Marx there is a prior step, the existence of individual values that diverge from market value. In addition, Ricardo has taken a further step than Marx. He has introduced exchange value and gone beyond the formation of DR by assuming the conditions for the equalisation of the rate of profit. This is not simply a divergence between the methods of Ricardo and Marx, it is an inconsistency in Ricardo's theory. For by introducing competition between capitals within a sector at the same time as competition between sectors of capital, Ricardo has simultaneously assumed that all capitals have equal rates of profit at the same time as assuming that they do not. It is purely arbitrary to presume that different rates of profit exist in one sector (and name the differences rent) and not in another, even if in agriculture there is a natural basis for such differences. Taken to its logical and consistent conclusion, Ricardo's theory must either allow the margin to determine the (exchange) value in every industry, or assume common techniques within each industry (including agriculture). In either case the theory of rent disappears. Perhaps this is not a surprising conclusion, because Ricardo's theory is drawn entirely at the level of factor ownership and natural conditions of production. It is irrelevant whether the farmer or another owns the land, the differential rent remains the same. Ricardo's is not a theory of landed property as a barrier to capital investment.

Paradoxically, it is Ricardo's errors which permit his theory of rent to parallel the appearance of Marx's theory of DRI at the same time as denying Marx's theory of AR. The neglect of the formation of market value from individual values (denying Marx's theory of surplus profits in all industries but their formation as DRI in agriculture) is coupled with the premature introduction of equal rates of profits between industries (denying the existence of surplus profits in agriculture, as a result of a low OCC, which do not enter into general equalisation). Ricardo cannot comprehend the basis of AR, since he has not understood how value diverges from exchange value in the absence of rent. In turning to rent theory, Ricardo forgets the difficulty he has confronted in the determination of exchange value by value and by capital advanced. He proceeds with value alone. Consequently any potential understanding of the source of AR is lost. Value is identified with exchange value with no differences in OCC present. Rates of profit are only equalised within agriculture by the formation of Ricardian DR, but are already presumed to be equalised between sectors by exchange at values.

Appendix II

Differential rent on the worst land

In the Ricardian theory, DR could arise on the worst land because of the difference between its average productivity and the productivity of the intensive margin. According to our interpretation of Marx's theory of DR, the Ricardian DR on worst land could arise in Marx's theory as a special form of DRII, with the proviso that for Marx the intensive margin is determined by an expanding minimum or normal level of capital whereas for Ricardo the marginal investment should be infinitesimal.

Marx devoted a chapter of Volume III of *Capital* to DR on the worst soil. It is remarkable for a correction that Engels makes to Marx's calculations, which does not reflect the usual arithmetical slip by Marx, but which changes the basis for DR calculation. Essentially Marx begins with the situation in Table 1.[16]

Table 1

Type of Soil	Acres	Total Price of Production	Output	Selling Price	Proceeds	Money Rent
A	1	3	1	3	3	0
B	1	6	3½	3	10½	4½

There is DR on land B, and the normal capital corresponds to the price of production of 3 on A. After a rise in the demand for corn, a further intensive cultivation takes place on B at decreasing productivity, depicted in Table 2. An extra capital associated with

Table 2.

Type of Soil	Acres	Total Price of Production	Output	Selling Price	Proceeds	Money Rent
A	1	3	1	3½	3½	½
B	1	9½	4½	3½	15¾	6¼

price of production 3½ produces an output of 1 on land B. This additional investment has a higher price of production than for the worst land A and regulates the selling price. The normal capital now corresponds to this 3½ on B. Rent then arises on A. Here we have DRII in the form of the Marxian 'intensive margin'. As such it appears similar to the Ricardian intensive margin in which rent is a result of capital accumulation and not a condition for it. It is perhaps to remedy this that Engels suggests the schema of Table 3. He argues as follows. B is charged a rent of 4½ and so

Table 3

Type of Soil	Acres	Total Price of Production	Output	Selling Price	Proceeds	Money Rent
A	1	3	1	3⅑	3⅑	⅑
B	1	9½	4½	3⅑	14	4½

becoming the regulating soil, it forms a selling price of 14 in costs (9½ + 4½) divided by output 4½, yielding 3⅑. This leaves rent ⅑ for soil A over its price of production. In terms of the numerical results, Engels' treatment is equivalent to an increase in the normal level of capital used, since B continues to bear the same rent despite an increase in the capital used. However, Engels' calculation is incorrect because rent is used exclusively to determine (regulating) price of production rather than derived from it as a surplus profit on the condition that the additional investment is made. That this is so is demonstrated by the fact that the capitalist farmer on B could make surplus profits by remaining at the previous level of cultivation since the production of the last unit produced exceeds the selling price (3½ as opposed to 3⅑). As Marx demonstrated the selling price must rise at least to 3½ to induce the additional capital on B.[17]

According to our interpretation of Marx's theory of DR it can only arise on the worst land in two circumstances. First, it may occur as already described in parallel to the Ricardian intensive margin.

> For as soon as differential rent II comes into force through successive investments of capital, the limits of the rising price of production may be regulated by better soil; and the worst soil (previously) the basis of differential rent I, may also yield rent (III, p. 739).

As a special case the intensive cultivation could occur on the worst soil itself, and with decreasing productivity the creation of differential rent would depend upon whether the additional capital becomes normal or not:

> It would depend to what extent a second investment of capital in the available soil A had become general, whether the price of production is equalised at the average price or whether the individual price of production of the second investment of capital becomes regulating (III, p. 744).

Second, DRII can arise on the worst soil if intensive investment takes place there without diminishing returns (which are necessary for the rent on the worst soil of the previous paragraph). If the additional capital were to become normal, the surplus profits would be eroded to form a reduction in the price of production as this becomes calculated on the average rather than the additional investment (III, p. 742/3).

Appendix III

Marx's theory of rent: a critique of interpretations

The main body of the text has established the basis for misinterpretations of Marx's theory of rent. On the one hand, there is the identification of Marx's theory of differential rent with Ricardo's, for a critique of which by Marx himself, see Appendix I. On the other hand, there is the supposedly arbitrary dependence in Marx of absolute rent upon the low OCC in the agricultural sector. By denying the exchange of agricultural commodities at value as the limit to absolute rent and by denying the dependence of AR on a low OCC, properly understood, the result is necessarily the displacement of absolute by monopoly rent.

The generality of the view that Marx's theory of DR is identical to Ricardo's cannot be over-emphasised. Those that do differentiate Marx and Ricardo tend to emphasise the latter's assumption of diminishing returns at the extensive and intensive margins. In contrast, it is argued that Marx pointed to the increasing productivity of additional capital, no necessity for the sequence of land taken into cultivation being from better to worse, and the general improvement on all lands. True, these assumptions diverge from Ricardo's and undermine the theory of the falling rate of profit associated with classical political economy, but they do not represent a break with the Ricardian theory of rent. They merely reorganise the technical assumptions on which it is based.

The effect of a Ricardian concept of DR is to deny the most crucial result of Marx's theory, that DRII is produced as a result of an obstacle to intensive cultivation of the land. Ball (1977) correctly adopts this point of departure from Ricardian interpretations of Marx's theory of rent. It is symptomatic that in doing so he displaces the Ricardian intensive margin of (additional) investments by the Marxian average (normal) investment. He also finds it necessary to draw the distinction between the formation of values in industry as the average and their formation in agriculture at the margin. In principle, then, Ball has discovered the specifics of DRII. In addition, he emphasises the role played by rent as a determinant rather than simply a result of the structure of capital accumulation. Where our analysis differs from, or more exactly develops, Ball's analysis is in the location of the surplus profits associated with DRII according to the determination of normal capital in agriculture. Ball always adopts the average productivity on each land as the standard by which to determine market value by the highest individual value. As we have seen, this would determine market value correctly only by way of an exception. In general, the normal capital could be established by a portion of the capital utilised on a particular land. Ball also follows Engels' procedure, outlined in Appendix II, of presuming that capitalists would invest on lands until average productivities were equalised, despite the loss of surplus profits on better lands, if landlords allowed them to do so by not charging rents. Although erroneous, this procedure has the advantage of permitting the role played by rent in forming the structure of capital accumulation.

If, with the notable exception of Ball's work, Marx's theory of differential rent is usually confused with Ricardo's, the theory of AR is almost universally rejected. For example:

> Marx's claim that we are dealing with monopoly rent if the price of the product exceeds its value is dubious. (Clarke and Ginsburg, 1976: p. 72.)

> Why the definition of absolute rent is limited to sectors with a low organic composition of capital, and why absolute rent cannot drive prices above value, is one of the more obscure and debatable points in Marx. (Edel, 1976: p. 105.)

Otherwise, those more faithful to Marx, tend merely to restate the conditions of existence for AR without bringing out the interconnections of these conditions with capital accumulation (rather than surplus value distribution) – see Murray (1977), for example. However, whilst the theoretical basis for Marx's theory of AR may be controversial for many, the Ricardian notion that it is determined by distributional struggle on the part of landowners is highly appealing (at the same time as destroying the limits placed on AR by the difference between value and price of production). In its most sophisticated form, this theory of AR is proposed by Ball (1976):

> To generate absolute rent, landowners have to intervene in the land market to alter the structure of rents from those which would have existed with differential rent alone. Ownership therefore gives landlords the potential to increase rents but an active role by them is necessary in order to realise his potential. This gives no simple criteria for the existence of absolute rent, such as those technical conditions suggested by Marx (p. 31).

Despite his assertion to the contrary, this is nothing other than monopoly rent, for the basis of the (absolute) rent is not to be found in the production of surplus profits within agriculture but is to be drawn from the social pool of surplus value. Symptomatically, Ball has extrapolated, from his considerations of DRII, the existence of a structure of rent prior to a structure of production. Logically, rent is indeed prior to production since it is a condition of the application of capital to the land. But it by no means implies that the structure of rents, or at least its limits, are independent of the production of surplus value within the sector. Marx, indeed, specifically asks whether non-differential rent on worst soil

> is necessarily a monopoly price in the usual sense, or a price into which the rent enters like a tax, with the sole distinction that the landlord levies the tax instead of the state . . . whether the rent paid on the worst soil enters into the price of the products of this soil . . . as an element that is independent of the value of the commodity (III, p. 758).

He answers in the negative and immediately refers to the distinction between value and price of production formation, the significance of which we have referred to in the main text.

Finally, but at length, we consider the work of Tribe (1977). He conducts a criticism of Marx's theory of rent at many levels. Most of these criticisms will be seen to be erroneous. The remainder need to be set in a broader methodological controversy as will become clear. Tribe agrees that Marx attempts to produce his theory of rent on the basis of the logical-historical method discussed in the main text:

> Marx . . . develops a theory of rent which is based on the extension of general principles of capitalism already worked out in the preceding analysis into the special case of agricultural production (p. 74),

and

> the existence of ground rent is left as an effect . . . which depends on the invocation of historical accident, both for its appearance and continued existence (p. 79).

Quite apart from the way in which Marx employs this method, Tribe objects to the method itself. The analysis of capital produces the existence of a landlord class which has otherwise been absent, suggesting that the analysis of capital itself be reconstructed – for otherwise the conditions of existence of the 'absent' class are untheorised, introduced exogenously by historical accident to the theory, and therefore not theorised as economic conditions of existence.[18] It is not our purpose here to defend Marx's method against this attack, except by bringing out the implications of the method of critique. Marx's analysis of landed property is based upon its intervention into the accumulation of capital. As a result, it is located in terms of its logical and historical relation to capital, both in terms of its effects and in terms of the historical preconditions for the creation and dissolution of these effects. If this method is denied because relations of production are being reconstructed at a more complex level, the same argument would apply to those other constructions that Marx makes by the same method. Commodity production leads to money and value, money leads to capital, capital leads to labour-power as a commodity, wage-labour leads to surplus value, surplus value leads to productive labour, productive labour leads to unproductive labour, and so on, as well as the chain being taken up in other directions (the logical and historical basis for other forms of capital such as interest bearing and merchant capital). Thus, it is not simply Marx's theory of rent that would fall by the wayside, the analysis of capital itself becomes a victim. In addition, it becomes displaced by a theory that would introduce all relevant considerations at the outset, for their subsequent introduction by their logical and historical relation to capital is prohibited. These relevant considerations must themselves be arbitrarily delimited and the analysis necessarily approaches closer and closer to a reproduction of the appearances of capitalist society.[19]

Tribe, however, does not limit himself to these general considerations. He also criticises the specifics of Marx's rent theory. We shall show that he does so by identifying Marx's theory of rent with Ricardo's. In other words, his critique is of Ricardo, not of Marx. He begins:

> Marx's *major disagreement* with Ricardo was that this differential rent was not the only form of rent, but rather that another form existed, absolute rent (p. 74).

In effect, Tribe identifies Marx's and Ricardo's theories of differential rent. We have already seen in Appendix I that this is incorrect and that by these errors Tribe will be unable to comprehend Marx's theory of absolute rent. Ricardo's theory of DR is a barrier to the construction of Marx's theory of AR. As a result Tribe nowhere discusses Marx's theory of DRII as a barrier to investment, but most significantly he unwittingly reproduces Marx's critique of Ricardo as a critique of Marx! Like Ricardo, Tribe bases DR on the inconsistent equalisation of rates of profit between and within sectors. Marx's theory of DR is based purely on competition within agriculture. Tribe refers to 'Marx's attempt to equate differential rent . . . with surplus profit arising in industrial production' in the context of 'the flow of capitals in and out of spheres of investment' (p. 78). Within the agricultural sector itself, Tribe correctly treats differential rent 'as analogous to surplus profit', continuing that 'a permanent surplus profit is a contradiction in terms' since 'if an "extra profit" does not become subject to tendencies which erode it as soon as it appears, then it is not a surplus profit in the accepted sense of the term.' All correct, and unfortunately for Marx 'the (permanent) existence of ground rent is not such an anomaly.' But Marx's theory of DR is based on the *pace* of erosion of surplus profits in agriculture, both for DRI and DRII (natural conditions and normal capital invested) and as Tribe admits unwittingly for DRII 'the possibility of gaining a temporary surplus profit for an innovating capitalist, no matter how temporary, is the general condition of capitalist expansion' so that the ' "general rate" (of profit) does not necessarily appear at any point in time, since it is continually in the process of formation and reformation.' No wonder that Tribe concludes 'Marx in this way takes over the elements of the Ricardian rent theory and explains the distribution of the differential "surpluses" as the outcome of the distribution of private property in land', for Tribe has cut away Marx's theory of DR based on the *production* of surplus profits.

Tribe goes on to argue 'as so often with Marx, whenever theoretical difficulties arise, resort is made to exhaustive computations' but 'no amount of adding and subtracting is going to solve theoretical problems' and 'this, however, *evades* the problem . . . since to compute differing magnitudes of ground rent gets us no nearer a clarification of its nature as an economic category.' In terms of our analysis, Marx has already solved the question of the basis of the DR, and his numerical examples are an ingenious approach to the problem of discovering the basis of the formation of market value in agriculture when DRI and DRII co-exist. As Tribe never discusses Marx's DRII nor understands the basis for DR in general, there is no problem in comprehending the source of his patronising attitude to Marx's arithmetic.

However, because Marx is unable to discover the source of rent in arithmetic, he has to resort to the alternative shenanigan – theoretical artefact. For Tribe 'absolute rent is a category introduced by Marx to cover the problem that differential rent alone cannot account for the fact that the least fertile piece of land does bear a rent' (p. 80). Of course, Marx can explain rent on the least fertile land by DRII (see Appendix 2). However, because for Tribe

> in the case of differential rent, Marx sought an explanation of the distribution of the surpluses resulting from the characteristics of agricultural production through the invocation of the notion of monopoly pricing, although this is merely an economistic account of property relations which depends for its effectivity on certain ambiguities in the term 'monopoly'. Absolute rent simply develops this idea by suggesting that the rent payable on the least fertile land . . . is the *direct* result of the intervention of landed property in capitalist production.

Thus, for Tribe, Marx's theory of AR is a theory of monopoly rent. Significantly, nowhere is there a discussion of the OCC in agriculture nor its relation to the transformation problem.

Appendix IV

The historical *transformation problem*

This topic is of significance for Marx's theory of rent because AR depends upon the existence of landed property as an obstacle to the equalisation of rates of profit between sectors. Recall Marx's theory of the transformation. At the first stage, market value is formed from individual values. At the second stage, prices of production are formed from market values. The distortion created by landed property at the first stage creates DR, although the Ricardian treatment of both rent and the transformation problem has tended to conceal this. The distortion created at the second stage is the source of AR. So much for the logic of the transformation problem and its relation to rent; the historical transformation problem concerns itself with the question of whether these stages correspond to particular historical epochs. Was there a stage, capitalist or otherwise, for which commodities exchanged at their values? Was this transformed into a stage where commodities exchanged at prices of production diverging from values? The significance for (absolute) rent theory is that the historical existence of these stages for industrial capital implies that landed property has the effect of holding back agriculture to the lower level of development.

It is quite clear that Marx's view is that there is a historical transformation. This follows not only from his comments upon the matter, but from the fact that these comments are often located in the context of rent theory:

> It is quite appropriate to regard the values of commodities as not only theoretically but also historically *prius* to the prices of production (III, p. 177).

> The conversion of values into cost-prices is only the consequence and result of the development of capitalist production. Originally commodities are (on the average) sold at their values. Deviation from this is in agriculture prevented by landed property (TSV II, p. 333).

In recent work Morishima and Catephores (M & C) have suggested that Marx would have modified his view.[20] Their argument is based on two factors. First, that value is a logical construct that aids an understanding of capitalism and therefore requires no historical underpinning. Secondly, that empirically no epoch has existed in which commodities in fact sold at value. They will be shown to be wrong on both counts.

M & C's concept of value is a technical one, a Ricardian labour theory of value, in which value is determined by labour embodied. Consequently, it is not the Marxian theory of value, which concerns the form value assumes in exchange. Further, it ignores the dependence of value on its social formation. Under developed capitalism, values are formed in a different way than for earlier epochs, because economic relations are constituted differently and this is reflected in different developments of technology, capital and labour mobility, forms of competition, etc. It is only here that socially necessary labour-time reaches its full fruition. The implication is that value is itself transformed in the historical movement from earlier epochs to fully developed capitalism. In other words, before we can ask whether commodities historically exchanged at their values, we have first to determine what values are historically.

M & C's concept of value, both for developed capitalism and earlier epochs, is labour embodied, as we observed earlier, calculated from the technical conditions of production, most explicitly on the basis of an input-output model of the economy. Consequently the value–price relationship differs only numerically according to the private ownership of capital by producers or not:

> These two economies (capitalism and [hypothetical] simple commodity production) show the same structure except for the ownership of capital, and this enables us to examine the effects of private ownership of capital upon equilibrium prices and the rate of profit.

In this way, M & C commit three errors. First, they incorrectly identify the Marxian with the Ricardian theory of value so that, for example, the transformation problem of Volume III of *Capital* is seen as the generalisation of the special case of Volumes I and II (commodities exchange at prices of production as a generalisation of exchange at values) rather than as a concretisation of value at a more complex level of analysis. Second, this (incorrect) concept of value for developed capitalism is imposed upon previous epochs. Third, and as a generalisation of the second error, the economic structure of developed capitalism is imposed upon previous epochs. The last point bears further discussion.

Having defined value technically, M & C can enquire what are the conditions for simple commodity production which would lead to exchange at value. The conditions towards which they strive are those of 'perfect competition', i.e. labour mobility between sectors, non-intervention of distorting merchant capital, full information about relative labour costs of different products, etc. Otherwise, any systematic divergence from these conditions would lead to a systematic divergence between value and market price. Naturally, no historical epoch can be found empirically which corresponds to these conditions, for they tend to be fulfilled only as capitalism reaches its full development – when the formation of prices of production brings a divergence from exchange at values. M & C thereby reject the 'historical' transformation and even go so far as to reject the existence of value prior to developed capitalism. It certainly strengthens their empirical argument, or rather renders it redundant, if values have no historical existence. If values do not exist historically one wonders why there is any need to look at the empirical evidence at all. There could not have been a historical transformation.

Under developed capitalism, the conditions of imperfect competition do indeed bring divergences between market price and price of production. What M & C do is to project this result onto the special case of simple commodity production for which the conclusion is that market prices diverge from values. That they can do so is a function of their concept of value as labour embodied. What they never ask is how is value formed. If they did so, they would find for developed capitalism that imperfect competition is a distortion in the formation of market prices, because for the value of advanced capitalism certain tendencies associated with 'perfect' competition are the basis for the real existence of value. Exactly the opposite applies to earlier epochs, where value is itself formed on the basis of 'imperfect' competition. For example, the immobility of labour that characterises feudal commodity production is not a condition of competition that distorts market price formation, it is a relation of production that is the basis for feudal value production (a social not a technical basis).

It might appear that these arguments lead to a tautologous definition of exchange at value for societies that are not a fully developed capitalism. This is false. Each commodity-producing society has a set of relations of production which determine both the conditions under which value is formed (what sort of value is produced) and the conditions which lead to a divergence of market price from value. What cannot be accepted, contra M & C, is that value is determined by the narrowest of relations, the technical, and the distorting conditions of competition constitute all other relations, these considerations to be applied to all societies. Once we accept that values are qualitatively different between epochs, or more exactly forms of organisation of commodity production, then the question is not whether there was a historical transformation but how. It is here that the division of modes of production into stages is of paramount importance not only for the original development of capitalism from pre-capitalist societies but also for the development of capitalism itself. As Marx observed for capital's historical transformation:

> What competition, first in a single sphere, achieves is a single market value and market price derived from the various individual values of commodities. And it is competition of capitals in different spheres, which first brings out the price of production equalising the rates of profit in the different spheres. The latter process requires a higher development of capitalist production than the previous one (III, p. 180).

Notes

* This paper was written whilst the author was in receipt of Social Science Research Council Grant HR5724/1 to study the effect of royalties on the UK inter-war coal industry.

1. References to *Theories of Surplus Value* will be denoted by TSV followed by part number. Reference to the three volumes of *Capital* will be by volume number.
2. See Appendix IV.
3. More specifically, Marx is less concerned with the average than with the 'normal' technique. The normal technique is itself socially established. It is often argued that the most (least) favourable technique forms the normal when there is an excess supply (demand). This is incorrect and only explains the divergence of market price from price of production. For Marx, the establishment of the least or most favourable technique as the normal would depend upon specific historical circumstances connected to the relations of production within the sector, for example, a predominance of independent commodity producers.
4. The creation of values and then prices of production is not a chronological but a logical process. Clearly values are formed simultaneously to the prices of production.
5. Between TSV and *Capital* III there is a change of terminology. Where in TSV 'cost-price' is used, in *Capital* 'price of production' is used. The latter is a better term since cost-price incorrectly suggests the exclusion of profit.
6. For a more detailed study of these stages of capitalism, see Fine and Harris (1979).
7. There is a terminological problem here. If we are conducting analysis at a level where prices of production have not been formed, then profit is an inappropriate category since it also has not been formed. The appropriate term is surplus value. Unfortunately, where individual values diverge, the appropriate terminology is the existence of 'surplus surplus value.' This is generally replaced by the less clumsy but methodologically incorrect term surplus profits. Where OCCs differ, correct terminology is the existence of excess surplus value in particular sectors. Both of these 'surplus profits' are to be distinguished from each other and from the surplus profits that arise through the competition associated with supply and demand. We will, however, use the term surplus profit throughout, despite its potential ambiguity.
8. This is an almost universal procedure in the application of Marx's theory of (agricultural) rent to urban rent. For a critique of this method of argument by analogy see Ball (1977). In this paper we are explicitly dealing with agricultural rent alone.
9. Fertility here is to be taken to include natural conditions of production as well as of location, etc. These conditions are themselves not exogenous but socially determined.
10. I have been guilty in this respect. See Fine (1975). For a critique of Ricardian interpretations of Marx's DRI, see Appendices I and III.
11. Although DRII does not explicitly figure in TSV, the index makes a small number of references to it precisely by the knowledge of its definition in *Capital* according to unequal applications of capital.
12. In fact, as Ball (1977) points out, Ricardo is driven to the conclusion that all values, and not just agricultural values, are determined at the intensive margin.
13. Some of the issues discussed here are taken up in Appendix II.
14. Marx never realised his goal of constructing a theory of monopoly price, precisely because he died before dealing with market competition. We cannot construct here a theory of monopoly price, but suggest that it would be defined in terms of the appropriation of surplus profits at the level of exchange between sectors rather than the appropriation of surplus profits as a result of their production within a sector.

15. For a discussion of the relationship between Marx and Ricardo's value theory, see Himmelweit and Mohun (1978). See also Fine (1979), Chapter 6.
16. The tables here are taken from *Capital* but have been abbreviated and exclude lands irrelevant to the argument.
17. Despite these problems with Engels' calculations, they do represent, by taking rent as a condition of the application of additional capital to land B, a definitive break with the Ricardian theory. Engels seems to have been influenced by Marx's calculations of the previous chapter in which non-profit maximising behaviour by capitalists is assumed since they are presumed in the absence of landed property to invest until average productivities are equalised even if this implies an erosion of surplus profits on the better lands. But Marx's construct here must be interpreted to be hypothetical with the purpose of demonstrating the limits imposed by rent to the application of capital to the land. Otherwise, it can be seen that Marx's example implies that landowners force capitalist farmers to maximise profits and allocate capital efficiently between lands by charging rents that prevent them from eroding surplus products!
18. Our representation of Tribe's criticism of Marx's method goes beyond his own presentation of it and is therefore open to the charge of misrepresentation. Tribe's critique, however, is extremely vague. In addition, the purpose here is not to assign arguments to particular individuals, but to present and criticise particular modes of argument.
19. Tribe's arguments seem to bring him close to the method adopted by Cutler, Hindess, Hirst and Hussain (1977) and (1978), for which privileged concepts are rejected. For a critique of their work, see Harris (1978) and Ball, Massey and Taylor (1979).
20. See Morishima and Catephores (1975), (1976) and (1978).

References

Ball, M. (1976) 'Marx's Theory of Rent and the Role of Landed Property', *Birkbeck Discussion Paper*, No. 48.
Ball, M. (1977) 'Differential Rent and the Role of Landed Property', *International Journal of Urban and Regional Research*, I.3.
Ball, M., Massey, D. and Taylor, G. (1979) '*Marx's "Capital" and Capitalism Today*: A Review Article', *Capital and Class*, 7.
Clarke, S. and Ginsburg, N. (1976) 'The Political Economy of Housing', *Kapitalistate*, Summer 4/5.
Cutler, A., Hindess, B., Hirst, P. and **Hussain, A.** (1977) and (1978) *Marx's 'Capital' and Capitalism Today*, Volumes 1 and 2, Routledge and Kegan Paul.
Edel, M. (1976) 'Marx's Theory of Rent: Urban Applications', *Kapitalistate*, Summer 4/5.
Fine, B. (1975) *Marx's 'Capital'*, Macmillan.
Fine, B. (1980) *Economic Theory and Ideology*, Edward Arnold, forthcoming.
Fine, B. and **Harris, L.** (1979) *Rereading 'Capital'*, Macmillan.
Harris, L. (1978) 'The Science of the Economy', *Economy and Society*, 7.3.
Himmelweit, S. and **Mohun, S.** (1978) 'The Anomalies of Capital', *Capital and Class*, 6.
Marx, K. (1971) *Capital*, Volume III, Moscow.
Marx, K. (1968) *Theories of Surplus Value*, Part II, Moscow.
Morishima, M. and **Catephores, G.** (1975) 'Is there a "Historical Transformation Problem"?' *Economic Journal*, 85.
Morishima, M. and **Catephores, G.** (1976) 'Is there a "Historical Transformation Problem"?: A Reply', *Economic Journal*, 86.
Morishima, M. and **Catephores, G.** (1978) *Value, Exploitation and Growth*, McGraw-Hill.
Murray, R. (1977) 'Value and Theory of Rent: Part I', *Capital and Class*, 3.
Tribe, K. (1977) 'Economic Property and the Theorization of Ground Rent', *Economy and Society*, 6.1.

DEBATE

On Marx's theory of agricultural rent: a reply to Ben Fine

Michael Ball

Ben Fine has added to the contemporary revival of interest in Marx's theory of rent in an article published in a recent issue of this journal (Fine 1979). His purpose was to suggest a new formulation of differential rent II (DRII), and to highlight its relation to absolute rent (AR). In this article I want to take issue with his analysis of DRII and, as a consequence, also with his defence of absolute rent. Rent theory, however, is not just about the niceties of categories of rent. Its central concern is to consider the impact of the rent relation on the production and distribution of surplus value. It is in the context of this wider question that debates over rent are likely to be resolved, so much of the argument here will consider it, rather than Fine's paper in isolation.

Capitalism and Rent

Capitalist ground rent is the revenue received by private landed property in capitalist societies. Whilst capitalism does not need private landed property for its existence (see Massey and Catalano (1978) ch. 2), this type of landownership does depend upon capitalism and its legal definition and defence of private property. The simple existence of landed property is, however, not sufficient to specify the class relations within which it operates. Owners of land can be individuals, enterprises, distinct social classes or even capitalist producers themselves. In the latter case, capitalists either receive rent in the capitalised form of a selling price for land or pay rent through land purchase. Whatever the class composition of landowners, nonetheless, land does not produce value; its ownership only enables landed property to appropriate surplus value in the form of rent. Surplus value has to be redistributed from capital to landed property.

Rent depends consequently on certain distributional mechanisms existing within capitalist societies. The analysis of rent must start, therefore, with the elaboration of those mechanisms; in other words, with questions about the distribution of the social product. Rent can be appropriated because landed property controls a necessary condition for production. Virtually every conceivable capitalist production process needs land (except such activities as deep-sea fishing). Landed property can consequently appropriate as rent surplus profits from capitalist producers.

The fact that rent is derived from surplus profit raises an immediate question for the analysis of rent. Surplus profits within the accumulation process generally tend to be only temporary; occurring when new production methods are introduced or monopoly positions achieved by a few capitals. Competition between capitals will erode away the conditions which create specific surplus profits. Yet rent depends on the existence of a specific surplus profit — that earnt on the land in question. That surplus profit has to be *permanent* for rent always to exist; although the magnitude of the surplus profit can change. The analysis of rent must consider consequently the mechanisms within the rent relation which limit the erosion of surplus profits.

This issue cannot be avoided as landed property has to appropriate *surplus* profits. It cannot get rent by forcing the rate of profit for capital invested on a land below the normal rate of return for capital, otherwise that capital would be invested elsewhere. Similarly, if rent forced the rate of profit below the normal one in a complete industrial sector capital would move wholesale out of that industry. Surplus profits themselves can exist only if market price is forced above price of production or if production on different lands generates different rates of profit. Even if the latter is the case, rent can be charged only until the rate of profit on capital invested on different lands is equal.

All analysis of rent has, therefore, to pre-suppose (a tendency to) the equalisation of rates of profit within and between different sectors of capital — unless exceptional circumstances can be specified which make such equalisation impossible. The initial basis of Fine's analysis of the categories of rent is consequently mistaken. He argues that differential rent operates at the 'level' of values and absolute rent at the 'level' of prices of production (PoP). Both must be considered instead in relation to PoP, for that is the only criterion against which to consider whether and why surplus profits exist and the mechanisms by which those profits are appropriated as rent. Absolute rent arises when market price is forced above PoP. Differential rent arises possibly for the same reason (see later) but predominantly because permanent surplus profits exist even though the commodity is sold at a PoP. (All Marx's tables on DR, for example, considered PoPs — not values.)

Raising questions about rent as a distributional effect within capitalism requires, however, an analysis that considers more than just distribution. This can be seen clearly with the case of differential rent, which occurs because distinct PoPs exist on different lands. PoPs diverge because of the differential effects of the application of capital to different land. Each land's PoP will depend on the amount of capital invested and its physical yield. So the surplus profit generated on any land will depend upon which land's PoP dominates in the determination of market price. This necessitates consideration of the formation of exchange value, and consquently an analysis of value.

For most industries little needs to be said beyond the analysis of value given by Marx in the early chapters of *Capital*. Value is determined by the socially necessary abstract labour required at the contemporary normal conditions of production. Capitals using techniques requiring less labour will earn surplus profits. Location on a better than normal site could be one of the reasons why less labour is required; either because less transportation is needed or because certain characteristics of the site (such as water-power) reduce the mass of commodities necessary as means of production. Such locationally based surplus profit can be appropriated as DR.

Normal conditions of production, however, obviously always include a locational element. So the impact of site location on profitability can only be evaluated in relationship to those normal conditions of production. With accumulation that norm will change, and so will the structure of locational advantage and DR. In other words, the appropriation of DR can only be evaluated in relation to the norm in the industry, and that normal condition of production determines value. Rent does not consequently have a direct effect on the determination of value nor, therefore, on PoP.

The situation in agriculture is different because of the peculiar characteristic of land as a condition of production. Things are grown in it rather than produced on it, and ownership of land is ownership of a non-reproducible condition of production. Non-reproducible in the sense that it is spatially fixed ('the monopoly by certain persons over definite portions of the globe'). A distinct relation between capitalist production and exchange is generated. Following from his analysis of the formation of market value in Chapter 10 of *Capital*, volume III, Marx argues (or, more correctly, asserts albeit with considerable justification) that exchange value in agriculture is determined on the 'worst' land production (the one with the highest PoP). Surplus profits in agriculture are therefore generated by a different process from that in manufacturing industry[1], and hence the need for a distinct theory of agricultural rent.

Values, moreover, are not fixed entities. Accumulation and the concomitant adoption of new methods of production will alter agricultural exchange values. So values in agriculture (and, therefore, surplus profits) are not based upon differences between lands but upon differences in the rate of accumulation on different lands. And, to make matters even more complicated, the level of rent can influence the rate of accumulation.

Rent theory shows (jumping ahead to conclusions yet to be reached) that it is precisely because the appropriation of rent can affect the rate of accumulation that rent itself can exist permanently. This is the mechanism by which landed property can stop the erosion of surplus profits. But to reach such a conclusion a complex series of factors have to be disentangled. It is the purpose of the different categories of rent (AR, DRI and II) to help sort out this complexity.

Fine, however, isolates each of these categories into distinct analyses in a way which makes it impossible to integrate them into an adequate overall theory of rent. I now want to show that his separation of DRI and II is conceptually impossible and that most of the important effects of DR on accumulation are missed.

Accumulation and differential rent

Marx's distinction between DRI and II is made to explore the effect of rent on accumulation. Accumulation does not take place evenly on different lands: more is invested in some land than others. DRI, in effect, assumes that no accumulation is taking place, that equal capitals exist on different lands. To explore the effect of rent on accumulation something called DRII is required.

DRI, then, is an abstraction, not from some pre-conceived notion of the real but from certain key features of the CMP as a theoretical object. The CMP *is* the accumulation of capital; a process, however, which is not smooth. It is undertaken by uncoordinated capitals and surplus profits, investment rates and the intensity of competition all vary for a whole series of reasons, one of which is spatial differentiation. Yet DRI assumes *equal* capitals are invested on different lands even though they each produce distinct amounts of surplus profit.

The purpose of this abstraction is to explore the inter-relation between a physical production process with its product (a use-value) under capitalist agriculture and a simultaneous value production process with its product (value). The approach is the same as that adopted by Marx when considering value and the origin of surplus value in *Capital*, volume 1. Yet the result is different as exchange value is shown to be determined by the 'worst' physical production process in existence.

With DRI, one thing that is not different is the size of the capital. But the same amount of capital invested in different lands will produce distinct results. The size of the physical output will vary as will, consequently, labour productivity. The production process is also unlikely to be the same; some lands require more drainage or fertiliser, others more labour. Some will require their products to be transported further distances to market. DRI does not abstract from such physical differences, so even if equal capitals are assumed to exist, their technical and organic compositions will vary. Each land will only have the same (or normal) capital in respect of its size, not its content. Normal technical composition and its value 'mirror', the organic composition, whilst valid for manufacturing industries, has therefore no meaning in agriculture. Each land has its own technical and organic compositions of capital. By unquestioningly transposing such concepts to the agricultural case, Fine has abstracted from the physical differences within agricultural production which generate the unique relation between production and exchange. By doing so, the basis for differential surplus profits and therefore differential rent has been removed.

There are not, however, simply physical differences between production on different lands. Each will also have different individual prices of production. All bar one (the worst) will be lower than the market price even though the same money capital has been expended on each. In value terms this means that whilst the value of capital invested is the same, the total value of each land's output is not, for exchange value is determined on the worst land alone. The rate of surplus value therefore differs substantially between lands, although the rate of profit does not as the rest of surplus value goes as rent. There is consequently no correspondence between actual embodied labour-time and the amount of value produced between lands. Marx chose to call this the creation of a false social value.[2]

Consideration of DRI has produced a number of important results which form the basis for all Marxist rent theory. In the first place it has shown that agricultural production under capitalism is different from other industries in the relationship between its use value and exchange value. Second, it has shown that capitalist ground rent can only be explained via this peculiar articulation between production and exchange. The magnitude of differential rent on any land can be found only by a comparison of its individual price of production with that of the worst land. If the price of production on the worst land changes, the rent on all lands will change. Either because the worst land's new price of production now constitutes the new market price, or because another land now becomes the worst. No land, or type of land, can be seen in isolation.

Once accumulation takes place the whole structure of rents could change even those on lands without the additional investment, *if* the worst (or ruling) price of production is altered. And this *if* is at the core of Marx's analysis of accumulation in agriculture and DRII. It is not possible *a priori* to assume that the market price will change with additional investments. So he runs through virtually every conceivable case to see whether it does, what happens to the structure of rents, and how accumulation is thereby influenced. The applicability of the results of each of these cases is obviously dependent on the existence of the conditions that constitute the case (e.g. rising or falling demand, rising or falling productivity etc.).

There is, therefore, a determinate sequence to Marx's argument on rent through DRI to DRII, although some of the justifications for that sequence are absent. The most important absence concerns the distinction between the determinants of market price and the rate of accumulation. For Marx, capital can be invested on a land as long as it does not raise the individual price of production on that land above that of the worst soil, and provided that the rent relation permits it. This is the case *even if* the additional output could have been produced more cheaply on other lands. Neo-classical economists would throw up their hands in horror at such economic inefficiency. Good reasons for Marx's distinction can be given, however, relating to the nature of land and landed property. But before they can be examined Fine's approach to DRII has to be considered for he has chosen to reject the sequence of Marx's argument and to treat DRII in isolation as a 'pure form'. To quote: 'Marx's discussion of DRII in volume III of *Capital* never undertakes an analysis of the type laid out here.' Fine (1979) p.254.

The isolation of DRII

The isolation of DRII by Fine is done by assuming that all land is the same and in unlimited supply. Then it is argued that additional investments generate economies of scale and, therefore, a lower price of production. If each plot does not receive the investment, the ones that do will generate surplus profits for their farmers which, in turn, can be appropriated as rent. Fine claims therefore that DRII must only exist temporarily until all the (equal) lands in cultivation have the new higher 'normal' level of investment

(p. 253). Because surplus profits accruing to farmers are reduced by DRII, they have less 'incentive' to invest additional capital and the rate of investment is slowed. Land property has, thereby, acted as a barrier to accumulation in agriculture.

The argument seems plausible, and Fine backs it up with the proof of a quote from Marx. Unfortunately the argument does not necessarily follow, and it is not what Marx said. At best it comes close to one out of fourteen cases considered by Marx.

The first problem is the initial assumption of equality between lands. For this to be the case, not only has fertility to be equated but lands also have to have the same transport costs to market, i.e. be locationally equivalent. The rent relation, however, arises because of private ownership of a non-reproducable means of production, and that non-reproductibility relates to the locational *uniqueness* of lands. 'Land property is based on the monopoly by certain persons over *definite* portions of the globe. . . ' (*Capital* III, p. 615, my emphasis). To assume that all land is equal and in unlimited supply is to negate a fundamental condition for the existence of the rent relation. This is why Marx repeatedly states that DRII cannot be treated in isolation from DRI[3].

Let us remain with this strange assumption, nonetheless, to consider the barrier to accumulation effect. In the first place, surplus profits are temporary so there is no necessary reason why they should ever be appropriated as rent. Nor would DRII exist if the investment was made on all lands. The only thing, therefore, that creates DRII is, what neo-classical economics calls, a capital constraint which lasts long enough so that profits can be appropriated by landowners as a *quasi-rent*. If this is the barrier to accumulation that distinguishes the dynamics of Marx's rent theory from Ricardian and subsequent marginalist approaches, it is hard to see what all the fuss is about. There is fortunately more to differential rent than Fine suggests.

The disincentive to investment is, moreover, only relative. It is still possible for surplus profits to be higher in agriculture than elsewhere after DRII is paid. The lack of incentive to invest only *definitely* comes into operation when the farmer earns less than the normal rate of profit. The disincentive would also disappear if the farmer directly owns the land, as surplus profits would remain as profits rather than being taken as rent or capitalised in the price of land. The conclusions about rent as a barrier to accumulation consequently can, at best, provide only a statement of the probable benefits to capital of leasehold enfranchisement[4].

Normal or worst?

Fine's main conclusions are reached within the confines of his 'pure forms' of DRI and II. He does, however, try to combine the two, but the way in which they have initially been separated makes the process difficult and confusing. For a start how is exchange value determined? Two distinct processes seem to exist: determination by the worst soil for DRI, and determination by the normal capital for DRII. The two cannot be the same for different amounts of capital will be invested on different lands. Fine suggests, for example, that each land type will have its own normal capital. So which normal will rule the market price?

Phrased in this way the whole notion of 'normal' sounds absurd. There is nothing 'normal' about the capital invested in agriculture as lands *differ*. Fine, however, still goes on to suggest that the concept of the normal capital is the most important for it sets the market price. He does this (in his appendix II) by using Marx's first attempt at explaining DR on the worst soil. Say there are two lands A and B, and additional capital is invested whose *marginal product* is less than that of the previous investments on A and B. It is suggested that this additional unit will determine market price. If this was the case, all lands will pay rent but this last unit of capital will not. This is the Ricardian intensive margin which Marx rejects almost as soon as he has stated it. But what is interesting at this stage is that Fine calls this last unit of capital *the* 'normal capital' (p 267). The concept of a 'normal capital' no longer even relates to the amount of capital invested on a particular land but to a part of it: the last part; even though it is 'normal' to invest some capital on this land before the last unit. The only function left for the word 'normal' seems to be one of obscuring the fact that the author is expounding the *Ricardian* theory of rent (albeit with the possibility of a capial constraint existing).

Marx did not have these problems over normal and worst to confront as he never separated out DRII and DRI. There in only one normal capital in agriculture: the average amount invested on the worst land. And the worst land always (apart from two inconsistent Ricardian statements, see below) determines the price of production. The average capital invested on the worst land is normal in that it forms a minimum level of investment for all lands. So at least this 'normal' capital has to be invested in better soils[5]. Marx gave no justification for this assumption and, it must be said, it is unecessary to his argument.

Marginal units of capital or average prices of production?

The effect of accumulation in agriculture on market price is a central issue in the discussion of differential rent, and it is controversial. Resolution of the problem is not helped by the fact that *two* distinct and contradictory views are expressed by Marx in the section on DR in *Capital.* The problem essentially is one of whether the ouput arising from additional investments of capital on the same land can have identifiable individual prices of production. If this is technically possible and represents the social process by which investment is undertaken, marginal units of capital will determine market price, and Marx's differential rent will fundamentally be only a modified version of Ricardo's.

The alternative is that the social process of accumulation in agriculture makes such an identification impossible, so that the capital invested on one land can only be seen as a totality whatever the level of capital applied to that land. If this was the case each unit of output from that land would have the same average price of production (calculated as total capital and average profit divided by total output) instead of different individual prices of production each depending on which unit of capital invested on the land that part of the ouput could be attributed. The diverse effects on rent and accumulation of the two approaches are considerable as can be seen from Marx's description of differential rent on the worst soil (*Capital* III, Chapter XLIV) where he first expounds the marginal unit of capital approach and then rejects it in favour of the average approach.

Fine, as we have seen, adopts the marginal unit of capital approach, arguing that it best represents the social process of accumulation. This, he argues (p. 267), is because the individual farmer will get maximum surplus profits by recognising the discrete returns from each additional investment. All farmers by analogy are the same, and so the implicit position is that individual behavioural responses determine the process by which market price is set. It is possible to argue, I believe, that the accumulation process in agriculture does not allow farmers to behave in this way, even if they wanted to. Marx, unfortunately, does not go into much detail about the social processes the effects of which he is trying to explore in the cases and tables concerning DR. He tends rather to make assertions and work out their implications. But before those social processes can be considered in more detail, it is important to clarify what Marx's assertions were and their implications.

Fine argues that Engels, rather than Marx, adopted the average price of production on each land approach. Engels is criticised for it, and so are subsequent writers (such as myself (Ball, 1977)) who are said to have followed Engels. This is, however, blaming Engels for an argument in *Capital* that Fine does not like. The need to consider the output from each land at an average price of production is given the status of a *law* by Marx[6].

The chapters on rent in *Capital* are, however, exceedingly confusing on this crucial point. Most of the text (and the tables of cases of DR) assumes the existence of an average price of production on each land. The introductory chapter on DRII (Chapter XL) nevertheless expounds Ricardo's approach of marginal units of capital determining market price[7], and, as we have already seen, so does Marx's first attempt at DR on the worst soil. Marx rejects his initial presentation of DR on the worst soil because it contravenes the law of the average price of production. But the dichotomy between the initial presentation of DRII and the rest of his argument is never recognised, let alone explained.

Disagreements over the two approaches, consequently, cannot be undertaken solely by reference to interpretation of Marx but by consideration of inconsistencies in the *text* of *Capital* itself. The existence and recognition of those inconsistencies should have beneficial consequences for the debate over rent. Discussion has to be over rent theory, and its relation to the concrete issues that it is trying to confront, rather than over sterile and dogmatic presentations of the word of Marx.

Differential rent as a barrier to accumulation

Recognition that surplus profits in agriculture will depend on the difference (if any) between the average price of production on a land and the current market price for that commodity has important implications for analysis of accumulation in agriculture. It enables a distinction to be made between the processes that determine accumulation on any land and those that determine the market price itself.

Accumulation on all but the worst land will be determined by its profitability at the current market price. In other words, it will depend on the effect the additional investment has on the price of production on that land relative to that on the worst soil. Accumulation on the worst soil, however, will directly influence the market price itself, and, as a result, will possibly alter the relative profitability of all lands currently in production. Competition will, in turn, influence the economic viability of production on the worst land. Lower cost producers on better lands can squeeze marginal producers out of production by undercutting their prices. The significance of that competition will depend on the state of the market. Gluts will reduce the market price, and bankrupt the highest cost producers. So a better land will become the 'worst'. Shortages, alternatively, will induce even higher cost lands into production. In the absence of such shortages or gluts, however, accumulation on the better lands will not affect production on the worst soil nor, therefore, the market price[8].

This distinction between accumulation and the formation of market price enables the role of land property through the appropriation of differential rent to be divided into three distinct effects. Each relates to the type of land in question: (i) accumulation in the better lands, (ii) accumulation on the worst land, and (iii) the movement to new lands. Presented in this way it can be seen that land property can intervene at a number of points within the overall accumulation process, even within the context of DR alone. So, its effect will 'depend wholly upon the circumstances' (*Capital,* III, p. 743). In other words, it will depend on the state of the class struggle. The 'circumstances' can vary considerably and so, consequently, can the ways in which rent acts as a barrier.

Before exploring the 'circumstances' in more detail, it is worth noting that this distinction between accumulation and price formation in agriculture is not possible within the marginal unit of capital approach. The distinction is only possible if market price is always determined by the worst land. In the marginal capital approach, however, it is not the worst land but the worst unit of capital that determines market price. And that capital could have been invested on *any* of the lands in cultivation. Investment and price determination, therefore, have to be treated as a simultaneous process leading to an equilibrium state. Any new investment will alter that equilibrium, and the new equilibrium will depend upon the relative marginal products of each land. Technical conditions determine consequently whether and where investment will take place and the surplus profits that can be made. Rent is, therefore, only a redistribution of surplus profit and not a barrier to investment; as it neither influences the structure of surplus profits nor their possibility. It is simply a deduction from a technically predetermined array of profit. The only possible interruptions to accumulation occur in the adjustment process to the new equilibrium. These interruptions, moreover, do not concern the theorisation of the rent relation itself. They consist instead of elements of 'realism' tacked onto the pregiven theory of rent: in the form, for example, of an unequal access to credit. To put it another way, class relations, which should be central to a Marxist theory of rent, have to be imposed upon a theory of rent which relies only upon technical conditions (differing marginal productivities) for its existence.

Returning to the examination of the 'circumstances' surrounding the appropriation of rent, it can be seen that accumulation in agriculture depends on the profitability of capitalist farming *and* on the need to pay rent. Landowners cannot wholly dictate the amount of rent charged, for farming has to be a viable option for the capitalist. They can, nonetheless, use favourable situations to help create surplus profits which can be appropriated as rent. Rents can be forced up at any given level of investment or, alternatively, investment can be restricted, slowing down the development of the forces of production and, thereby, generating surplus profits. The ability to do either will depend on the state of the class struggle: between farmer and landowner, farmer and agricultural worker, and capitalist and non-capitalist producers. It is possible to examine a whole series of situations where rent acts as a barrier to accumulation. With agriculture, it is useful to cite some of the cases presented by Marx in *Capital*.

1. *Rent represents a barrier to the equalisation of prices of production in agriculture*. This example has been discussed at length elsewhere (Ball, 1977). In essence, Marx argues that capitalist farmers will continue as farmers and accumulate as long as they earn the prevailing normal rate of profit on their total capital. Farmers on better lands consequently will invest more capital as long as their price of production is less than the market price. There will, therefore, be a tendency for average prices of production to be equalised; with better soils having more capital invested upon them and the worst soils being competed out of production. Rent retards this process of equalisation as farmers on better soils have to make sufficient surplus profit to pay rent. The need to pay rent means, therefore, that less investment will take place. The point is most clearly seen with a decreasing productivity of additional capital (which is the case being considered by Marx when this effect is raised, *Capital*, III, pp. 733–737)[9].

2. *The gradual improvement of the worst soil*. This is the case when additional investment lowers the price of production on the worst soil. Normally, the market price would fall correspondingly, but Marx suggests (*Capital*, III, p. 743) another possibility; *if* the investment is gradual, and demand is increasing. The first lands to have the new investments would earn surplus profits, compared with their unimproved equivalents, which their landowners could appropriate as rent. Marx then suggests that all owners of that type of land might force their tenants to pay that new level of rent. They could do this if the additional capital was invested *and* the market price did not fall.

In this case, landed-property has forced up the market price, increased the surplus profits on all lands and thereby altered the structure of accumulation. It is noteworthy that Marx classified this particular exercise of landowner's monopoly power as *differential* rent[10]. Many of the staunchest defenders of absolute rent seem to think that such an active response by landowners can only be contemplated within the confines of absolute or monopoly rent.

3. *The impossibility of no rent land.* It was argued earlier that farmers will produce as long as they earn the going rate of profit. But no surplus profit means no rent. This is in contradiction with the notion of land-property, which will always demand a rent in return for the use of land. This point is one of the conditions of existence for absolute rent (AR) but is not solely relevant to AR. In situations where DR = 0, landowners could also compel their tenant farmers to switch to other crops which yield a surplus profit and, therefore, a differential rent. The farmers might not be too happy about this change, particularly if their expertise and fixed capital were geared to the old rather than the new crop. In this case, the amount of land under use for the crop in question would be reduced or, conversely, the expansion of the acreage under that crop restricted[11].

Other examples could be cited but hopefully the discussion has been long enough to show that there is more to differential rent than just one simple effect: historically specific circumstances have to be investigated; albeit within the theoretical framework of Marxist rent theory.

Absolute rent

Absolute rent (AR) is the category of rent discussed by Marx which has been subjected to the strongest criticism. The controversy centres on the adequacy of the mechanism for appropriating rent that Marx is describing with the category AR.

According to Marx, there are two necessary conditions for AR to exist. The first is that no other mechanism for appropriating rent will generate a rent for the landowner on the land in question. DR is zero, for example, because it is the worst land or, more correctly, *potentially* the worst land as the landowner will not let it without a payment of rent. The second condition for AR, Marx argued, is the existence of a low organic composition of capital (OCC) in agriculture. Industries with relatively low OCCs will produce commodities with prices of production (PoP) below their values. By demanding a payment for rent on otherwise no rent land landowners are, in effect, intervening in the competitive process by which market price is determined by PoP. The need to pay AR forces market prices above PoP. All lands will generate more surplus profits at this higher market price, and their landowners can, in turn, appropriate those profits as rent. So the need to pay AR on the worst soil in cultivation means that all lands have to pay that level of AR. Marx then argues that the limit on the ability to force market price above PoP will be the value of commodity. Hence, the need for a low OCC in agriculture for the existence of AR.

The argument about the need for a low OCC has been the centre of most of the controversy about AR. Marx gave no adequate justification for it, and many subsequent commentators have argued that the commodity's value is an entirely arbitrary limit. Once it is accepted that the intervention of landowners can cause market price to rise above PoP, they suggest, what is to stop it rising above value as well in some circumstances? The real limit to the rise in market price is the ability of landowners to exercise their monopoly control over land: a monopoly control which is the basis of *all* forms of rent. This power of landowners will be limited by the state of the class struggle; in particular, the economic and political conditions faced by the classes involved in the production and exchange of agricultural commodities.

Fine comes to the defence of Marx against such criticisms. He dismisses them by labelling the discussion as 'Ricardian' (p. 270), and stating that they have mistaken monopoly rent for absolute rent (pp. 258–9). He does, however, recognise that Marx provides no adequate justification for the need for a low OCC, and attempts to plug the gap by positing a relationship between DRII and AR.

In doing this, he reverts to the assumptions of the 'pure form' of DR II – and unlimited supply of land of equal quality to which is applied unequal amounts of capital. Investing on land already in cultivation will raise the OCC in agriculture, he suggests, whereas the movement to new lands will not. So, for a given increase in the total capital invested in agriculture a move onto new land will produce a larger additional amount of surplus value than it would if it were invested on current lands. At this stage the argument becomes exceedingly unclear, but the gist of it is that if you invest more on the current lands the surplus profit will go as DRII, and if you invest on the new land AR has to be paid. No farmer will pay an AR greater than DRII for otherwise it would have been cheaper to have invested on the current lands. So Fine claims that the limit put in AR by DRII is equal to the difference between value and PoP.

I must confess to have hopelessly lost the thread of Fine's argument. I am also bewildered by the apparent absence of the transformation of the input values into PoP as well as the output values (Marx's famous transformation problem), and by what seems to be a confusion between a change in the difference between value and PoP (caused by a rise in the OCC of whatever size) and the absolute size of the initial difference between the two. The most important consideration, however, is not the formal intricacies of Fine's model but the implications of the approach for the *mechanisms* by which landowners appropriate rent, in particular, the monopoly/absolute dichotomy.

In the first place, Fine's discussion of AR takes place within a rarified world of equal lands. Its applicability is then implicitly assumed to hold within the real world that is being modelled. This process of abstraction has already been criticised and it was pointed out there that the assumption of equal lands denies the possibility of any mechanism for the appropriation of rent; let alone that for absolute rent.

Consideration of unequal capitals on unequal lands raises, furthermore, the question of the efficacy of relating differential rent to absolute rent in the way done by Fine. DRII, he argues, relates to intensive cultivation of current lands, and AR to extensive cultivation by moving onto new land. The former, he suggests, raises the OCC, and the latter does not; because on the one the size of capital rises above the normal and on the other just the normal amount of capital is used. Hence, the link between the two types of rent and the OCC. There are a number of problems here: an increase in the mass of capital does not necessarily result in the OCC rising[12], nor is the investing of a greater than normal capital on the new land an impossibility (e.g. especially on the 'newest' of lands: those reclaimed from the sea).

The new land, moreover, could also generate a differential rent. Consideration of unequal capitals on unequal lands results, therefore, in the collapse of the intensive/extensive investment and leads to the DRII/AR dichotomy.

Rather than concentrating on the choice between investing on two different lands, the focus should be on the possibilities for appropriating rent on the new land in question. Consideration should be on the mechanisms open to the landowner to charge a rent. And they will relate to the price of production on that soil compared to the market price (i.e. the PoP on worst soil in cultivation). One of Marx's major objections to Ricardo's theory, after all, was to the latter's view that new land would be progressively worse (i.e. its DR = 0). There is no basis for Ricardo's belief, as Marx showed with endless examples: it all depends on the circumstances. Absolute rent is historically contingent. Fine is trying to compare the marginal productivities of capitals invested on different lands directly in his relation between DR11 and AR. Even though it does not work, by doing so he is placing himself firmly within the marginal unit of capital approach. Once again technical differences (e.g. productivities of capital, differences in OCC) are substituted for social relations. No explanation of the mechanism by which AR can be appropriated is required, for it can be simply read off from its technical conditions. Hence, the ease with which Fine feels he can dismiss others who have tried to explore those mechanisms.

Farmers, however, do not choose between investing 'intensively' or 'extensively'. That the 'extensive' margin for sheep farming is somewhere in New Zealand, for example, is hardly of much interest to the Welsh farmer who is wondering whether to invest more capital. The choice is more likely to be between sheep farming and a caravan site, than of emigration to New Zealand. Competition in the market and the movement of capital, moreover, will not lead to investment on only one type of land. Investment could take place on many different lands at the same time. It all depends on their PoPs relative to the market price, on what is happening to the market price, and on how much rent they have to pay.

It is in relation to market price that the mechanism by which AR is appropriated can be seen. Landowners refuse to let their land at no rent. So *if* DR = 0 on that land the owner will hold the land idle until the market price rises sufficiently to generate surplus profits on that land to pay the rent (i.e. AR). Landowners can do this as they can control the supply of the agricultural commodity by withholding land from cultivation until a rent is paid. The significance of this withholding effect, and therefore the size of AR, will depend on the control by landowners over land than can be used for cultivation and the state of the market (rising, static or falling prices). The difference between PoP and value has no influence on this mechanism; value as an upper limit is a total irrelevance.

To what extent is this discussion considering a monopoly rent? Monopoly is central to the argument; as it is for *all* considerations of rent. A monopoly 'by certain persons over definite portion of the globe' is the basis of land property and rent. The discussion is also considering an *active* use by landed property of their monopoly: withholding land until a rent is paid. But, once again, so does the examination of any form of rent. Surplus profits are not automatically transformed into rent. The appropriation of rent helps, in addition, to generate the surplus profits in the first place. The active intervention by landed property to create rent is seen just as much in the case of differential rent as it is in the mechanism described for absolute rent.

A reference to monopoly does not consequently distinguish

forms of rent. One particular type of monopoly can, however, be distinguished from the mechanisms generating both DR and AR. This case is when the producer of an agricultural commodity has a monopoly over its supply. Here, a high market price (and surplus profits) will exist independently of the rent relation. The need to pay a rent would consequently just be the re-distribution of a pre-given mass of surplus profit. A good example is a vineyard producing a rare wine. This mechanism has been categorised by some as *monopoly* rent (e.g. Edel, 1976).

To dismiss criticism of the necessity of a low OCC for the existence of AR as reducing the concept of AR to a monopoly rent, as Fine does, is therefore to miss the point. It ignores the crux of the problem posed by the different categories of rent: the examination of the mechanisms by which rent is appropriated and the economic conditions which enable that appropriation to take place (and which, in turn, rent helps to create). Perhaps the controversy could be resolved by calling AR 'absolute rent' when market price is below value, and calling it 'monopoly rent II' when market price is forced above value. It would, nevertheless, be mere semantics as the mechanism described by AR has not changed in the slightest[13].

Criticism of the origin of surplus profit as the basis for the existence of AR does not mean that considerations of the origin of surplus profit have no relevance for the analysis of rent. The basis for the surplus profits might have important implications for the state of class struggle in agriculture. In specific historical circumstances the level of rent might depend on the ability to depress the wages of agricultural workers below the value of labour-power. This will increase farmers' surplus profit and, therefore, rent. This was a common feature of nineteenth-century British agriculture, for example, as Marx describes in his introductory chapter on rent. Similarly, farmers might be forced to accept less than the average rate of profit. Leasehold conditions might also result in the farmer's fixed capital reverting to the landowner at the end of the lease. Non-capitalist relations would further exacerbate such effects[14]. But, here, the origin of surplus profits are describing a process of class struggle, and not simply a technical relation.

Accumulation in Agriculture

The need for a theory of capitalist ground rent is obvious. Landed property appropriates rent. How is it done and what effects does it have? The importance of the theory of rent consequently is not just as a theoretical exercise but results instead from the historical and political role of landed property in the development of capitalism. The effects of landed property have to be theorised within the framework of historical materialism and its analysis of the CMP. That analysis is obviously an 'abstract' one but, even so, the concept of landed property has to be a simplified one for analysis to be possible. Many important features of landed property as a theoretical object have to be ignored by any theory of rent. That theory, however, should still be able to confront those features and be compatible with them.

When considering agricultural rent examination of accumulation in agriculture has to be considered. And it is a highly simplified process of accumulation that is examined. In *Capital*, cases (rising or falling productivity, etc.) are considered in total isolation, and conclusions deduced from them. This raises the question of their wider applicability, and their compatibility with a more comprehensive analysis of accumulation in agriculture. This question, for example, has been at the centre of the criticisms of Fine's analysis of rent.

The problem is not one of the 'realism' of an assumption but one of producing an adequate theorisation of the process of accumulation in agriculture. Accumulation in agriculture is different from that in other industries, and the reason for this can be explained within rent theory: the nature of one of the conditions of production (land), the different articulation between production and exchange, the role of landed property, etc. That explanation, however, does not go far enough. More is required. It does not explain, for example, what the coercive force of accumulation does to investment in agriculture, nor whether accumulation is even, in fact, a coercive force. The marginal unit of capital approach would suggest it is not – agricultural capital chooses where it goes.

Certain features of accumulation in agriculture have consequently to be theorised, and the theory of rent has, at least, to be compatible with them even if it does not consider them directly. Some brief and tentative suggestions of the nature of some of these features will now be given to conclude the paper.

An important characteristic of agricultural production, which has to be encompassed within the theory of rent, is location. Capitalism (or any other mode of production) cannot ignore the effects of spatial differentiation. But the effects of locational specificity and their importance are not fixed like physical co-ordinates. Capitalism can, and does, overcome many of the problems for accumulation thrown up by spatial differentiation: through changing modes of transportation, or the distribution of population, or methods of production, etc. Agricultural capital, however, faces a particular problem in that one of its principal means of production, land, is locationally fixed. They are farms. They have soils of a particular type although ones that can be changed within limits and at great cost. And they face particular climates whose effects can again only be changed at great expense. Farm sizes can be altered, but basically farms have relatively fixed characteristics and accumulation likewise has to be locationally fixed. A capital either accumulates on that land or goes out-of-business. Whether it makes a profit depends on keeping the price of production on its land below the market price for the commodity in question, and on the rent (if any) that it has to pay.

The market price itself will be determined by a process of competition between different lands/farms (in the way described for DR). If new methods of production start to change the market price, all farms will have to adopt them or find some other way of reducing prices of production. In no sense are farmers immune from the coercive effects of accumulation.

Capital can only be invested on land by a particular capitalist enterprise (as long as it has effective possession). Access to finance consequently becomes crucial to the speed at which methods of production change and, therefore, to the extent of the competition between different lands. Those enterprises will invest as long as they make a profit and, where necessary, will try to get credit to do so. Capital cannot, therefore, float freely between lands, flitting from one with the current highest marginal product to next, and so on. Individual social agents invest and accumulate, not an all-seeing computer.

Added to these features is another characteristic of accumulation which rent theory tends to ignore: the uncoordinated nature of accumulation and the massive fluctuations in both output and prices that result. Variations in weather conditions compound these fluctuations. An agricultural capital does not know from year-to-year, therefore, how much output they will produce nor the price they can get for it. They have to guess. Speculative decisions have to be made over the choice of crop and the level of investment. Neat arrays of marginal products and fixed market prices do not enter the accumulation process.

Various nation states have tried partially to shield their agriculture sectors from the problems which beset accumulation. Attempts have been made to circumvent foreign competition, fluctuations in prices and the barrier posed by rent to investment through import controls, price supports, investment subsidies and the encouragement of owner-occupation. None of these measures, however, can alter the process of accumulation. They can only make it more profitable, or less uncertain.

The picture of accumulation in agriculture is consequently far more complex than the treatment it gets in rent theory. This does not necessarily lead to a rejection of that rent analysis, as long as the latter can be extended to encompass those features. It is difficult, I would suggest, to do that with the marginal-unit-of-capital approach. That approach depends on too many assumptions which are directly at variance with the process of accumulation. Once that approach is rejected, however, rent inevitably has to be regarded as a barrier to accumulation. This can be seen within the average price of production approach, which is broadly compatible with the features of accumulation described above. But there is no need to slavishly assume that capitals in agriculture will always tend to accumulate until the price of production on their lands is equal to the market price. It all depends on the circumstances.

What is needed (to close on a cliche) are more studies of concrete situations.

Notes

1. The necessity of this distinction between agriculture and manufacturing industry has not been elaborated here. Hopefully it will become clearer as the argument progresses. An attempt at a more detailed elaboration and justification for the distinction is given in Ball, 1977.
2. It is false in the sense that it would not be there if landownership and capitalism were not there. Like certain of his distinctions between productive and unproductive labour in *Capital*, volume II, analogies are being made with other modes of production and the results are then being applied *within* capitalism. It is difficult to see how other modes of production are more 'true' than the CMP. Within the CMP this is how social value is produced in agriculture, and it should be examined as such.
3. 'In the study of DRII, the following points are still to be emphasised. First, its basis and point of departure, not just historically, but also in so far as concerns its movements at any given period of time, is DRI, that is the simultaneous cultivation side by side of soils of unequal fertility and location; . . .' *Capital*, III, p. 676.

'The combinations of DRII, *which presupposes DRI as its basis*, will now be taken up.' *Capital*, III, p. 684, my emphasis.
4. Fine's quote from Marx, on p. 253, used to validate his barrier argument is unfortunately a misquote. It comes from the second case (falling price of production) of DRII considered by Marx in its third variant (rising rate of productivity of additional capital). Nowhere there does Marx talk of restrictions on the investment of capital, nor about a single type of land, and he is talking about the effect of investment on the worst land, A, which determines the market price.

'In the same way, a certain minimum capital is required for every individual branch of industry in order that the commodities may be produced at their price of production.

If this is minimum is altered as a result of sucessive investments of capital associated with improvements on the same soil, it occurs gradually. So long as a certain number of acres, say, of A, do not receive this additional working capital, a rent is produced upon the better cultivated acres of A due to the unalterd price of production, and the rent from all superior soils, B, C and D, is increased. But as soon as the new method of cultivation has become general enough to be the normal one, the price of production falls; the rent from the superior plots declines again, and that portion of soil A that does not possess the working capital which has now become the average, must sell its product below its individual price of production, i.e. below the average profit.' *Capital*, III, p. 706.

By merging the paragraphs, editing out all reference to other lands, and emphasising the word 'gradually', Fine has succeeded in altering the meaning substantially. The first sentence by Marx in the second paragraph, for example, does not conclude that there is a barrier to accumulation but reads instead like a truism.

5. See the quote in footnote 4 and the following statement a paragraph later in Marx's text, where the worst soil A has fallen out of production because cheaper lands can now satisfy demand.

'. . . A no longer competes in the production of this particular product e.g., wheat. The quantity of capital which is now required, on the average, to be invested in the better soil B, the new regulator, now becomes normal: and when one speaks of the varying fertility of plots of land, it is assumed that this new normal quantity of capital per acre is employed.' *Capital*, III, p. 706 and *passim*.

6. To show that it is more than an isolated statement by Marx more than one quote will be given.

1. 'It shows, secondly, that differential rent, in so far as it arises from successive investments of capital in the same total area, resolves itself in reality into an average, in which the effects of the various investments of capital are no longer recognisable and distinguishable, and therefore, do not result in rent being yielded from the worst soil, but rather: 1) make the average price of the total yield for, say, an acre of A, the new regulating price and 2) appear as alteration in the total quantity of capital per acre required under the new conditions for the adequate cultivation of the soil; and in which the individual successive investments of capital, as well as their respective effects, will appear indistinguishably blended together. It is exactly the same with the individual differential rents from the superior soils. In each case, they are determined by the difference between the average output from the soil in question and the output from the worst soil at the increased capital investment – which has now become normal.' *Capital*, III, p. 705.

2. When rejecting his first approach to DR on the worst soil:

'But from the point of view of differential rent, a peculiar difficulty arises here owing to the previously developed law – according to which it is always the individual average price of production per quarter for the total production (or the total outlay of capital) which acts as the determining factor.' *Capital*, III, p. 741.

3. When considering an investment on the worst soil A when the productiveness of successive investments is increasing:

'The additional capital per acre of soil A, however it is applied, would be an improvement in this case, and would make the original portion of capital more productive. It would be ridiculous to say that $\frac{1}{3}$ of the capital had produced 1 qr and the other $\frac{2}{3}$ – 4 qrs. For £9 per acre would always produce 5 qrs, while £3 would only produce 1 qr.' *Capital*, III, p. 743.

7. The marginal unit of capital approach is most clearly expressed in the following statement:

'If the same capital of £10, which is shown in Table 1 to be invested in the form of independent capitals of £2½ each by various tenants in each acre of the four soil types A, B, C and D, were instead successively invested in one and the same acre D, so that the first investment yeilded, 4 qrs, the second 3, and the third 2 and the fourth 1 qr (or in the reverse order), then the price of the quarter furnished by the least productive capital, namely = £3, would not yield any differential rent, but would determine the price of production, so long as the supply of wheat whose price of production is £3 were needed.' *Capital*, III, p. 678.

8. The meaning of the 'worst' soil in this context can be seen to be the land with the highest price of production. This need bear no relation to its innate natural fertility as the price of production will depend on the amount of capital invested in the land and that land's location in relation to major markets. Worst, therefore, refers to a social process – the level of accumulation at a point in time – evern though that social process has a 'natural' base i.e. land.

9. Fine seems to think that Marx never made this point, and criticises Engels for 'erroneously' using it (Fine, 1979, p. 267 and 269). That Engels was simply reiterating Marx's argument can be seen from the following statement by Marx:

'For a long time, then, additional capital with under-productiveness, or even increasing under-productiveness, might be invested until the individual average price per quarter from the best soils became equal to the general price of production, until the excess of the latter over the former – and thereby the surplus-profit and the rent – entirely disappeared.' *Capital*, III, p. 735.

Fine's claim is more surprising in view of the fact that he actually uses (p. 257) a quote from the section where Marx is discussing this effect. The quote is used to back up a repeated assertion that rent is a barrier to accumulation (Fine, pp. 256–7). To make a reference to *Capital* for a detailed exposition of a process, whose effects only are being considered, seems reasónable. But, to quote approvingly a conclusion that rent is a barrier having rejected the mechanism by which that conclusion has been reached can only be regarded as remarkable.

10. When talking about this possibility Marx concludes:

'Thus, as was previously seen to be the case for the better soils when the productiveness of the additional capital decreased, it would again be the transformation of surplus-profit into ground-rent, i.e., the intervention of property in land, which would raise the price of production, instead of the differential rent merely being the result of the difference between the individual and the general price of production.' *Capital*, III, p. 743.

11. Marx cites this example when considering the free importation of grain:

'Even if grain were freely imported from abroad, the same result (i.e. interference with the determination of market price by the average price of production on the worst soil, MB) could be brought about or perpetuated by compelling farmers to use soil capable of competing in grain production regulated from abroad, for other purposes, e.g., pasturage, so that only rent bearing soils would be used for grain cultivation,. . .' *Capital*, III, p. 743.

12. A general tendency for manufacturing industry is being unquestioningly transposed to agriculture. Whether the TCC, or the OCC, rose would depend on the type of land and the type of process being used. Different lands will have different OCCs it was argued earlier. A switch of capital from one type to another could consequently easily result in the overall OCC falling. Similarly, additional capital on one land could easily be *all* variable capital, lowering the OCC, e.g. the benefits of hand-weeding or picking a delicate crop, or more workers to tend a valuable herd.

13. Quotes from Marx could be used to justify the distinction, if desired. In *Capital*, III, p. 775 he first distinguishes monopoly price on the market

from that generated by rent, and then goes on to relate the latter to AR: 'Here then, the monopoly price creates the rent. On the other hand, the rent would create a monopoly price if grain were sold not merely above its price of production, but also above its value, owing to the limits set by landed property to the investment of capital in uncultivated land without payment of rent.'

Why, however, the price will only be a monopoly one above value and not above PoP is difficult to understand.

14. 'Such is the case, e.g., in Ireland. The tenant there is generally a small farmer. What he pays to the landlord in the form of rent frequently absorbs not merely a part of his profit, that is, his own surplus labour (to which he is entitled as possessor of his own instruments of labour), but also a part of his normal wage, which he would otherwise receive for the same amount of labour. Besides, the landlord, who does nothing at all for the improvement of the land, also expropriates his small capital, which the tenant for the most part incorporates in the land through his own labour.' *Capital,* III, p. 625.

References

Ball, M. (1977) 'Differential Rent and the Role of Landed Property', *International Journal of Urban and Regional Research*, 1. 3.

Edel, M. (1976) 'Marx's Theory of Rent: urban applications.' In *Housing and Class in Britain*. London: Housing Workshop of CSE.

Fine, B. (1979) 'On Marx's Theory of Agricultural Rent', *Economy and Society*, 8. 3.

Marx, K. (1971) *Capital*, Volume III, Moscow: Progress Publishers.

Massey, D. and **Catalano, A.** (1978) *Capital and Land: Landownership by Capital in Great Britain*. London: Edward Arnold.

DEBATE

On Marx's theory of agricultural rent: a rejoinder

Ben Fine

In responding to Michael Ball's criticisms of my article I feel it is first necessary to emphasise two points of agreement. The first is that there can be no general theory of rent (or agricultural rent) as, for example, in neoclassical theory where the structure of rents emerges from technical and market conditions and rents are appropriated by those who happen to own the land. Rather, the formation of rent is contingent upon an historical element that must be incorporated into the theory according to the social relations actually associated with landed property. Secondly, we agree that rent is a distributional form corresponding to the relations of landed property and that these relations act as a barrier to capital accumulation so that rent cannot be seen solely or even primarily as a distributional relation. It is Ball's intention to show that despite my analysis and protestations to the contrary, that I depart from these propositions and that the logic of my position is Ricardian. Here I hope to show that the agreement between Ball and myself remains whilst there are differences that persist which I will seek to clarify and justify in so far as I am responsible for them.

The necessity of an historical element in the theory of agricultural rent renders a dispute of the type between Ball and myself problematic, because we have both been theorising at an abstract level in the absence of specific considerations of historical developments in the form of landed property and capital's relation to it. Differences may be produced by virtue of a divergence between the sort of landed property relations that each has in mind. Here, however, I believe I have been more consistent than Ball. My analysis was based on the dominance of the capitalist mode of production over agriculture the implications of which are spelt out in general terms in a quotation from Marx reproduced on page 248 of *Economy and Society*, Vol. 8 no. 3. Ball, in contrast, varies the stage of development of capitalist agriculture analysed, referring at times to non-capitalist relations (p. 320) and at other times to accumulation through hand-weeding (fn. 12) denying the tendency for the technical composition of capital to rise because of differences in land qualities and crops. It is on this basis that he rejects my 'transposition' of categories drawn from the analysis of industrial capital to agricultural capital, although his own analysis also contains its own transposition of a less systematic kind. The first major difference between us then concerns the validity of such a transposition. To pose the question in a different way: does the intervention of landed property render invalid the structure of economic relations associated with industrial capital in general or does it merely modify the effects that these relations produce? If the answer is the former, then my analysis is redundant, and clearly so, since the first part of my paper was concerned to exposit the structure of economic relations to which agricultural capital is bound in a society dominated by the CMP. But the question cannot be settled theoretically, for as we have observed, it is an historical question concerning the actual status of landed property in the society concerned. Ball might like to deny that the economic relations that I transpose from industry to agriculture can be transposed in reality in the presence of landed property, but he does not do so explicitly. Rather he tends to argue that the result of my transposition is to produce for agriculture an analysis that fails to distinguish it from industry. Indeed, he goes further, not only are industry and agriculture rendered identical, each is analysed in terms of a Ricardian, at times a Marshallian, equilibrium.[1]

Most of the differences between Ball and myself are derived from a disagreement over transposition. My transposition has the advantage of clarity. The structure of market value and price of production is used to produce the categories of differential and absolute rent in correspondence to the pace and structure of accumulation. Ball's transposition is more uncertain. Prices of production, profit equalisation, and the formation of surplus profits are taken for granted but the structure of economic relations connecting these and other categories is far from clear, particularly concerning surplus profits which is an ambiguous term as I pointed out in my article. My analysis allows a ready identification of the different forms of rent with the production of surplus value. Ball's does not.

Nevertheless, Ball does make criticisms that I am prepared to accept, although they represent more of a need for improved exposition. Ball is quite right to argue that my construction of DRII is purely ideal.[2] To assume unlimited supplies of equally fertile land is to deny the basis of rent. However, the exposition had a purpose and was deliberate. The whole recent tradition of Marxist rent theory has treated DRII as comparable to the Ricardian intensive margin.[3] My intention was to undermine that tradition as simply as possible and to some extent on its own terms. To do this I took differential levels of capital application in their simplest form, emphasising increasing size of capital as opposed to infinitesimally small increments of capital. Having done so I made quite clear that DRI and DRII were not 'simply additive', 'a more complex analysis is necessarily involved' (Fine, 1979: pp. 254–5). Ball's suggestion that DRII is treated 'in isolation as a "pure" form' (p. 309) is unfortunate. What I showed, in agreement with Ball's supposed criticism, is that DRI and DRII could not be treated in isolation and brought together because of the indeterminacy of worst land and normal capital. The way I discussed the interaction of DRI and DRII was also perhaps unsatisfactory. First, there was the use of the word 'temporary' for the surplus profits corresponding to the DRII produced by unequal capital applications. As Ball points out (p. 305), 'surplus profit has to be *permanent* for rent always to exist; although the magnitude of the surplus profit can change. The analysis of rent must consider consequently the mechanisms within the rent relation which limit the erosion of surplus profits.' My analysis did show how DRII would be reproduced as well as eroded by the process of capital accumulation. This cannot be treated separately, however, from the potential pattern of land usage corresponding to DRI. Again as Ball observed, rent is charged as a piece and not according to its component parts in political economy.

Second, my treatment of differential rent as a whole was perhaps misleading because of the use of 'normal' capital on the worst land, an obvious misnomer since, however market value of agricultural produce is determined, the corresponding production process will not be employing a normal but rather a unique size of capital. In addition, my argument conducted in these terms perhaps gives the impression that the worst land and the normal capital are prior to and determine the structure of rents (but see Fine, 1979 p. 256 for the opposite view) as in Ricardian theory. This is only true in the mathematical sense of determination, once we know which land and capital determine value then the structure of rents is determined, but there is the prior determination of that land and capital.[4]

The remarks in the previous paragraph do not reconcile a difference which remains between Ball and myself. He accords the formation of market value by the highest average price of production (i.e. on the worst land) the status of a law, albeit a law that 'all depends on the circumstances' (p. 323). He then imposes this law on agriculture, a transposition which is far more dogmatic than any produced by me, and criticises what he considers to be the only alternative law, marginalism. I am presumed to hold to the latter theory and Marx is caught holding both theories. But Ball is wrong to argue that market value is necessarily determined by the law of highest production price or by the law of additional unit of capital. There is no law at all. At times, price of production will correspond to the total application of capital to the worst land, at other times will correspond to the productivity of additional units of investment.[5] Nor does the latter instance require that it is an individual rather than a social act that determines value, for it is a question of which capital on which land corresponds to value rather than which determines it.

Ball's insistence on the law of highest average price of production creates its own peculiarities, particularly the view that farmers are forced to make investments as individuals that reduce their profits. This is not to deny that social forces on farmers are prior to their individual motivation and the former are determinant, nor that conditions may render farmers unaware of the most profitable options, but that they should otherwise deliberately forego profits to allow the 'laws' of political economy to operate is implausible.

In his concluding remarks, Ball considers those elements which are necessary for the development of rent theory, particularly emphasising locational and spatial factors. To these I would add the form and distribution of landed property. More generally, any factor which potentially raises profitability is the basis for landed property's intervention and the formation of a rent. This merely returns us to our starting point, that the theoretical point of departure for rent theory must be those relations which make such interventions possible and significant. My analysis attempted to demonstrate the possibility of intervention on the most systematic basis, that is according to the increases in profitability brought about by the process of capital accumulation. Ball perhaps finds this approach too narrow, waiting upon, for example, any proximate cause that raises prices and potentially rent. Neither approach is wrong as such and each has its virtues, the one emphasising the necessary connection between accumulation and rent formation, the other emphasising the diversity of the forms in which landed property can intervene. As Ball observes, 'it all depends on the circumstances.'

Notes

* This paper was written whilst the author was in receipt of Social Science Research Council Grant HR5724/1 to study the effect of royalties on the UK inter-war coal industry.

1. Ball's critical zeal has clearly got the better of him. The very worst my transposition can produce is an agriculture identical to industry. As my analysis of industry appears acceptable to Ball and does not include equilibrium states, it is unclear how my analysis of agriculture can do so. Here we have an example of a method of criticism by Ball which might be termed 'guilt by association'. It litters his paper and is a barrier to understanding. Where similar concepts are drawn from different theories they are used to classify the theories as identical. Consideration of additional units of investment makes you Ricardian, marginalist and ultimately neo-classical, differential access to credit locates you in the theory of Marshall, etc.

2. The same applies to my exposition of the formulation of absolute rent.
3. Ball is himself a most notable exception.
4. There is a clear analogy here with the neo-Ricardian/Sraffian determination of value mathematically by predetermined production relations. This determination is mathematical, not causal.
5. Ball seems to suggest that the notion of the productivity of additional investment is invalid, since a production process is a totality that cannot be separated into parts. This is correct but the results of two unequal applications of capital are quite clear and can be subtracted the one from the other.

Reference

Fine, B. (1979) 'On Marx's theory of agricultural rent', *Economy and Society* 8, 3.

DEBATE

The historical transformation problem — a reply

George Catephores

In the August 1979 issue of *Economy and Society,* in a brief Appendix to his interesting paper on Marx's theory of agricultural rent,[1] Ben Fine saw it fit to accuse Morishima and myself of serious misconduct in our study of the historical transformation problem.[2] He claimed that we could be shown wrong on two counts and guilty of three errors. The two counts were: (a) our claim that value is a logical construct for the analysis of capitalism and as such requires no historical underpinnings and (b) our associated claim, presented against a thesis by Engels seconded by the late R. L. Meek that empirically no epoch has existed in which commodities actually exchanged at labour determined values. The three errors consisted of (1) our *alleged* identification of the Marxian with the Ricardian theory of value; (2) our imposition of this incorrect concept of value upon precapitalist epochs and (3) of our further imposition of the economic structure of advanced capitalism upon such epochs.

Before I can plead guilty to this crushing indictment, I beg the prosecution to consider the following points:

First, our critic nowhere demonstrates that the labour theory of value does require historical underpinnings in order to aid our understanding of the structure of capitalism. But this is what he ought to have done if he wanted to show M and C positively wrong. Pending such demonstration I reserve my admission of guilt on count (a).

Second, our critic nowhere sticks his neck out to assert that there has been some actual historical epoch (say between 1000 and 1400 AD or any other dates) in which products of labour did exchange according to labour determined ratios. But this is what he ought to have done if he wanted to show M and C wrong in what they said – i.e. that on the existing historical record they could perceive of no such epoch. Pending such assertion and demonstration, I reserve my admission of guilt on count (b) also.

But, of course, Ben Fine does not mean that we were wrong in what we literally said. Rather he asserts that we were wrong in what we did not say for not having said it. In particular he would have liked us to have adopted, or rather anticipated, (since his paper was published after ours), his own new interpretation of the historical aspects of the labour theory of value. He finds that we did not do so and from this he concludes that he has shown M and C wrong. I find this way of proving someone wrong really extraordinary.

Ben Fine's suggestion for a new approach is best summarized in his own words.[3] 'Each commodity producing society has a set of relations of production which determine both the conditions under which value is formed (what sort of value is produced) and the conditions which lead to a divergence of market price from value'.

If this statement is intended to supply the labour theory of value with the historical underpinnings missed out by Engels and Meek, then surely it is unduly squeamish. Engels, the originator of the historical line of defence of the labour theory of value made no bones about what he intended to argue:[4]

> The Marxian law of value holds generally, as far as economic laws are valid at all, for the whole period of simple commodity-production that is up to the time when the latter suffers a modification through the appearance of the capitalist form of production. Up to that time prices gravitate towards the values fixed according to the Marxian law and oscillate around those values . . .

In our article this is the position we essentially concentrated against, although we discussed it in the more sophisticated, cautious but in the end no less committed form in which it appeared in the work of the late R. L. Meek.[5] Engels' (and Meek's) position is clearcut and relevant, so it is possible to support or reject it on the basis of the historical record. By contrast, it would be meaningless to present any evidence of non-proportionality of exchange rate of commodities to labour embodied in them against Ben Fine's view, because he rules out the relevance of such evidence by definition.

However, while Engels' thesis, if supported by evidence, would indeed provide serious underpinnings to the labour theory of value, the same cannot be said about Ben Fine's proposal. In its present form at least, (and disregarding his hasty formulation and his polemical tone that can do no justice to so serious a problem) his thesis can contradict nothing that we have said; it might even be thought to support many of our points. We would not necessarily object to someone showing to us that some other 'sort of value' was produced in precapitalist epochs, but we might point out to him that the 'sort' we were talking about was not just any sort of value but labour-determined value. Not much more can be said about Fine's new idea, in its present sketchy form, except that its implications seem very doubtful. I would, myself, think twice before putting down on paper the expression 'feudal value'.[6] I suspect Marx's eyebrows would have been raised to a rather steep angle had he been able to read this neologism.

Ben Fine also accuses M and C of identifying the Marxian with the Ricardian theory of value; of adopting a technical, Ricardian labour theory of value, which is not Marx's because his theory of value was concerned with the form value assumes in exchange; and of ignoring the dependence of value on its social formation.

I find this hasty identification of a technical definition of value with the Ricardian theory totally objectionable. The concept of value used by M and C is certainly technical without for this reason being any more Ricardian than it is Marxian. Marx also uses a technical definition of value, in so far as he determines the value of a commodity by the quantity of labour embodied in it in the production process. In this he coincides with Ricardo and, although he has criticised various other aspects of Ricardo's development of the value concept, I have yet to discover one word of such criticism against the embodied labour idea. In fact, Marx's greatness as a theorist is demonstrated not least by his perception that, under capitalism, social relations become objectified and therefore operate as technical relations, 'technical' referring here to the functioning of a reified economy, to which the labor theory of value exclusively applies. Both his celebrated fetishism of commodities and his definition of labour-power amply, I think, illustrate this point.

Operating with such a technical concept of value, Marx was able to show the compatibility of exploitation of labour with the existence of a free, perfectly competitive market. In Morishima's work,[7] and in the joint M and C work, this aspect of the labour theory of value and of the transformation problem, historical or otherwise, has always been at the centre of interest. Given that, I find it hard to understand how anybody could tax us with neglect of the social presuppositions or implications of the value concept or describe our approach as merely Ricardian.

I also find it rather surprising to hear from somebody who has co-authored a very useful book on re-reading *Capital*[8] – a book in which the primacy of production in Marx's analysis is, quite rightly, heavily emphasised – that Marx's theory of value, by contrast to the Ricardian, is concerned with the form value acquires in exchange. Marx's theory of value is concerned with the form value acquires in exchange *in addition to* its quantitative determination by labour embodied in the production process. To suggest, as Ben Fine seems to me to be doing, that the form-aspect is the only or the mainly important one would, in my opinion, be a serious mistake.

On the other hand, I would not deny the very great interest of studying the historical evolution of the form of value, particularly the money form. This obviously has had a career of its own in empirical history. Could it be that Ben Fine's emphasis on the form of value in his understanding of Marx's labour theory of value and his defence of the historical reality of the value concept are mutually conditioned? If so, I would again point out to him that for Marx the quantitative determination of value is at least as important as its form. It is of the former only (i. e. the quantitative determination by labour) that, together with Morishima, we could find no historical trace.

To end, the last two alleged M and C errors, our imposition of an extraneous value concept and of the extraneous structure of advanced capitalism upon precapitalist epochs, can be dispatched rather quickly. We imposed nothing because we did not intend to analyse the historical past. We merely wanted to point out some of the most glaring incongruences between precapitalism and capitalism so as to illustrate our claim that the concept of value determined by labour embodied in commodities could not possibly fit to the past. In particular we did not extrapolate backwards from the conditions of monopolistic capitalism to the lack of competition in the precapitalist era. Rather, we compared the mercantilist past of capitalism with its free trade era. Our reference to lack of competition was therefore in the same vein as that by Marx, when in a speech on free trade,[9] he said: 'All those laws developed in the classical works on political economy, are strictly true under the supposition only that trade must be delivered from all fetters, that competition be perfectly free . . . '.

Notes

1. Ben Fine (1979).
2. Michio Morishima and George Catephores (1975) and (1978).
3. Ben Fine (1979), p.276.
4. Frederick Engels (1971), p.899–900.
5. R. L. Meek (1956), pp.94–107.
6. Ben Fine (1979), p.276.
7. Michio Morishima (1973) particularly chapters 5 and 6.
8. Ben Fine and Lawrence Harris (1979).
9. Karl Marx (1976), p.289.

References

Engels, F. (1971) 'Supplement to *Capital*, Volume Three', in Karl Marx, *Capital*, Vol. 3, Progress Publishers.

Fine, B. (1979) 'On Marx's Theory of Agricultural Rent', *Economy and Society*, 8.

Fine, B. and **Harris, L.** (1979), *Rereading Capital,* Macmillan.
Marx, K. (1976) 'Speech of Dr Marx on Protection, Free Trade, and the Working Classes' as reported by F. Engels in 'The Free Trade Congress at Brussels', in *Collected Works,* Vol. 6, Lawrence and Wishart.
Meek, R. L. (1956) 'Some Notes on the Transformation Problem', *Economic Journal,* 66.
Morishima, M. (1973) *Marx's Economics,* CUP.
Morishima, M. and **Catephores, G.** (1975) 'Is there a "Historical Transformation Problem"?' *Economic Journal,* 85.
Morishima, M. and **Catephores, G.** (1976) *Value, Exploitation and Growth,* McGraw-Hill.

DEBATE

On the historical transformation problem

Ben Fine

In a short rejoinder to a short reply to a fourth appendix to an article on Marx's theory of agricultural rent, I cannot hope to settle questions concerning the historical transformation problem. Instead I will attempt to focus on the differences which exist between Catephores and myself. Catephores brings to the fore my criticism of Morishima and Catephores (M and C) on two counts and three errors. Let us begin with the errors. First, I argue that M and C identify Marxian and Ricardian value theory and Catephores denies this by suggesting two things. First, that the presuppositions for the existence of value are necessarily present in M and C's theory but secondly there is a technical definition of value as labour embodied that is neutral between Ricardo and Marx. This is, in fact, precisely the neo-Ricardian position on value, that in some way the social relations necessary for the existence of value can be evaporated to leave a technical definition as labour embodied.[1] Catephores' view that not a word of criticism exists against the embodied labour idea is simply astonishing in the light of the extensive debate that has raged for and against this position.[2]

The second error is that M and C impose this notion of value on other epochs. I do not see how he can deny this. A *logical* and a *historical* notion of value as labour embodied is put forward as a virtue by M and C to investigate whether this value has been identical to price during any period of history. The third error is a corollary of the second as a result of this investigation. M and C impose the economic structure of advanced capitalism on less developed stages by treating the *relations* between production, distribution and exchange as if they were the same even if they allow the conditions within these spheres of economic activity to vary (more or less competition, free flow of labour and commodities etc.). This is analogous, for example, to treating slavery as a special case of capitalism in which we simply have no labour mobility. In contrast, we must emphasise that what constitutes production, distribution and exchange has first to be determined prior to a calculation of what constitutes value. Indeed, as Marx makes clear in the *Grundrisse* (see the Introduction) and elsewhere, there is a role for an analysis of production (and labour) in general (as suggested by the notion of labour embodied) but only in the context of its incorporation with an analysis drawn from a specific stage of development of production. Before this is done, it is not even possible to identify what is the labour to be added up in the embodiment because production itself has not been located. What is production for a slave society, for example, may be reproduction for capitalism. Even in advanced capitalism, what constitutes value production is open to question (and struggle) as is evidenced by the existence of nationalised industries, for example, for which a logical analysis based on embodied labour can provide no answers particularly in the absence of historical underpinnings. In short, M and C's use of a logical (technical) construct of value contains an error of method, for an ideal construct is imposed not only on earlier epochs but also upon advanced capitalism itself. As observed earlier, the logical, ahistorical concept of value has not been drawn from the society to be analysed, even if certain presuppositions are presumed for its existence, so that the idea of value is analysed rather than its real existence.

So much for the three errors. On the two counts, the first concerns the question of whether value is purely a logical construct and requires no historical underpinnings and we have already attempted to indicate a negative answer. The second count concerns the challenge to me to identify an epoch during which commodities exchanged at values. As perhaps I hope I have made clear, this challenge presents a need to analyse nothing short of the economic relations of the societies concerned. It is not open to the M and C confrontation of an ahistorical notion of value with the facts of history, a task that confusedly leads Catephores to state in the same paragraph that 'we did not intend to analyse the historical past' but 'rather, we compared the mercantilist part of capitalism with its free trade era.' However, whilst evading the task of pinpointing dates, my original article did make clear the conditions necessary for the divergence of values and prices under the capitalist mode of production, and that is that the competition between capitals of different sectors should not be subordinated to the competition within sectors and this requires the establishment of the monopoly stage (and in particular the credit system as a means of capital mobility). Indeed, production of commodities which exchange at their values can still be identified in the contemporary world particularly in the underdeveloped economies where precapitalist or underdeveloped capitalist relations persist, although the value itself may be determined by advanced capitalist methods.

Finally, I close with two further comments. My criticism of M and C should not be seen as a defence of either Engels or Meek who were originally the object of criticism for M and C. In particular, there are considerable doubts about Engels' interpretation of the logical-historical method and his application of it to the historical transformation problem.[3] He seems much closer to M and C than to Marx and constructs ideal modes of production to justify the historical existence of value which allows M and C quite rightly to deny their existence.[4] Second, Catephores criticises me for emphasising the form of value, but he does so with perhaps an over-formal understanding of this as price. The form of value concerns not only its creation by labour but also its *formation* through exchange. This has price as its final result but the mediation between price and value is not subject to an invariant set of economic relations and it is these which have to be analysed before value can be determined let alone compared with price.

Notes

1. Catephores makes clear that his objective is the neo-Ricardian one, to place 'at the centre of interest' 'the compatibility of exploitation of labour with the existence of a free, perfectly competitive market.' This, as the Sraffians have shown, can be done with no reference to value at all so that the concept becomes redundant. See Fine (1980) for the distinction between neo-Ricardians and Sraffians.
2. See Fine and Harris (1979) for a survey, but also Elson (1979) and Himmelweit and Mohun (1978) for more recent contributions.
3. Engels (1971) argues that the logical order of concepts corresponds to their historical order. This is both incorrect and at odds with Marx who states and shows the opposite in many places. See the Introduction to the *Grundrisse* where he seems to assert that the logical and the historical order of development of particular categories either tend to occur in the same or opposite sequence.
4. Banaji in Elson (1979) argues that Engels requires careful interpretation. Weeks (1980) goes further accusing Engels of neo-Ricardianism, further arguing that for value to exist it requires the relations of advanced capitalism.

References

Engels, F. (1971) 'Supplement to *Capital*, Volume Three'. Progress Publishers.
Elson, D. (1979) *Value: The Representation of Labour in Capitalism*, CSE Books.
Fine, B. (1980) *Economics Theory and Ideology*, Edward Arnold.
Fine, B. and **Harris, L.** (1979) *Rereading 'Capital'*, Macmillan.
Himmelweit, S. and **Mohun, S.** (1978) 'The Anomalies of Capital', *Capital and Class*, No. 6.
Weeks, J. (1980) *Value, Capital and Social Relations*, manuscript.

CHAPTER 6

Sraffa versus Ricardo: the historical irrelevance of the 'corn-profit' model*

Gilbert Faccarello

Sraffa's interpretation of Ricardo's theory of the profit rate in the *Essay on Profits* (Ricardo, 1815) has so far been widely accepted, and not only by the so-called 'neo-Ricardian' or 'Sraffian' school. It has been suggested, however, that while this interpretation is simple and suggestive, it is more of a projection on Ricardo's work of ideas developed in Sraffa's *Production of Commodities by Means of Commodities* (1960) than a careful exegesis of the Ricardian system itself. Perhaps the most well-known expositor of this view to date is Samuel Hollander (1973, 1975, 1979). Unfortunately, Hollander's point is part of an attempt on his part to build another comprehensive interpretation of Ricardo, probably at least as ahistorical as Sraffa's, from the point of view of neo-classical economics.[1]

This essay tries to map out a way to preserve Hollander's point about the invalidity of Sraffa's analysis but also rejecting his 'neo-classical' reading by choosing the following route: instead of reading Ricardo with modern eyes one should try to locate the Ricardo–Malthus encounter in the context of an emerging clash between Ricardo's natural price notion versus Malthus's demand and supply framework. Once one sees this as the context of Ricardo's statements it will be clear that Sraffa's model not only is at variance with the inner logic of Ricardo's 1813–15 texts but also represents a misreading of the dialectic of the Ricardo–Malthus correspondence from which it draws some of its crucial evidence. It would appear that Sraffa took over some of Malthus's misunderstanding of Ricardo's approach to prices.

I Ricardo's correspondence (1813–15): a first view

Ricardo's early conception of the variation in the profit rate is to be found in two oft quoted letters from 1813 and 1814. The first one is addressed to Malthus and underlines the effects of the war upon income distribution. It states that despite capital accumulation, the increased rate of profit is only due 'to improvements of agriculture both here and abroad' and 'new facilities in the production of food' (17 August 1813, in Ricardo (1951–5) vol. 6, pp. 94–5). Several months later, Ricardo clarified the terms of the outstanding dispute in a second letter (to Hutches Trower, 8 March 1814, *ibid*., pp. 103–5). The starting-point seems identical for both protagonists.

> Interest rises only when the means of employment for Capital bears a greater proportion than before to the Capital itself, and falls when the Capital bears a greater proportion to the arena, as Mr Malthus has called it, for its employment [*ibid*., p. 103].

In other words, the profit and interest rates depend, on the one side, on the amount of *money* capital invested in production and, on the other side, on the *real* capital (labour and means of production) commanded by the sum advanced (and which can also be defined by the amount of commodities it can produce). These two elements are called by Malthus 'supply' and 'demand' of capital, terms about which Ricardo does not agree.[2] This disagreement about terminology is of course meaningful, and the dispute runs precisely on the problem which lies behind it. Put succinctly, Ricardo does not think that it is possible to produce too many commodities, except by accident: thus, fluctuations in the market prices cannot influence profits in the long run. If capital is scarce with respect to the means of employing it (following Malthus's words which Ricardo will soon give up), i.e. if commodities could be produced (or produced in greater amounts) because of the demand for them, the only way for increasing the quantity of capital is to make its constituting elements, e.g. food, cheaper. The sums of money released in this way can, *ceteris paribus*, be employed to increase real capital; profits will in any case be increased.

> I contend that the arena for the employment of new Capital cannot increase in any country in the same or greater proportion than the Capital itself, unless there be improvements in husbandry – or new facilities be offered for the introduction of food from foreign countries; – that in short it is the profits of the farmer which regulate the profits of all other trades – and as the profits of the farmer must necessarily decrease with every augmentation of Capital employed on the land, provided no improvements be at the same time made in husbandry, all other profits must diminish and therefore the rate of interest must fall [*ibid*., pp. 103–4].

It is thus sufficient to set forth the principle of diminishing returns on land as far as capital accumulation goes on to be led to the following: increased difficulty in the production of food induces a fall in the over-all profits through a fall in the profits of the farmer. Let us examine what happens in agriculture. Assuming an unchanged real wage rate, increased difficulty in the production of (agricultural) wage goods causes a rise in their prices, a general increase of (nominal) wages and decrease in the profits of the farmer.

> The capitalist 'who may find it necessary to employ a hundred days labour instead of fifty in order to produce a certain quantity of corn' [Malthus's example] cannot retain the same share for himself unless the labourers who are employed for a hundred days will be satisfied with the same quantity of corn for their subsistence that the labourers employed for fifty had before. If you suppose the price of corn doubled, the capital to be employed estimated in money will probably be also doubled – or at any rate will be greatly augmented and if his monied income is to arise from the sale of the corn which remains to him after defraying the charges of production how is it possible to conceive that the rate of his profits will not be diminished? [to Malthus, 25 July 1814, *ibid.*, pp. 114–15].

The same mechanism will take place everywhere in the economy. Thus, it is not in fact the falling profit of the farmer which induces a perequation in all other trades, but rather the monetary wage increase. The context of the different statements is never ambiguous, nor is the connection made by Ricardo between the two seemingly conflicting formulations. 'It is by the rise of the price of corn that all other profits are regulated to agricultural profits' (to Malthus, 17 March 1815, *ibid.*, p. 194).

To this opinion, Malthus answers quite ironically (5 August 1814, *ibid.*, p. 117).

> If the nominal price of corn be doubled, and the nominal amount of capital employed, be not quite doubled which you seem to allow be the case, instead of saying 'how it is possible to conceive that the rate of profits will not be diminished' I should say how is it possible to conceive that it should not be increased?

The objection is well grounded indeed. It points out strikingly that important questions concerning the variations in the profit rate remained unsettled: (1) why should the farmer's profit rate fall? The money capital is greater for the same physical product, but the price of this product is rising; (2) why should the profit rate decrease in the other activities? Money wages are rising, but in accordance with the adding-up theory of value that Ricardo was accepting at that time ('the prices of all commodities must increase if the price of corn be increased' (25 June 1814, *ibid*., p. 114)), the prices of *all* commodities increase: thus, there is no reason why the profit rate should fall; (3) does not the above argument apply to agricultural prices also? They first rise because of an increased difficulty of production (the amount of wages and profits paid at their natural rates are greater than before), but should they not increase a second time, following the rise of the money wages?

We know how Ricardo settled the question by substituting a 'deductive' theory of value (based on the 'difficulty of production' bound to the only labour spent in the production processes of commodities) for the Smithian 'adding-up' one, and by a qualified acceptance of Malthus's theory of rent. He can then assert that when money wages rise following an increased difficulty in the production of food, the profit rate in all trades must fall (the prices of all commodities other than agricultural ones being constant) and that the same happens in agriculture because of the existence and increase of rents. This was stated in the *Essay on Profits*.

II Ricardo's correspondence: a second view

Before examining the 1815 pamphlet, I should like to go back to the controversy of the previous year. This will, I think, make it possible to understand the post-*Essay* dispute better.

At first sight, the controversy seems to centre on the relevance of 'Mill's law'. It seems to Ricardo that the demand for commodities depends on those very circumstances that act on production. Income and production go *pari passu* and each factor affecting the latter also lessens the former (to Malthus, 26 June 1814, *ibid*., p. 108). Malthus's answer (6 July 1814, *ibid*., pp. 109–12) is important and characteristic of his approach. I must therefore quote it at length before commenting on it. The dissension between the two authors will then appear in a different and hopefully more suggestive light.

> You observe that in the case supposed [of restrictions on corn's importations], there would be less production and less demand with the *same* capital; but surely there would be *much less capital*. There would be a smaller quantity both of corn, and of all other commodities, and every monied accumulation would command less labour and less product. The question then seems to be whether production or demand would decrease the fastest?

and . . . in my opinion the dearness of labour would have more effect in diminishing capital than in diminishing revenue.

'I can by no means agree with you in thinking that every thing which diminishes produce, tends to diminish the power of paying for the commodities wanted.' Thus far, the objection bears on Mill's (or Say's) law, with the following indication: the increased price of corn would induce a decrease in the real capital and in that way a disequilibrium between the (unchanged) demand and the (diminished) supply of commodities, all other things being the same.

Malthus goes on emphasizing the fact that the profit rate depends on the state of demand and supply for 'in this question that great element of effective demand . . . must always have great influence. I think you overlook it too much.' The

rate of production, or more definitely speaking, the proportion of production to the consumption necessary to such production, seems to be determined by the quantity of accumulated capital compared with the demand for the product of capital, and not by the mere difficulty and expense of procuring corn.

Having already taken into account the effects of restrictions on corn's importation, the author is now to meet the second case evoked by Ricardo: an increased difficulty in the production of food.

If it is necessary to employ a hundred days labour instead of fifty, in order to produce a certain quantity of corn, there seems to be no reason whatever that the person who possesses an accumulation sufficient to make the necessary advances should have a less remuneration for his capital. The effects of a great difficulty in procuring corn would in my opinion be, a diminution of capital, a diminution of produce, and a diminution in the *real* wages of labour, or their price in corn; but not a diminution of profits; although unquestionably low profits might accompany a great difficulty of procuring corn, if at the same time . . . there was a great abundance of capital. In short all will in my opinion depend upon the state of capital compared with the demand for it.

The effect mentioned by Ricardo is thus considered as unusual, and only associated with a situation where there exists a 'great abundance' of capitals competing with each other in search of one of the many fields of investment left and satisfying themselves with a diminished rate of profit.

This letter, however, states the two ways by which demand and supply can influence the profit rate, by distinguishing demand and supply of *commodities* from those of *capital.*

The working of demand and supply of commodities remains here quite implicit. But it is very well known. It is analysed by the protagonists in the same manner. A change on the side of demand, not (or not immediately) followed by the reaction of supply, induces price changes which themselves induce variations in the sectoral rates of profits. Capital migrations will then restore the uniformity of the profit rate by provoking changes on the supply side. But opinions of course differ as for ulterior specifications.

The working of the demand and supply of capital is a more intricate problem, which is really the focus of the dissensions. In contradiction with the previous case, which only allows for the disturbance due to demand, everything being the same, the present case deals with the effects induced by changes on the supply side, with initial unchanged demand. We must here distinguish the two Ricardian situations of a rise in the price of corn due to restrictions on importation and a rise induced by an increased difficulty of production (this latter sometimes follows from the former). If Ricardo thinks they lead to an identical result (fall in the profit rate for a given real wage rate), Malthus argues in quite a different way:

> 1 Restrictions on importations at first cause a rise in the price of food, which acts on *all activities*, and the disequilibria thus induced are cancelled by the working out of a *price adjustment.* The rise in the price of corn induces an increase in money wages, and capitals engaged in the production process are suddenly reduced in real terms. Supply of commodities thus decreases, while the demand for them is, by hypothesis, to remain unchanged or to diminish in a lower proportion. Following Malthus's theory of value, prices of commodities increase, maintaining the profit rate at its previous level, or even at a higher one.[3]
> 2 As regards an increased difficulty in the production of food, it only has a real effect on *one activity* (agriculture), disequilibria being at first cancelled by a *quantity adjustment.* As a matter of fact, an increased difficulty of production on land does not immediately alter prices, demand and supply of agricultural products being unchanged. The profit rate on land only is affected and, as a consequence, the farmer withdraws part of his capital from that activity, inducing a fall in supply of agricultural commodities. But two phenomena are to occur simultaneously, which are at variance with the previous tendency. First, an excess supply of labour arises, and a new equilibrium state is

reached only through a decrease in the real wages. Second, this fall of real wages lessens the demand for agricultural products and thus tempers the rise in agricultural prices due to a depletion of supply. On balance, a new equilibrium position is to prevail, Malthus says, with a lower real (but the same nominal) wage rate, so that the initial profit rate is not affected, neither on land nor in all other trades.

We can of course imagine other analytical cases. It remains that the views of the two authors are at variance with each other. The dispute *apparently* centres on the part played by demand and supply, in the perspective of the acceptance or the rejection of Mill's law. A common analytical framework seems to exist, within which the discussion is embedded. As a consequence, the particular views expressed by the two authors seem at last to consist in a matter of personal (more or less grounded) opinion about the permanence of the acting economic forces. When Malthus again objects that

> in stating the cause of high profits you seem to me to consider almost exclusively the expense of production, without attending sufficiently to the price of produce, and greatly to underrate the wants and tastes of mankind in affecting prices, and consequently in affecting the means of profitably employing capital [9 October 1814, *ibid*., p. 141],

Ricardo simply answers that he does not think to underrate these factors which 'frequently occasion large profits on *particular* commodities for *short* periods' (23 October 1814, *ibid*., p. 147; my italics).

The basic question is not clarified after the publication of the *Essay on Profits.* In 1817, Ricardo is still writing that

> It appears to me that one great cause of our difference in opinion, on the subjects we have so often discussed, is that you have always in your mind the immediate and temporary effects of particular changes – whereas I put these immediate and temporary effects quite aside, and fix my whole attention on the permanent state of things which will result from them [1951–5, vol. 7, p. 120].

It is still a matter of personal and subjective judgment ('Perhaps you estimate these temporary effects too highly, whilst I am too much disposed to undervalue them'). But there is a shift in 1818 when the true motive of the dispute eventually arises: 'I confess it fills me with astonishment to find that you think . . . that *natural price*, as well as *market price*, is determined by the demand and supply' (30 January 1818, *ibid*., p. 250). Ricardo is now perfectly aware of being in opposition, as a defender of the natural price theory, to the economists who claim that a concept of a normal price determined independently of demand and supply is irrelevant or even meaningless.

> In saying this do you mean to deny that facility of production will lower natural price and difficulty of production raise it? . . . I may be so foolishly partial to my own doctrine, that I may be blind to its absurdity. I know the strong disposition of every man to deceive himself in his eagerness to prove a favourite theory, yet I cannot help viewing this question as a truth which admits a demonstration and I am full of wonder that it should admit of a doubt. If indeed this fundamental doctrine of mine were proved false I admit that my whole theory falls with it (*ibid*., pp. 250–1).

III Sraffa's interpretation

Sraffa's well-known interpretation of the early Ricardian theory of profits (Sraffa, 1951, section 4) is illustrated by the simple scheme of the 'corn-profit model', in which one agricultural product (called 'corn' or 'wheat') is the only basic commodity. The rate of profit is thus independent of the methods of production prevailing in any other trade and of the price system itself. Ricardo, Sraffa says, would have supported this theory in some lost paper of 1814, during a conversation with Malthus . . . and in the famous Table of the pamphlet.[4] He would also have given up his views (and simultaneously adhered to the labour theory of value) under the attacks of Malthus after the *Essay* was published.[5] This summary of Sraffa's position is sufficient for our purpose and obviously sets an important problem to the historian of economic thought: is such a retrospective interpretation sufficiently well grounded, that is, could it be supported not only by the relevant texts but also by the analysis of the inner logic of the 1813–15 dispute, such as has just been attempted? To answer this question, we must first sum up Sraffa's arguments which proceeds from two sources:

1 From the correspondence of these years:

(a) *letters from Ricardo:* assertion that the profits of the farmer regulate the profits of all other trades (to Trower, 8 March 1814); and a sentence which states that 'the rate of profits and of interest must depend on the proportion of production to the consumption necessary to such production' (to Malthus, 26 June 1814);

(b) *letters from Malthus:* the proposition that

> in no case of production, is the produce exactly of the same nature as the capital advanced. Consequently we can never properly refer to a material rate of produce . . . [It] is not the particular profits or the rate of produce upon the land which determines the general profits of stock and the interest of money [to Ricardo, 5 August 1814];

a critique of the *Essay*'s table (to Ricardo, 12 March 1815 and to Horner, 14 March 1815) and precisely of the 'corn' expression of circulating capital, whereas this capital also includes 'tea sugar clothes ecc. ecc. used by [the] labourers'.

2 From the pamphlet itself: Sraffa's sole evidence here is an excerpt from the table in which all numerical examples are quantities of 'corn'. Following the author, this suggests that 'both capital and the "neat produce" are expressed in corn, and thus the profit per cent is calculated without need to mention price' (Sraffa, 1951, p. xxxii). I can even add to this a second argument: a footnote in the *Essay* resumes the question under examination in the terms of the letter to Trower quoted above: 'I am only desirous of proving that the profits on agricultural capital cannot materially vary, without occasioning a similar variation in the profits on capital, employed on manufactures and commerce' (1951–5, vol. 4, p. 12). I shall start with the arguments related to the pamphlet. Those excerpted from the correspondence are considered in the following section.

There is a striking feature in the first half of the *Essay*, where the famous table appears: corn is only a *numéraire* by means of which different kinds of capitals are estimated. This has already been noted by many commentators, and is unquestionable. Ricardo always makes it clear that capital is 'estimated in quarters of wheat' and includes fixed as well as circulating capital (see for example *ibid*., p. 10, and the footnote, pp. 15–16). What should be emphasized here is that this reasoning in *real terms* forms the first step in the argumentation: Ricardo is interested in showing that, as far as cultivation of land goes on, rents rise at the expense of profits. We can call this the *real effect* of the extension of cultivation. But then follows a second step to take into account a *price effect*, i.e. the variation in relative prices to the advantage of agriculture, and particularly, again, to landlords. The price effect thus *strengthens* the real effect, and acts in the same way.

> Not only is the situation of the landlord improved . . . by obtaining an increased quantity of the produce of the land, but also by the increased exchangeable value of that quantity. If his rent

> be increased from fourteen to twenty-eight quarters, it would be more than doubled, because he would be able to command more than double the quantity of commodities, in exchange for the twenty-eight quarters [*ibid*., p. 20].

'It follows then, that the interest of the landlord is always opposed to the interest of every other class in community' (*ibid*., p. 21). I shall show that Malthus's objection to the pamphlet does not relate to a supposed 'corn-profit model' but precisely to this dissociation between the two effects he thinks irrelevant.

It remains, then, to come back to the expression of the *Essay* which restates the terms of Ricardo's letters to Trower. The context shows unambiguously that it must be accepted in the broad sense of a fall of the general profit rate due to the rise in the price of food, and not to the decrease in the profits upon the land: 'general profits on capital, can only be raised by a fall in exchangeable value of food' (*ibid*., p. 22).

> A fall of a price of corn, in consequence of improvements in agriculture or of importation; will lower the exchangeable value of corn only – the price of no other commodity will be affected. If, then, the price of labour falls, which it must do when the price of corn is lowered, the real profits of all descriptions must rise; and no person will be so materially benefited as the manufacturing and commercial part of society [*ibid*., pp. 35–6].

IV The grounds of an opinion

Sraffa's first argument excerpted from Ricardo's letters relies, however, on the literal interpretation that the profits of the farmer regulate all other profits. We should notice here that Malthus's objection is mentioned in the *same* letter to Trower and is related by Ricardo himself.

> To this proposition Mr. Malthus does not agree. He thinks that the arena for the employment of Capital may increase, and consequently profits and interests may rise, altho' there should be no new facilities, either by importation, or improved tillage, for the production of food; – that the profits of the farmer no more regulate the profits of all other trades, than the profits of other trades regulate the profits of the farmer, and consequently if new markets are discovered, in which we can obtain a greater quantity of foreign commodities in exchange for our commodities, than before the discovery of such markets, profits will increase and interest will rise . . . A cheaper mode of obtaining food will undoubtedly increase profits says Mr. Malthus but

> there are *many other circumstances* which may also increase profits with an increase of Capital. The discovery of *a new market* where there will be *a great demand* for our manufactures is one [1951–5, vol. 6, pp. 104–5; my italics].

According to Ricardo, Malthus's objection is not directed to the supposed physical homogeneity of capital and product in one activity, but rather (and more logically) to the point at issue on the preceding years: the part played by demand and supply in the determination of prices and the profit rate. Malthus claims that a discovery of new markets, i.e. an increase in demand, will induce a rise in the profit rate. As a matter of fact, the price of those commodities the demand for which is increased will rise. Migrations of capital from other activities towards those sectors where prices (and profit rates) first rise will induce a supply shortage in these activities, and thus similarly a rise of prices and the rate of profits, until a new equilibrium is reached.

Against this, Ricardo not only argues that excess demands or supplies are temporary and cannot raise the sectoral profit rates in a permanent way above their 'normal' level determined by the difficulty of production on the land, but also that migration of capital does not take place easily, especially if capital is invested in agriculture, where it is absolutely necessary to satisfy an incompressible demand. The context of the letter to Trower and the correspondence with Malthus supports this interpretation. I shall add that this line of theoretical analysis is taken up again in the *Essay* (pp. 24–5) with the terms of the letter to Trower recurring, and in the *Principles* (Ch. 6). The basic difficulty remains the incompatibility of the two approaches, i.e. the natural price 'problématique' and the approach which is grounded on the symmetric working of demand and supply.

As far as the second piece of evidence (namely that the rate of profit 'must depend on the proportion of production to the consumption necessary to such production') is concerned, it is by no means relevant. This definition relates to the 'produce rate' only from which the rate of profit can be known. If this expression had been specific to the 'corn-profit model', it would have been very surprising to find it currently employed by Malthus himself (see the letter to Ricardo quoted above (6 July 1814) in which the context shows that this produce rate is expressed in value terms and not in physical ones).

The evidence quoted by Sraffa from Malthus's letters seems to be more decisive. I shall first come back to the objection addressed to Ricardo's table, and examine Sraffa's own assertion that

> the feature of calculating the advances of the farmer in corn is

> singled out by Malthus as 'the fault of Mr. Ricardo's table'; since circulating capital did not consist only of corn, but included 'tea sugar cloaths ecc. for the labourers'; so that *a rise in the relative price of corn would 'afford a greater surplus from the land'* [1951, p. xxxii, n. 4; our italics].

The last sentence simply means that Malthus's remark, again, has not much to do with the supposed homogeneity of capital and product in agriculture; but rather with the dissociation which Ricardo has made between a real and a price effect. Malthus's very acceptable objection is that the price effect does not strengthen the real one, but is not even an autonomous effect. The distortion of relative prices structure to the advantage of agriculture does not simply favour the landlord, but also the farmer, who gets the non-agricultural items of his capital from the other activities in exchange for *a lower quantity of corn.* Consequently, the figures of the table, showing the different quantities invested on the land 'estimated in quarters of wheat', cannot remain unchanged when cultivation is extended to land of a worse quality. Ricardo's calculations are thus faulty, and the compared evolution of rent and profit rates is greatly affected. To sum up, *in 1815 Malthus only repeats what he had said before, and points out again the analytical difficulty which induced Ricardo to give up the Smithian adding-up theory of value.* It is thus by no means certain that an increased difficulty of production induces a higher amount of capital with respect to the product. Indeed, the evolution of the profit rate in agriculture is *indeterminate.*[6]

Sraffa's thesis seems further supported by the second quotation excerpted from Malthus's letters (to Ricardo, 5 July 1814):

> In no case of production, is the produce exactly of the same nature as the capital advanced. Consequently we can never properly refer to a material rate of produce. . . . [It] is not the particular profits or rate of produce upon land which determines the general profits of stock and the interest of money.

We can, however, interpret this sentence in a different manner from Sraffa's, and at the same time explain the probable origin of the 'corn-profit model' which, it must be said, lies either here or nowhere else in the writings of that time.

First of all, note that Sraffa neglects to quote two sentences of Malthus, which are to be found between the first two (refutation of the idea of a physical rate of return) and the last one in the passage I have just quoted. The last sentence thus appears as a logical conclusion of the previous ones, and the truncated passage results in that way a critique of Ricardo's supposed thesis, which it is not if we restate it unabridged. One missing sentence is the following: 'The more I reflect on the subject, the more firmly I feel convinced, that it is the state of capital, or the general profits of stock and interest of money, which determines the particular profit upon the land.' Here, Malthus not only mentions the interconnection of the different sectors in the determination of the profit rate but also and more fundamentally all his thesis that this rate is determined by the 'state of capital', i.e. the 'quantity of capital' compared with 'the means of employing it'. Clearly this is a restatement of the demand and supply theory, once again.

The other missing sentence, which we quote here in italics, argues in a similar way. 'Consequently, Malthus writes, we can never properly refer to a material rate of produce, *independent of demand, and of the abundance or scarcity of capital.*' We must conclude again that Malthus's critique does not test the logical coherence of his adversary's views, which is never the case in this controversy, but consists in reading Ricardo's writings through Malthusian spectacles. This remark is important if we recall the long period of reciprocal misconception between the two authors.

Another important point can be emphasized. It is striking that a very specific theory like the 'corn-profit model', the occurrence of which would have been rather surprising in that time (remember the Physiocrats on whom discredit was thrown, especially by Smith), reaches us in such an indirect way, and that absolutely no writing of Ricardo remains to attest it. It is also disconcerting that the arguments excerpted from the correspondence, which mainly consist in a remark made by Malthus and written *by Ricardo* to Trower, has not brought about a clear restatement of the supposed theory, just as Ricardo usually did every time one of his principles was questioned. Unless it is assumed, of course, that all the papers or letters in which such a clarification was made have been lost, just as the leaves of the 1814 *Notes* and the words of the conversation with Malthus (Sraffa's references) have been blown away by the wind. . . . Last but not least, it is also surprising to note that the *only* indications which support Sraffa's thesis, related or not by Ricardo, *proceed from Malthus.*

My conclusion is then an obvious one. If indeed such a corn-profit model was really formulated, it took shape, for a brief period of time, in Malthus's fancy. This theory, to suppose again it really was formulated before Sraffa, only results from the incapacity of Ricardo's opponent to grasp correctly the natural price approach he was fighting against. To Malthus, imbued with demand and supply theory, the idea of a normal price determined independently of demand and basically different from a market price was inconceivable (just as the determination of the natural price by the interaction of demand and supply was not acceptable to Ricardo). Ricardo's refusal to take demand into account appears to him *as a simple refusal to consider prices themselves,* the two concepts being closely associated in his mind. All this could but induce him to impute to Ricardo the purpose of arguing in *physical terms* only. The fact that Sraffa's evidence is all bound to the discussion of the demand and supply principle in price and profit determination corroborates our interpretation. In a letter quoted above (9 October 1814), Malthus blames Ricardo for not considering the working of demand on prices and writes:

> The profits of stock, or the means of employing capital advantageously may be said to be accurately equal to the price of produce, *minus* the expense of production. And consequently whenever the price of produce keeps a head of the price of production the profits of stock must rise. . . . It is not the *quantity* of produce compared with the expense of production that determines profits (which I think is your proposition) but the exchangeable value or money price of that produce, compared with the money expense of production [1951–5, vol. 6, pp. 140–1].

To which Ricardo unambiguously replies:

> You say 'that I seem to think that the state of production from the land, compared with the means necessary to make it produce, is almost the sole cause which regulates the profits of stock, and the means of advantageously employing capital'. This is a correct statement of my opinion, *and not as you have said in another part of your letter, and which essentially differs from it,* 'that it is the *quantity* of produce compared with the expense of production, that determines profits' [23 October 1814, *ibid.*, p. 244; my italics].[7]

Sraffian economists see themselves as the modern heralds of the anti-Neoclassical fight. It is thus ironical that their conception of the Ricardian theory in part falls into the trap set by Malthus's misconception.[8]

Notes

*I am indebted to Istvan Hont, Philippe Mongin and Antoine Rebeyrol for helpful discussions and comments.

1. An estimation of the 'merits' and/or 'demerits' of S. Hollander's analysis goes beyond the purpose of this article. On the whole, it is true that this analysis 'will stimulate a reassessment of the "orthodox" interpretations, and this can only help the cause of scholarship' (Peach, 1981, p. 247). But Hollander's interpretation is nevertheless established on a very 'narrow basis'.

I thus agree with K. Tribe's opinion (Tribe, 1981, p. 463), especially when he argues that

> one of the most general reasons for the study of the history of economics is to establish the unevenness and incommensurability of diverse theoretical systems, the resistance of such systems to uniform principles of coherence, the heterogeneity of the manner of setting up and solving various problems. Hollander's approach on the other hand results in the steady obliteration of difference, and promotes the view that neo-classicism is a truth to which all other theoretical systems merely tend.

2. As writes Malthus (6 July 1814, in Ricardo (1951–5), vol. 6, pp. 111–12):

> In short all will in my opinion depend upon the state of capital compared with the demand for it. This will be the prime mover, and it is this which will determine the profits which a capital employed in agriculture shall yield, whether the land be naturally rich or naturally poor, much worked or little worked. The demand for capital depends, not upon the abundance of *present* produce, but upon the demand for the future products of capital, or the power of producing something by means of capital which shall be more in demand than the produce actually employed.

To this formulation, taken up by Malthus in his *Principles,* Ricardo objects (*Notes on Malthus, ibid*., vol. 2, p. 331): (a) that 'the temptation to increase capital does not arise from the demand for its products, for that never fails', and (b) that

> what Mr. Malthus calls a demand for capital I call high profits – capital is not bought and sold, it is borrowed at interest, and a great interest is given when profits are high. Mr. Malthus' language appears to me in this instance 'new and unusual'.

3. If the capitalist in the Cotton or Woolen manufacture be obliged to pay more for the labour which he employs, owing to restrictions upon importation, he will not be able to work up the same quantity of goods with his capital; the goods will in consequence rise in price, and his profits, from the general scarcity of capital, will be increased [letter to Ricardo, 5 August 1814, in Ricardo (1951–5), vol. 6, p. 117].
4. Although this argument is never stated by Ricardo in any of his extant letters and papers, he must have formulated it either in his lost 'papers on the profits of Capital' of March 1814 or in conversation [Sraffa, 1951, p. xxxi].
5. In the *Principles,*

> it was now labour, instead of corn, that appeared on both sides of the account – in modern terms, both as input and output: as a result, the rate of profits was no longer determined by the ratio of the corn produced to the corn used up in production, but, instead, by the ratio of the total labour of the country to the labour required to produce the necessaries for that labour [Sraffa, 1951, p. xxxii].

A corollary of Sraffa's thesis is the unimportance of the theory of price as regards profits before 1817. The two previous sections sufficiently prove that it is not the case, and I do not examine this point further in this paper.

6. Pray think once more on the effect of a rise in the relative price of corn, upon the whole surplus derived from land already in cultivation. It appears to me I confess, as clear as possible that it must be increased. The expenses estimated in Corn will be less, owing to the power of purchasing with a less quantity of corn, the same quantity of fixed capital, and of the circulating capital (Malthus to Ricardo, 12 March 1815, in Ricardo (1951–5), vol. 6, p. 185).
7. Among the Sraffian literature, the work of N. De Vecchi (1976) is a kind

of exception: the book has a careful analysis of the Ricardo–Malthus debate. It is thus surprising to read the author's desperate attempts to make Ricardo and Sraffa agree with each other.

8. As a matter of fact, Sraffa is more artful.

   It should perhaps be stated [he argues (1960, p. 93)] that it was only when the Standard system and the distinction between basics and non-basics had emerged in the course of the present investigation that the above interpretation of Ricardo's theory suggested itself as a natural consequence.

References

De Vecchi, N. (1976) *Valore e profitto nell'economia politica classica*, Feltrinelli, Milan.

Faccarello, G. (1983) *Travail, valeur et prix: une critique de la théorie de la valeur*, Anthropos, Paris.

Hollander, S. (1973) 'Ricardo's analysis of the profit rate: 1813–15', *Economica*, XL, pp. 260–82.

Hollander, S. (1975) 'Ricardo and the corn profit model: reply to Eatwell', *Economica*, XLII, pp. 188–202.

Hollander, S. (1979) *The Economics of David Ricardo*, Heinemann, London.

Peach, T. (1981) Review of Hollander, *The Economics of David Ricardo*, *The Economic Journal*, 91, pp. 244–7.

Ricardo, D. (1815) *An Essay on the Influence of a low Price of Corn on the Profits of Stock*, in Ricardo, D. (1951–5), vol. 4, pp. 1–41.

Ricardo, D. (1951–5) *The Works and Correspondence of David Ricardo*, Cambridge University Press, London.

Sraffa, P. (1951) Introduction to the *Works and Correspondence of David Ricardo*, in Ricardo, D. (1951–5), vol. 1, pp. xiii–lxii.

Sraffa, P. (1960) *Production of Commodities by Means of Commodities, Prelude to a Critique of Economic Theory*, Cambridge University Press, London.

Tribe, K. (1981) 'Ricardian histories', *Economy and Society*, 10, pp. 451–66.

DEBATE

On the economics of Ricardo and Sraffa

Note on Gilbert Faccerello 'Sraffa versus Ricardo: the historical irrelevance of the "corn-profit" model', *Economy and Society*, vol. 11, no. 2.

Ben Fine

Sraffa's (1960) contribution to economics has been examined and debated in great depth in two separate but related areas. The first concerns the critique of neoclassical theory as is indicated by the subtitle of the book, *Prelude to a Critique of Economic Theory*, and its preface. The second involves the debate surrounding the legitimacy and interpretation of Marx's value theory. This application never seems to have been intended by Sraffa. Nevertheless, those following him have seized upon his analysis to refute and reject Marx's value theory.[1] The controversy has been focused upon the so-called transformation problem although it has significance for most of Marx's major propositions, particularly the law of the tendency of the rate of profit to fall.[2]

The intention here is not to examine these debates.[3] It is to bring to the fore an area that has been neglected in the controversy surrounding Sraffian economics, the interpretation of Ricardo.[4] Sraffa himself was the main editor of Ricardo's works and wrote an interpretative introduction to them that has been highly influential.[5] Sraffa's followers have always taken the implications of his work much further than he has himself, and possibly much further than he would wish. Even though there is only less than two pages in Sraffa (1960) on the relevance of this work for Ricardo, it has been used to interpret Ricardo by the Sraffians. It is this interpretation which has remained relatively unchallenged.[6]

For this reason, Faccarello's (1982) contribution is to be especially welcomed. He challenges in detail Sraffa's own interpretation of Ricardo and hence, by implication, anyone who would take it further. The extent of the cavalier attitude of the otherwise cautious Sraffa is revealed in his dependence upon evidence of this type:

> Although this argument is never stated by Ricardo in any of his extant letters and papers, he must have formulated it

> either in his lost 'papers on the profits of Capital' of March 1814 or in conversation. Sraffa (1951) p. xxxi.

As Faccarello reveals, the argument to which Sraffa refers is one more likely to have been formulated by Malthus as the only possible way that he could understand Ricardo's theory of price in which demand played no part. For Malthus, dependent upon the interaction of supply and demand, this must imply a one commodity world and lead to a corn-profit model. It is this interpretation of himself by Malthus to which Ricardo is responding. This both explains why it is not Ricardo's argument and why it might appear to be so.

Such is the elegance of Faccarello's critique. However, he confines himself to this issue of Ricardo's economics, as indeed does Sraffa in his *Introduction,*[7] prior to Ricardo's more mature thought for which a labour theory of value has been both adopted and been found problematical. As a result the question of the Sraffian interpretation of Ricardo's mature economics is left unaddressed by Faccarello. Nor does Faccarello address the question directly of why Sraffa should have been bent towards the particular (mis)interpretation that he adopts.

The second of these questions is rather easier to answer than the first. One major characteristic of the Sraffian system is that it deals in economic categories as things, as a technical relationship between inputs and outputs. It is, of course, one of the criticisms of the Sraffian system that this reification is extended to the category of labour itself.[8] Accordingly, the interpretation of Ricardo (and necessarily Marx) is liable to suffer from the same process of reification. As a result the 'cornification' of Ricardo, treating his economics as a corn-corn or a corn-profit model, is a natural interpretation for Sraffa and the Sraffian system.

In his mature thought, Ricardo became committed to a value theory based on labour time and remained so despite the problems that this created for the theory of price and profit within his system.[9] The problems concern the divergence of price from such simply conceived value once account is taken of factors such as the differing durability and compositions of capitals. Sraffa suggests that the labour theory of value permits Ricardo to abandon the supposedly previously held corn-corn model and to rely upon value theory in its place. In his *Principles*, however, with the adoption of a general theory of value, it became possible for Ricardo to demonstrate the determination of the rate of profit in society as a whole instead of through the microcosm of one special branch of production:

> as a result, the rate of profits was no longer determined by the

> ratio of the corn produced to the corn used up in production, but, instead, by the ratio of the total labour of the country to the labour required to produce the necessaries for that labour. Sraffa (1951) p. xxxii.

Here Sraffa appears to leave the matter in his *Introduction*, but for Sraffians the problems of Ricardo's price theory are to be corrected by their own system. As in the critique or correction of Marx's transformation of values into prices, this involves the abandonment of value theory based on labour time. The result is that Ricardo's mature thought is also subject to 'cornification' at the expense of his own emphasis upon labour. Propositions concerning distribution, for example, based in Ricardo on the division of value between capital and labour are replaced by propositions concerning the division of the net produce of the standard commodity between the two classes.[10] The standard commodity reduces the many commodity model of the economy to one as if it were a corn-corn model. Consequently distribution can be analysed in terms of this thing (or more exactly this composite bundle of things) without any special reference to labour or value. Ricardo's supposed problem of finding a uni-dimensional axis on which to measure distribution has been solved just as his problematic based on labour time has been abandoned.

The cornification of Ricardo by Sraffians is also apparent from their tendency to identify their standard commodity with the invariable standard.[11] Ricardo observed that relative prices would change as a result of wage changes and he wished to minimise this variation by the choice of a money commodity as an invariable standard that was produced by an average composition of past and present labour. Ricardo was acutely aware that such an invariable standard could only serve as an approximation. By contrast the standard commodity is an exact theoretical solution to an entirely different problem, of finding a commodity which is produced hypothetically by a sequence of uniformly declining labour inputs expended in the periods extending into the indefinite past.[12] The two standards cannot be identified.

In conclusion, it is hoped that Faccarello's critique of the significance of Sraffa's contribution to the assessment of Ricardo's economics has been widened further.

Notes

1. Most notably in the case of Steedman (1977).
2. The Sraffian critique of this is associated with Okishio (1961).
3. For the author's views on the Sraffian critique of neoclassical economics, see Fine (1980) Chapter 5. For value theory see Fine (1980) Chapter 6 and

Fine and Harris (1979) Chapter 2. For the law of the tendency of the rate of profit to fall see Fine (1982) Chapter 8 and Fine and Harris (1979) Chapter 4. See also Steedman *et al* (1981), Elson (1979) and Weeks (1982).

4. Sraffa (1926) also made a major contribution in his discussion of economics of scale. This has been neglected altogether although it would be important to assess how this informs and is informed by his economic thinking as a whole.

5. See Sraffa (1951).

6. A major exception is Hollander (1979) who simply reads Ricardo through a neoclassical retrospective.

7. Sraffa (1960) p. 93 also appears to refer only to premature value theory in Ricardo.

8. Consider the title of Sraffa's book: *Production of Commodities by Means of Commodities*!

9. In a draft of manuscript whose completion was interrupted by his death, Ricardo wrote 'that the greater or less quantity of labour worked up in commodities can only be the only cause of their alteration in value is completely made out as soon as we are agreed that all commodities are the produce of labour and would have no value but for the labour expended upon them'. Ricardo (1951b).

10. The use of the standard commodity to interpret both the early and mature work of Ricardo led me (Fine (1982) Chapter 3) in the pursuit of the critique of the Sraffian interpretation of Ricardo confusingly (and erroneously) to run together the two periods of Ricardo's thought as if he always held a value theory based on labour time rather than earlier holding to the more general principle of difficulty of production (but with the exclusion of demand). See Faccarello (1982).

11. Sraffa (1960) is himself guilty of this but, as usual, to an unknown degree. He merely observes that 'the conception of a standard measure of value as a medium between two extremes also belongs to Ricardo' p. 94. The fact, however, that ham lies between the two extremes of bread in a sandwich does not identify it in any other way with other categories of medium and extremity. Sraffa makes an association and no more although he does go on to observe a paradox. Continuing the above quote: '. . . and it is surprising that the standard commodity which has been evolved from it here should be found to be equivalent to something very close to the standard suggested by Adam Smith, namely "labour commanded", to which Ricardo himself was decidedly opposed.' The paradox is easily resolved, since Sraffa's standard has little to do with Ricardo's (or Adam Smith's). Here Sraffa also reveals a tendency to read 'the connection of this (i.e. his) work with the theories of the old classical economists' by cornifying them. In the two and a half pages of Appendix D, *References to the Literaure*, he manages to do it to a remarkable number of authors. He proceeds by extracting what can be interpreted to be Sraffian within them.

12. Broome (1978) cast doubts on the invariability of the standard commodity. See also Fine (1982) Chapter 3 where the difference between the Ricardian and Sraffian standard is examined in more detail. At more of a methodological level, it is to be observed that the standard commodity of Sraffa serves as an ideal construction for expositional purposes and its validity

as a category of political economy has to be established separately. Do the classes struggle over the distribution of the standard commodity? By contrast, Ricardo addresses himself to the immediate workings of the economy. What is the money commodity that would minimise price variations as a result of wage changes? The nature of Ricardo's answer (and of his question) is determined by his treating all economic categories at the same empirical level whilst remaining committed to a value theory based on labour-time. Sraffians do much the same other than to abandon the value theory. In this light, it is unfortunate that Sraffians are often termed neo-Ricardians because of their belief in an inverse relationship between wages and profits. This is a term best reserved for those who support this proposition but continue to defend value theory based on labour-time. See, for example, the critique of Steedman (1977) by Armstrong, Glyn and Harrison (1978).

References

Armstrong, P. A. Glyn and J. Harrison (1978), 'In Defence of Value: A Reply to Ian Steedman', *Capital and Class.*

Broome, J. (1978), 'The Allegedly Invariable Value of Sraffa's Standard Commodity', *Birkbeck Discussion Paper*, 64.

Elson, D. (ed.) (1979), *Value: The Representation of Labour in Capitalism*, London: CSE Books.

Faccarello, G. (1982), 'The Historical Irrelevance of the "Corn-Profit" Model', *Economy and Society.*

Fine, B. (1980), *Economic Theory and Ideology*, London: Edward Arnold.

Fine, B. (1982), *Theories of the Capitalist Economy*, London: Edward Arnold.

Fine, B. and **L. Harris** (1979), *Rereading 'Capital'*, London: Macmillan.

Hollander, S. (1979), *The Economics of David Ricardo*, London: Heinemann.

Okishio, N. (1961), 'Technical Change and the Rate of Profit', *Kobe University Economic Review.*

Ricardo, D. (1951a), *Principles of Political Economy and Taxation, The Works and Correspondence of David Ricardo*, vol. 1, London: Cambridge University Press.

Ricardo, D. (1951b), *The Works and Correspondence of David Ricardo*, vol. 4, London: Cambridge University Press.

Sraffa, P. (1926), 'The Law of Returns under Competitive Conditions', *Economic Journal.*

Sraffa, P. (1951), 'Introduction' to Ricardo (1951a).

Sraffa, P. (1960), *Production of Commodities by Means of Commodities*, London: Cambridge University Press.

Steedman, I. (1977), *Marx after Sraffa*, London: New Left Books.

Steedman, I. et al (1981), *The Value Controversy*, London: New Left Books.

Weeks, J. (1982), *Capital and Exploitation*, London: Edward Arnold.

CHAPTER 7

Note: A dissenting note on the transformation problem

Ben Fine

What is the Problem?

The so-called transformation problem of values into prices and of surplus value into profit has been one of the most controversial topics of Marxist political economy. The divergence of prices of production from values was seen as the Achilles heel of the labour theory of value even before the publication of Volume III of *Capital.*[1] Subsequently, it has invariably proved to be the grounds on which bourgeois economics has dismissed Marxism, preoccupied as this economics is with the precise calculation of prices, for which a *labour* theory of value is irrelevant given the role played by other factors of production (and demand). Even within Marxism, there has been, associated with the Sraffian school, a dismissal of the labour theory of value on the grounds of the transformation problem.

Much ink has been spent on this problem despite its lack of immediate application to economic or political issues. It has proved the ground on which deeper conceptual matters have been raised and occasionally resolved. These have particularly concerned the notion of value and its place in Marx's thought and in any valid analysis of capitalist society.[2] The purpose of this paper is to argue that, whatever the merits of these debates, they have misrepresented Marx's own contribution to the subject. This is an astonishing claim, given the attention paid to Marx's exposition, but it is one that is easily summarised. Discussion of the transformation problem has examined the implications for prices of differing compositions of capital across sectors of the economy. This has, however, invariably focused upon differences in the *value* composition of capital, whereas Marx's analysis is concerned almost exclusively with the *organic* composition.

This error in interpreting Marx is not a simple misreading of 'value' wherever 'organic' appears. It is a failure to recognise that there is any distinction between the value and organic compositions so that the organic composition is treated as if it were the value composition. It is essential then to outline Marx's notion of the composition of capital. He distinguishes between the technical, organic and value compositions and does so within a few pages of embarking upon the transformation problem. The technical composition reflects the differing rates of physical means of production to living labour. When this is assessed in value terms the organic composition results:

> A definite number of labourers is required to produce a definite quantity of products in, say, one day, and – what is self-evident – thereby to consume productively, i.e., to set in motion a definite quantity of means of production, machinery, raw materials, etc. . . .This proportion forms the technical composition of capital and is the real basis of its organic composition. III p. 145.

Marx proceeds to explain that the value differs from the organic composition in that the same technical process may employ raw materials of different values. Then the technical and organic compositions are the same but the value compositions differ across the sectors:

> For instance, certain work in copper and iron may require the same ratio of labour-power to mass of means of production. But since copper is more expensive than iron, the value relation between variable and constant capital is different in each case, and hence also the value-composition of the two capitals . . . . The value composition of capital, in as much as it is determined by, and reflects, its technical composition, is called the organic composition of capital.

Engels appends a footnote pointing out that these distinctions were inserted into the third edition of volume I of *Capital*. There and elsewhere in *Theories of Surplus Value*, Marx's distinction is seen to go further. For whilst the distinction between value and organic composition is clear enough where the same material process is involved in production but with materials of different values (copper and iron to make plate, silver and gold to make jewellery), the same is not true of different production processes such as construction and agriculture. Marx further distinguishes the organic and value compositions in a dynamic context in which, as capital is accumulated, the increasing use of raw materials etc. in one sector as opposed to another is the basis of comparing technical and organic compositions whereas the value composition allows, in addition, for the changing values brought about by such technical changes.[3] This ties the organic composition to changes in the production process and the value composition to the resulting formation of values after the intervention of exchange. For example, an increasing organic composition of steel, resulting in increasing productivity, will tend to reduce the value composition in all steel using sectors but have no direct effect on their organic compositions.

Because Marx discusses the transformation problem in terms of the organic composition he is concerned with the following problem: what is the effect on prices of differences across sectors in the quantities of raw materials worked up into commodities irrespective of the values of those raw materials? The transformation problem as traditionally concerned would wish to take account of differences in the values of raw materials. Usually, following on from this, account is also taken of the differences in the prices of raw materials (which differ from the differing values).

Given Marx's problem, there are two sensible ways of proceeding, both of which he adopts. The first is to assess advanced capital at its value rather than at its cost. Then, if one capital works up four times more raw materials than another it will have an organic composition of four times. A simple example illustrates this together with the consequential formation of the rate of profit and prices of production

Sector	c	v	s	p*
I	80	20	20	150
II	50	50	50	150
III	20	80	80	150
Total	150	150	150	

* Prices of production are based on c + v marked up by the rate of profit which is formed by dividing aggregate s by aggegate c + v.

Alternatively, it can be presumed that constant and variable capital have already been assessed at cost prices so that advances are made in money form. In this instance, the table above remains the same but the quantities are expressed in pounds or whatever. In other words, money magnitudes directly represent magnitudes of labour and raw materials during the course of the production process. Outside production, in exchange, the prior purchasing price of inputs and the subsequent selling price of outputs do not represent labour-time directly.

Marx recognises this divergence between value and price of inputs in a number of places (p. 161, p. 164, p. 173/4, p. 207 and also in TSV III p. 167). In the second of these references, he simply observes that 'our present analysis does not necessitate a closer examination of this point'. There are two reasons that can be put forward for this. The first is that qualitatively, prices and rates of profit prior to production must have been formed already:

> The prices which obtain as the average of the various rates of profit in the different spheres of production added to the cost prices of the different spheres of production, constitute the *prices of production*. They have, as their prerequisite the existence of a general rate of profit. p. 157.

Quantitatively, Marx is aware that differing value compositions have the same effect upon prices as differing organic compositions (and turnover mines) – see p. 144–5 – so that a separate consideration of this would not appear to be urgent.

Observations and implications

The most frequent criticism made against Marx's treatment of the transformation problem is that he got it wrong and in order to get it right value theory has to be abandoned or is irrelevant. Hopefully, I have shown that Marx did not get wrong the problem that *he* posed, although it differs from the one which he is presumed to have failed to solve. It is not surprising that the solution to one problem is inappropriate as the solution to another. It is worth exploring the difference between the two problems further.

Marx did not transform the value of inputs, presuming that this had already been done, since profits and prices of previous production are the preconditions of continuing production. It follows that the prices of production and rate of profit resulting from Marx's transformation can differ from the cost prices (and rate of profit) which are their antecedents. This will reflect the changing conditions of production intrinsic in any analysis based on the organic composition. It is for this reason that price of production is such an apt name, since it is the price resulting from differences in production processes. Cost price represents value considerations also (reflecting differences in value composition and turnover time) and is different both conceptually and quantitatively from price of production. Presumably, price of production must have been a carefully chosen terminology by Marx. In the *Theories of Surplus Value*, written prior to volume III of *Capital*, Marx never uses the term price of production, but uses various other terms including cost price! Whilst this is thought to reflect the lack of standard terminology amongst his contemporaries, the usage finally decided upon for *Capital* does not appear to be accidental.

In contrast to Marx his critics and many supporters, transform both output prices simultaneously. This reflects the rejection of a given set of prices and rate of profit prior to production. Rather input and output prices are determined simultaneously and as equal to each other. For this problem, there is no need for a distinction between the organic and value compositions and the latter alone suffices, better expressed in price and not value terms. The absence of the organic composition is marked by an equilibrium analysis whereas this is not essential to Marx's problem. Further, for Marx, the equality in aggregate between surplus value and profit and between value and price is immediate and accounted for in absolute quantities of labour time, whereas this cannot be so for his critics, giving rise to the normalisation problem in determining absolute rather than relative prices.

The interpretation of Marx's transformation offered here, integrates this part of his analysis into what follows and what has gone before in *Capital*. In volume I of *Capital*, Marx analyses the production of (relative) surplus value by the use of machinery and this is reflected in a rising organic composition, the variability of which is the starting point for his transformation. Volume II of *Capital* analyses the exchange between sectors which is the basis upon which reproduction rests. The first part of Volume III examines profit as the form of surplus value in exchange and the second part deals with the transformation problem. Part III of Volume III turns to the law of the tendency of the rate of profit to fall. It does so by relying upon the rising *organic* composition for the law as such and upon the formation of the value composition for counteracting tendencies.[4] For Marx, it is the internal contradiction between the law as such and counteracting influences which is of significance. A further use of the organic composition is made by Marx in his treatment of absolute rent, an analysis which is crucially dependent upon the relationship between changing productivity and price formation.[5]

By contrast, the traditional view of the transformation problem can take value and surplus value as given without analysing how it is produced or how it is exchanged. Just as this treatment extinguishes the distinction between the organic and value compositions by use of an equilibrium analysis, so discussion of falling profitability becomes an exercise in comparative statics where the tensions between (surplus) value production and circulation are eliminated.[6] Within this framework, absolute rent is also impossible other than as a monopoly rent with no systematic connection to the organic composition.

Finally, a new light is shed upon the historical transformation problem, Marx's idea that for an undeveloped or pre-capitalist economy, commodities exchange at their values.[7] It has generally been presumed that Marx had in mind a zero rate of profit, equal value compositions of capital or impediments to competitive exchange across sectors. Given the association of such economies with little or no development in the use of machinery little change is to be expected in the organic composition. On the interpretation suggested here, continued exchange at value is an immediate result.

Notes

1. See Engels's postscript to Volume III.
2. For an assessment of the debate, see Fine and Harris (1979) and for a colloquium of competing views, see Steedman *et al.* (1981).
3. For a more extended treatment of the distinctions between the compositions of capital and for reference to Marx's discussion of them, see Fine and Harris (1979) and Fine (1979).
4. For this interpretation, see Fine and Harris (1979) and Weeks (1982).
5. See Fine (1979) and Fine (1982).
6. See Fine (1982).
7. See the debate between Fine (1980) and Catephores (1980) for example.

References

Catephores, G. (1980) 'The Historical Transformation Problem – A Reply', *Economy and Society*, Vol. 9 (3).
Fine, B. (1979) 'On Marx's Theory of Agricultural Rent', *Economy and Society*, Vol. 8 (3).
Fine, B. (1980) 'On the Historical Transformation Problem', *Economy and Society*, Vol. 9 (3).
Fine, B. (1982) *Theories of the Capitalist Economy*, London: Edward Arnold.
Fine, B. and **L. Harris** (1979) *Rereading 'Capital'*, London: MacMillan.
Marx, K. (1972) *Capital*, Volume III, London: Lawrence & Wishart.
Marx, K. (1969) *Theories of Surplus Value*, Part II, London: Lawrence & Wishart.
Steedman, I. *et al.* (1981) *The Value Controversy*, London: Verso–NLB.
Weeks, J. (1982) *Capital and Exploitation*, London: Edward Arnold.

CHAPTER 8

The logic of prices as values*

Guglielmo Carchedi

Abstract

There are two major lines of criticism moved at Marx's approach to the transformation of values into prices. The circularity critique holds that constant and variable capital appear in Marx's numerical examples as inputs at their individual values and as outputs at their social, transformed value (or price of production). This critique is rejected as being foreign to Marx's methodology. Rather, the problem, when correctly formulated, is why and how the value incorporated in the constant and variable capital at the moment of their realization as outputs can differ from the value appropriated by them at the moment of their realization as inputs (and vice versa). The infinite regression critique submits that Marx's approach implies following the formation of value step by step backward *ad infinitum*. This critique too is rejected on logical grounds and it is submitted that the problem, rather, is that of bringing up to the present the value which has been formed in the past. After the transformation problem has been thus reformulated, a solution is provided. Seen from this angle, which I argue is Marx's own, there is no inconsistency in Marx's numerical examples.

Introduction

Marx's transformation of values into prices has been the object of hotly debated controversies since Böhm-Bawerk's attack (1973) on the third volume of *Capital*.[1] In short, to compute the price of production (PrPr) of commodities, Marx adds to the constant capital (c) and variable capital (v) needed for those commodities' production the average rate of profit (Marx, 1967c, p. 164). Two types of critique have emerged as the most influential. The first is the *circularity critique*. On the one hand, c is said to be an individual value, i.e. a value not yet transformed into a price of production. On the other hand, the same c is itself a product of other production processes and, when sold, must be sold at its price of production. There is, so runs the argument, a logical mistake, a circular reasoning which is why the conditions of equilibrium cannot be respected any longer (Sweezy, 1968). The second type of critique is complementary to the one just mentioned. This is the *infinite regression* argument, according to which to compute the value of a commodity we must know the value of c, but to know the value of c we must know the value of the c which went into its production in the previous period, and so on in an infinite series of steps backwards in time. In what follows, I intend to analyze Marx's approach and both the circularity and the infinite regression critiques. In the process of answering these two types of critique, I shall put forward a consistent interpretation and solution of the tansformation problem.

1 Marx's 'solution' of the transformation problem

Let us start with a few basic concepts. Marx works with the following ones. The *individual value* of a commodity is given by its value before its realization (sale) on the market. One example of individual value is the value actually expanded in a commodity's production. Another example is, as we shall see, an already realized (social) value which must undergo a new social realization either because it must be sold again – as a product or as a part (input) of it – or because its average conditions of production have changed since its previous realization. The individual value is a potential social value, a social value before its realization through exchange. The *social value* constitutes itself at the moment of the commodity's realization and is the value of the commodity produced under average conditions of production, given a certain distribution of society's purchasing power among the various branches. The social value can take several forms according to the scope of the problematic, i.e. according to the comprehensiveness of the analysis. Marx considers three forms. First, the *market value* which 'on the one hand . . . is to be viewed as the average value of commodities produced in a single sphere and, on the other, as the individual value of the commodities produced under average conditions of their respective sphere and forming the bulk of the production of that sphere' (Marx, 1967c, p. 176). The market value is then the social, i.e. average, value when reference is made to a single branch, taken in (artificial) isolation. Competition within that branch tends both to create different rates of profit (the countertendency) and to equalize them (the tendency) thus producing the market value. But the different branches compete also with each other since 'capital withdraws from a sphere with a low rate of profit and invades other, which yield a higher profit' (Marx, 1967c, p. 195). The equalization of the rates of profit in this case results in the formation of *prices of production*. The price of production in a certain branch, then, differs from the market value because the equalization of that branch's rate of profit is now subject to the influence also of other branches.[2] In this case, the social, i.e. average, value is given by the price of production rather than by the market value. As is well known, the formation of the prices of production is due to the fact that under capitalism, profits 'are not distributed in proportion to the surplus value produced in each special sphere of production, but rather in proportion to the mass of capital employed in each sphere, so that equal masses of capital, whatever their composition, receive equal aliquot shares of the total surplus value produced by the total social capital' (Marx, 1967c, p. 194). The price of production is thus computed by adding to constant and variable capital (the *cost-price*) the average rate of profit computed on the cost-price itself. Finally, the price of production is, in its turn, the centre 'around which the daily *market prices* fluctuate and tend to equalize one another within definite periods.'[3]

Against this background, given three branches of production, the transformation of individual values into prices of production is carried out by Marx as follows (Marx, 1967c, p. 164)

Table 1

	c	v	s	Value	PrPr	PrPr-Value
I	80	20	20	120	120	0
II	90	10	10	110	120	+10
III	70	30	30	130	120	−10
	240	60	60	360	360	0

where c = constant capital; v = variable capital; s = surplus value; PrPr = price of production; and where the average rate of profit ($\bar{p}$ = 60/300 = 20%) is used to compute the surplus value accruing to each capital of 100, i.e. to compute the PrPr. Therefore, the total value produced is equal to the total value distributed on the basis of a PrPr equal to 120. In this case, thus, the equalization of the rate of profit takes place through the equalization of the PrPr in all three branches and it will be around this level that the market price will fluctuate.

The usefulness of this procedure is that it isolates the essence of the problem, i.e. it shows that even when the rate of profit in the three branches is the same, there is inherent in the equalization of the rates of profit through the price mechanism a transfer of value or unequal exchange, from lower composition capitals (in this case branch III) to higher composition capitals (in this case branch II). In other words, the higher organic composition of capital in branch II will cause less production (in percentage terms) of surplus value than, but appropriation of more surplus value through redistribution from, branch III. Unequal exchange is thus inherent in and is the specific feature of the transformation problem. Or, again, the equalization of the rate of profit, the fact that all capitals (branches) must appropriate the same rate of profit (20%) on the total capital invested, takes place through a PrPr that ensures that part of the surplus value produced by the less productive branch (i.e. III) is transferred to, appropriated through distribution by, the more productive branch, i.e. II. *The height of the organic composition of capital* is here an *index of productivity* and the transfer of value to the more productive, higher composition, capitals is the way capitalist society rewards the introduction of capital intensive technologies, and thus stimulates a constant growth in the organic composition of capital. It is my contention that this is the purpose of Marx's scheme illustrating the formation of prices of production: to show the unequal exchange inherent in price formation and rewarding the most productive capitals at the expense of the least productive ones; i.e. to show how the price mechanism makes possible the functioning of competitive capitalism.[4]

2 The circularity critique

Perhaps the most well-known line of critique and discussion around the transformation problem, is that originated by Böhm-Bawerk (1973) which, with the reply by R. Hilferding (1973) and the seminal contribution by von Bortkiewicz (1973), has been brought to the attention of a wide readership by the classical work of P. Sweezy (1968). Building upon that discussion, Sweezy points out that, after the transformation has been carried out, (a) the value incorporated into a commodity and the value appropriated through its sale do not coincide any longer, something which 'results in the violation of equilibrium of Simple Reproduction' (1968, p. 114) and (b) in the computation of prices of production, 'the capitalists' outlay on constant and variable capital are left exactly as they were in the value scheme; in other words the constant capital and the variable capital used in production are still expressed in value terms' (1968, p. 115). This second point has been later formulated in more modern terminology as follows: inputs are expressed as values but outputs are expressed as prices of production; this is a logical flaw since the same commodity is bought as an input and sold as an output at the same price. In terms of table 1 above, the constant and variable capital entering the transformation process are said to be individual, embodied, labour. However, inasmuch as they are outputs of their respective branches, they are social, i.e. transformed values, prices of production. Looking again at table 1 above, suppose that I produces means of production, II produces wage goods, and III produces luxury goods; then I sells its product at 120 (the price of production) but a portion of that product is bought by I for a value of 80, another portion by II for 90, and yet another by III for 70, i.e. for total of 240. The means of production are sold at prices of production but bought at their individual values. For Sweezy, (b) is the source of the violation mentioned in (a). By far the most influential solution is that offered by von Bortkiewicz (1973).

2a The von Bortkiewicz answer

Von Bortkiewicz' solution, reduced to its essentials, assumes a situation of simple reproduction, given the three above-mentioned sectors, i.e.

$$\begin{aligned} c_1 + v_1 + s_1 &= V_1 \\ c_2 + v_2 + s_2 &= V_2 \\ c_3 + v_3 + s_3 &= V_3 \end{aligned}$$

where c, v and s are respectively constant capital, variable capital and surplus value and where the subscripts refer to the branch producing means of production (1), wage goods (2), and luxury goods (3). If demand equals supply then

$$\begin{aligned} c_1 + v_1 + s_1 &= V_1 = c_1 + c_2 + c_3 \\ c_2 + v_2 + s_2 &= V_2 = v_1 + v_2 + v_3 \\ c_3 + v_3 + s_3 &= V_3 = s_1 + s_2 + s_3 \end{aligned}$$

The assumption is then made that with the transformation of values into prices of production the price of the means of production becomes x times greater than their value, that of the workers' articles of consumption becomes y times greater than their value and that of the capitalists' luxury goods becomes z times higher than their value. If we call the average rate of profit in price terms r, then the model of simple reproduction transformed in prices of production becomes

$$\begin{aligned} c_1 x + v_1 y + r(c_1 x + v_1 y) &= (c_1 + c_2 + c_3)x \\ c_2 x + v_2 y + r(c_2 x + v_2 y) &= (v_1 + v_2 + v_3)y \\ c_3 x + v_3 y + r(c_3 x + v_3 y) &= (s_1 + s_2 + s_3)z \end{aligned}$$

Bortkiewicz obtains thus three equations with four unknowns (x, y z, and r). In terms of mathematics, to solve this system we must supply a fourth equation. In terms of economics, this means that we must choose between two equally undesirable solutions. Either we assume that the total of prices equals the total of values, but then the equality between surplus value and profit is not respected any more; or we assume that the total of profit equals the total of surplus value but then the total of prices and of values will not coincide any more. The two equalities do not hold, in general, at the same time. After Bortkiewicz, many other authors have worked out improved or more complete, equally 'consistent', solutions which, however, share with Bortkiewicz' solution the same characteristic of severing either the equality between prices and values or that between surplus value and profits. The significance of this is almost unanimously played down. Yet, if the former equality does not hold, it makes no sense any more to speak of 'transformation' of values into prices (which is precisely what Marx set out to do and is, as we have seen, fundamental for an understanding of capital reproduction and accumulation); and if the latter equality does not hold, profits do not come necessarily any more from surplus value and the theory of exploitation is dealt a fatal blow. Both conclusions are devastating for the Marxian value theory.[5]

2b Why von Bortkiewicz was off the mark

It should be pointed out right away that there is a basic *logical mistake* which invalidates the Bortkiewicz-inspired critique and 'solution': the tieing of the transformation problem to the reproduction schemes and thus the collapsing of one type of problematic into a *different type* of problematic. These schemes concern themselves with 'the reconversion of one portion of the value of the product into capital and the passing of another portion into the individual consumption of the capitalist, as well as the working class' (Marx, 1967b, p. 394). In other words, these schemes concern themselves with the redistribution of the social product (in terms of use and exchange value) *after* that product has been *realized* through sale, in such a way that the *equilibrium* conditions of simple (or expanded) reproduction are met. The point that this has nothing to do with Marx' transformation problem is not new. It was already made in 1948 by J. Winternitz (1948). Winternitz' solution, however, even though applicable to expanded reproduction, is not more satisfactory and in line with Marx's approach than Bortkiewicz' solution. In fact, Winternitz, instead of tieing the transformation problem to the reproduction schemes, considers it in the light of the input-output framework, in this followed by most commentators on the transformation problem, from Seton, who generalized Winternitz' three-departments model to N commodities,[6] onwards. But to consider the transformation of values into prices as an input-output scheme does not come closer to the problem as posed by Marx than Bortkiewicz and Sweezy did. Both inputs and outputs are commodities whose value has already been produced and realized so that – obviously – a commodity must be sold (as output) and bought (as input) at the same price (market price). To consider constant and variable capital as inputs in an input-output sense, means to have already left the transformation problem behind, to deal with *already realized* values; it means to disregard the interplay between the individual and social values of c and v both as inputs and as outputs.

But the nature of the problem under consideration is totally different. The problem is neither the analysis of how specific products must be used in the following period as constant and variable capital for equilibrium (under conditions of simple or expanded reproduction) to hold; nor the analysis of how this period's products (outputs) enter the production of the economy's several departments in the following period as inputs. The transformation problem is the problem of *why and how the value incorporated in c and v at the moment of their realization as outputs differs from the value appropriated by them at the moment of their realization as inputs* (and vice versa). *This* is the *definition* of the problem. This definition seems to be the same as the one submitted by Marx's critics, but it is not. The reasons why the two formulations are not the same as well as the reasons for choosing this formulation will become clear after the two basic critiques have been discussed and rejected. As far as the *boundaries of the problematic* are concerned, my thesis will be that the transformation problem is first of all a problem of *logic*, it concerns itself with the logical problem of why and how values exist only inasmuch as they at the same time can manifest (realize) themselves; why and how they must manifest themselves in a modified, social, form, i.e. as prices of production; and why and how realized social values can become again individual (or potential social) values. Secondly, I will submit that the transformation problem depicts a real transformation, a real process. This process must be seen both as a *chronological sequence* of different moments of distribution (realization), thus as a chronological sequence of transfers of value, and as a *logical sequence*, i.e. within each of these moments individual values precede logically (but not chronologically) the social, realized values. Finally, the *solution* is summarised at the end of section 3 and for reasons of exposition will be given in three steps, of which two arise from the discussion of the circularity critique and the third one from the discussion of the infinite regression critique.[7]

2c Redressing the balance in favour of dialectical logic

I have argued above that the problem is one of dialectics. The proper interpretative scheme has been developed elsewhere.[8] Here I will only mention what is strictly necessary for the purpose of this article. First of all, a distinction must be made between determination in the last instance (which deals with possible conditions of existence or of supersession) and realized determination (which deals with the realization of some of those possibilities). As far as *determination in the last instance* is concerned, given two instances, A and B, A is said to determine in the last instance B if B is a potential condition of reproduction (existence) or of supersession of A. A cannot then be theorized independently from B, as if B did not exist, not even as a first approximation to a more advanced stage of research in which A and B will be considered together. Rather, B must be considered to be a potential condition of reproduction of supersession of A, and thus inherent in A, from the very beginning of the theorization (but not necessarily from the beginning of the exposition). But determination in the last instance does not explain the *realization* of one or some of the several possibilities. If A calls into existence B as a condition of its own existence (or supersession), B in its turn reacts upon and modifies A. The theoretical explanation of how this is possible is provided in my above-mentioned works. All that can be said here is that *both* A and B realize themselves in their mutual interrelation, i.e. they constitute themselves reciprocally in the act of their realization and this realization is at the same time their reciprocal modification. These are some of the concepts dealing with realization in general. This is only a necessary but preliminary stage. The next stage in dealing with realization is to inquire into the specific mechanisms, or processes, through which the specific categories of phenomena realize themselves.

Particularly important is the question of how particular categories of individual phenomena realize themselves as social phenomena. In the context of this article, the question becomes that of the realization of individual values into social values. It could be submitted that prices of production (the social values of commodities in a capitalist economy, if the assumption is made that the prices of production coincide with market prices) are the determined instance, the conditions of existence of values. This interpretation would seem to be supported by Marx when he says that values 'lie beneath the prices of production and . . . determine them in the last instance' (1967c, p. 208). This, however, raises two objections. First, if there were a relation of determination between individual values and prices of production, both instances would realize themselves and they would do so in a modified way. In fact, what is realized is neither, but rather the market prices. Second, even if we assumed an equality between market prices and prices of production, the objection still remains that it is not values *and* prices of production which realize themselves, but values *as* prices of production. We must therefore conclude that individual values realize themselves in a modified form, as social values, i.e. as prices of production.

There is then no relation of determination between values and prices; rather the structure of the prices of production is the concrete, social, form (when it coincides with the market prices) taken by the structure of individual values due to these values' interrelation with all other social phenomena through the process of, and at the moment of, exchange. Individual values are the *potential*, not yet realized, social values and the prices of production are the *realized* social values, the form taken by the individual values through, and at the moment of, exchange. This interpretation is consistent not only with the discussion carried out by Marx; it is also consistent with the concept, to which Marx keeps coming back, that the prices of production are a modified form of value. This holds for all commodities, including those which are inputs for the production of other commodities, i.e. c. In other words, c cannot appear in table 1 as an input at its embodied value and must appear as an output at its price of production. This is the *first step* in the solution of the transformation problem: the explanation of why and how c as an input cannot appear at its embodied value and, therefore, the indication that its individual value as an input must already be a transformed value. In short, the *individual* value of c as an input cannot be its *embodied* value.

But there is also a second mistake inherent in the circularity critique. First of all, it is important to underline that there are *two* production periods. The former is the period in which c is the output, the latter is the period in which c is the input of a new output, say of *a*. The circularity critique collapses these two periods into just one. A real, and thus temporal process, is reduced to one in which two production periods are superimposed. But the producer of c realizes its (social) value when c is sold (as output) while the producer of *a* realizes the social value of c as input when *a* is sold. That is, *the moment of realization of c as output is not the moment of realization of c as input*. Thus, what is inconsistent is not Marx's procedure, but the application of the logic of the input-output scheme (i.e. to consider that c realizes its value both as output and as input at the same moment, i.e. when c is sold by the producer of c and bought by the producer of *a*) to that procedure. It should thus be clear that while I use the terms 'input' and 'output', I apply a totally different reasoning than that implicit in the input-output tables.

Since two production periods and thus two moments of realization are collapsed into one, the illusion is created that c is exchanged at both its individual and social value. To unravel the skein created by the circularity critique we must clearly see two things. First, the transformation problem depicts a transformation process and thus a chronological sequence of processes of production of value and surplus value and of moments of realization/distribution not only of surplus value but also of the value of c as an input. Secondly, within each of these moments of realization there is chronological contemporaneity (individual values can manifest themselves only as social values) which is at the same time a logical sequence (the individual values precede logically the social ones). This complexity is reduced by the circularity critique to the absurd accusation that there is implicit in Marx's procedure the notion that c appears (realizes itself) *both* as an individual *and* as a social value and that therefore it is bought and sold at different prices (values). In the last analysis, the circularity critique makes the *double mistake* of considering as a chronological sequence what in fact is a chronologically contemporaneous process (the realization of individual values as social ones) and of considering as a chronologically contemporaneous process what is in fact a chronological sequence (the realization of the social value of c both as an input and as an output). For Marx, on the other hand, the value of c can appear only in its realized, social form and (contrary to the logic inherent in the input-output tables) the moment of c's realization as an output is chronologically different from the moment of its realization as an input. Thus, the social value which realizes itself at time t, i.e. when c is sold as an output and bought as an input, is its PrPr as output and not as input (since this latter realizes itself only at time t + 1, when *a* realizes its social value). But since t is the moment at which both the previous production process ends and the new one begins, *the social value of c as an output enters the new production process as the individual value of c as an input*. But this individual value neither is embodied value (it is rather an old price of production, an already transformed value) nor it is a price different from the price at which c has been sold as an output. This is the *second step* in the solution of the transformation problem: the explanation of why the individual value of c as an input is its PrPr as the output of the previous period. But, since table 1 refers to time t + 1, the time of *a*'s realization, the value of c which appears in it cannot be its individual value (the old PrPr) but must be its social value. This will be determined in the next section.

There is thus no mistake in the transformation procedure of which Marx would have been aware but did nothing about.[9] The mistake is the critics' who do not understand Marx's dialectical method and who misinterpret a mathematical example aimed at showing how, under developed capitalism, values must realize, transform themselves into prices of production through the mechanism of the equalization of the rate of profit, i.e. aimed at showing how surplus value must be redistributed at the moment of realization in order for the rate of profit to be equal, as if it were a perverse input-output table depicting a type of transaction, in which the same commodity is bought by someone and sold by someone else at different prices. The mistake is to apply the logic of the input-output tables (which collapses the two moments of realization/distribution into just one but separates realization from distribution) to Marx's numerical examples in which realization and distribution of surplus value are chronologically contemporaneous but in which there are two chronologically different moments of realization/distribution (the first is the realization of c as an output, when c is sold, and the second is the realization of c as an input, when *a* is sold). The mistake is thus not only to consider Marx's solution of the transformation problem as a mathematical computation. The mistake is to do this without making explicit the methodology which supports it, thus leaving room for the implicit or explicit adoption of a different method which in turn changes the meaning and significance of that computation.

3 The infinite regression critique

But, it can be argued, if c is already expressed as realized, social value, computed as a PrPr, then to compute the value of c (i.e. the value of the means of production going into the value of a certain commodity, say *a*) we must go back to the previous period and from there to the previous one, thus falling into infinite regression. As J. Robinson puts it:

> the constant capital was produced in the past by labour time working with then pre-existing constant capital and so on, *ad infinitum* backwards. It therefore cannot be reduced simply to a number of labour hours that can be added to the net value of the current year. And there is no advantage in trying to do so. (1972, p. 202)

This highly sophisticated piece of methodology is wrong at least on two accounts. As far as *method* goes, the principle which must be adopted, and which is the only one which makes scientific research possible by avoiding infinite regression both in time and in logical causation, is that the choice of the starting point must be both subjective and objective. It is subjective in the sense that it depends upon the purpose of the research so that the starting point *need not* be analyzed in terms of its antecedents. It is objective because the starting point *could be* analyzed and *must be* analyzable *by the same laws* which govern the phenomena of which that point is the starting one. In other words, we could apply the same principles to the study of the starting point itself if (for reasons of historical analysis or because of the need to widen the logical chain of causations and not because of methodological considerations) we decided to go further back in time or in the chain of causations in the inquiry of the phenomenon under consideration. The value of c is given and need not be determined if the aim is to compute the value of *a*.

From the point of view of *determination*, it is necessary to consider the transformation process as a real process and thus as a sequence of real processes. As we know, the value of c has been produced in a certain period and is realized at a certain moment, say t, and is thus expressed as its PrPr at moment t. Therefore, c is sold as output and bought as input at its PrPr. There has been a production of value and of surplus value and a redistribution of that surplus value at the time c is sold as output and bought as input. In short, the individual value of c expresses itself as social value at the time of its realization as a product. Now a *new* production period starts and c enters in it as an input. The product, *a*, realizes its social value at time t + 1. The social value of c, now considered as an input, as an element of *a* at time t + 1, will be the value given by the socially necessary labour time at time t + 1 both to *re*-produce c and to produce *a*.

More specifically, if the average conditions of production of c change between t and t + 1, the value going into the value of *a* will be the one given at time t + 1; and if a certain producer of the commodity *a* has employed more (or less) c than it is socially necessary to produce *a*, then the value going into that particular *a* will be that of the average quantity of c at time t + 1. Thus, c is a social value in the double and interrelated sense that (1) it, as we have seen, as an output of the previous production process, is an individual value that cannot but realize itself as a social value, it counts as the quantity of labour socially necessary (i.e. average labour) to produce it (rather than the amount of labour actually spent to produce it) at the moment of its realization as an output; and (2) as an input in the present production period, it counts only as the quantity and quality of c employed in *a*'s average production process and produced according to c's average production process at the time of *a*'s realization. If it is not the average quantity and quality of c needed for a certain production process, if more (or less) socially necessary labour time is used at t + 1 to produce c than it was needed at time t, then the transfer of value will apply not only to the surplus value produced but also to the c which deviates from its average value. As Marx puts it in *Capital*, Volume I:

> if the capitalist has a foible for using golden spindles instead of steel ones, the only labour that counts for anything in the value of the yarn remains that which would be required to produce a steel spindle, because no more is necessary under the given social conditions (quoted in Nichols, 1980, p. 52).

This is the *third and last step* in the solution of the transformation problem: the explanation of why the social value of c as the input in the present production period is the modified quantity of its social value as the output of the previous period. It is this value which appears in table 1.

To sum up, from the point of view of method, the infinite regression critique makes no sense because the value of c is given and we do not need to determine it, but we could, if we wanted to, by following the procedure outlined above. From the point of view of value determination, the critique makes even less sense because the value of c as an input of *a* is its value at the time of *a*'s realization, i.e. the *re*-production value of the average quantity and quality of c needed to produce *a*. The question is not that of following the formation of value step by step backwards *ad infinitum* but that of bringing up to the present the value which has been formed in the past. Or, in other words, to counter the infinite regression movement, we first 'stop' it by means of the above mentioned methodological principle and then 'reverse' its direction by means of the above mentioned principle of value determination.

It should be now clear why Marx, after having performed the transformation as in table 1, says that also the c going into a commodity's cost-price (i.e. c + v) should be computed at its price of production (1967c, p. 208). For Marx the question is not whether the c of a commodity of average composition is expressed as an individual value or as a price of production: if it goes into a commodity of average composition, the surplus value contained in it will be equal to the average profit and its individual value will be equal to its price of production. In other words, Marx considers deviations of individual values from prices of production in c as input in the context of the question as to whether these deviations affect the price of production of a commodity of average composition (of which c is an input). The answer is no, as shown above. This is not the question to which the critics address themselves and according to which c is bought as an input at its (individual) value and is sold as an output at its price (of production). When Marx considers c as an input, he addresses himself to a completely different question, namely whether a deviation of the value of c as an input from its price of production affects the price of production of *a*; but since this deviation can manifest itself only when *a* is exchanged, the problem posed by Marx is in fact the one formulated above in section 2b, i.e. why and how the value incorporated in c as an output differs from the value appropriated by it as an input.

We can now summarize *the solution to the transformation problem*. The value incorporated in c as an output can differ from the value appropriated by it at the moment of its realization, say t, because of the transformation process as depicted in table 1. If we are concerned with the transformation of values into prices of production at time t + 1, it is methodologically correct to take this price of production as given. But whether or not this price of production coincides with its value at the moment of its realization as an output (t), the possibility arises of a deviation of this price of production at time t from its price of production at time t + 1 (the moment of its realization as an input), if the average conditions of production of c change between t and t + 1. Thus, the value of c as an input is determined by the PrPr of c in the preceding period (a given social value which need not be determined because of specific methodological reasons) as modified by the change in the average conditions of production of c in the present period. Thus c is not an individual value: if it is sold as an output at the end of the previous period and bought as an input at the beginning of the present period (the two moments coincide chronologically) it must be bought and sold at its social value. Or, c is a social (i.e. average) value because it is a realized social phenomenon. This is the answer to the von Bortkiewiczian critique: individual values can manifest themselves on the market only as social values, production and realization are distinct but indissolubly tied moments, a commodity sold (as output) and bought (as input) on the market is valued at its price of production at the time of its realization. But c as an input of the present period will realize its social value only at the end of the present period when the output, *a*, of which it is an input, will be sold, will realize its social value. If its individual value does not correspond to its social value (if, e.g, more than the average c has been used to produce a certain *a*), it must *count as* social value (i.e. realize itself as social value) because, when *a* is realized, what the market gives the producer of *a* is not only the average rate of profit, but also the average c needed for the production of *a*. Thus, what goes into the present period's product is the PrPr of c as given in the previous period and as modified in the present period. There is no need to go backwards *ad infinitum* either.

As long as the *dialectic* between individual and social values is lost sight of, i.e. as long as c as an input is considered to appear as an individual value and as an output is considered to be an *immutable* social value, a realized social value *which cannot become again an individual value*, i.e. as long as c as an input is not seen as a previously produced and realized value the magnitude of which, however, can change if its conditions of production change, the way is open to the two above mentioned critiques. There is a peculiar 'division of labour' between the circularity critique and the infinite regression critique: each specializes in a mistaken interpretation of the relation between potential and realized social values. The circularity critique does not see that c as an output of the previous process and thus as an input of the present process is a transformed social value. The value of c as an input cannot be given by the labour embodied in it: its individual value is already a transformed value (an old PrPr). This value must appear in table 1 as a modified social value, as the modification of that old PrPr, the social value of c as an output. The infinite regression critique does not see that, when c enters the present production process as the input of a commodity *a*, *its realized social value becomes again a potential social value, an individual value* (which, as such, cannot appear in table 1 which depicts the situation at the time of *a*'s realization). This individual value, this previous social value, will become again a social value (the new PrPr) only when the output, *a*, of which c is an input, will realize *its* value. In short, the circularity critique mistakes the PrPr of the previous period for labour embodied in the present period while the infinite regression critique mistakes the same PrPr for an immutable magnitude which is not modified by changes in the average conditions of production in the present period.

In the last analysis, neither type of critique sees (1) that c can have at the same time both an individual (but not embodied) value and a social value if we consider that moment, t, which marks the end of the previous production process and the beginning of the present production process; and (2) that this does not mean that c is bought at its individual value and sold at its social value, i.e. at two different prices: when it is sold by the producer of c to the producer of *a*, it is bought and sold at its PrPr, or social value, at time t. In short, *while c must be bought and sold at the same price, this price is at the same time its social value as an output (and this is why the transaction is carried out on the basis of this price) of the previous period and its individual (but not embodied) value as an input of the present period.*

4 Summary and conclusions

It can now be seen that the individual values (120 for branch I, 110 for branch II, and 130 for branch III) in table 1 above are the values given by how much surplus value has been added to the average, socially necessary, quantity and quality of c and v, before this surplus value is redistributed through the equalization of the rate of profit (the same reasoning applied to c can now be extended to v too). At the moment of the realization of c and v as outputs of the previous period there is a redistribution of surplus value, i.e. the formation of PrPr's through the equalization of the rates of profit. A certain redistribution of income takes place through the price mechanism. But the sale of c and v as outputs marks also the beginning of a new production period in which c and v are now the inputs. If the conditions of production of c and v do not change, the PrPr does not change either. If they do change, c and v have to adjust their social value at the end of the present production period, when the product, *a*, is sold. If, say, c has become cheaper, the producer of *a* will realize less value in proportion to the fall in c's value to the advantage of the other producers with whom our producer exchanges *a*. In the new, present, production period, the social value of c has to adjust itself to the new condition, it becomes the average cost of re-producing (under the new condition) c. Therefore, the individual values of 110, 120, 130 *are already social as far as c and v are concerned*, both as outputs of the previous period (since c and v are sold as outputs and bought as inputs, they are valued at their social magnitude, they must be PrPr's, realized social magnitudes) and as inputs of the new production period (since they transfer to the commodity of which they have become inputs only the average social value, i.e. only the average cost of production of the average quantity and quality of c and v needed under the new conditions of production). The values of 110, 120 and 130 are individual only inasmuch as the surplus value component is concerned since redistribution of surplus value has not been carried out yet.

This approach could be, mistakenly I think, criticized as relating solely to the sphere of exchange since the c and v entering the computation of the prices of production are already social values, prices of production. But this is not so. I do establish a link between production and exchange, between the individual and social value of c and v. My approach differs from the usual one in that this link is a logical (in terms of dialectical logic) rather than a mathematical one. I explain why the individual values of c and v cannot appear as such, must appear as social values, and how the individual value of *a* is transformed into its social value, i.e. how the value of c and v as inputs as well as the surplus value produced by using these inputs are redistributed in the act of exchange. Production and exchange are two distinct, but indissolubly tied moments of the same process. Both are necessary (even if the former, production, is the determinant one and the latter, exchange, is the determined one) for individual values to be able to express, realize, themselves, i.e. to become social phenomena. If this approach is followed, the way is open to mathematics, to the computation of how capitals with different organic compositions can realize amounts of surplus value different from those produced by them.[10]

It becomes thus clear how much Marx has been misunderstood on this score. The approach which is usually (but mistakenly) submitted as being Marx's own rests upon the mathematical relation between *two realized forms of value*, the individual and the social. But to treat individual values as if they were realized social phenomena is nonsensical in terms of Marx's problematic. Yet, it is this assumption which is behind the approach which is mistakenly attributed to Marx and upon which the critique is based, according to which commodities as inputs are exchanged at individual values and as outputs are exchanged at social values, i.e. at their prices of production. We can now see the importance of the emphasis placed upon the fact that prices are not determined by values but rather are their concrete form of existence. Far from being a philosophical quibble, this result allows us to stress the mistake made by all those who attempt to incorporate the Bortkiewicz-inspired approach within a Marxist framework, i.e. the concept of the determination of prices by values. To hold that inputs manifest themselves as individual values (i.e. not transformed into social values) and that outputs manifest themselves as prices of production (i.e. transformed form) implies that one should regard individual values as an already realized form (which determines another realized form, prices of production). But social phenomena do not appear first as individual phenomena and then as social ones; nor do they appear simultaneously both as individual and as social forms (where the former determines the latter). Rather, social phenomena are the social form of individual ones, the latter can express themselves only as the former.

There is no circularity and this because of two reasons. First, inputs, when sold by their producers as outputs at the end of the previous production period, must be valued at their social value or PrPr. It is on the basis of this PrPr that the producers of those inputs get a certain share of the societal wealth. Secondly, inputs, when bought by the new producers at that PrPr, will retain that social value or acquire a new, modified, social value at the moment of the product's realization, according to whether their conditions of production change or do not change. And there is no need to regress backwards *ad infinitum* either because for the determination of the value of this year's product (*a*) it is enough to take the value of c as socially *given* by the previous conditions of production and as *modified* by the present conditions of production. If we want to determine the value of c in the previous period, we can apply the same principles I have just outlined. But this is something we need not do if we are concerned with the value of the present year's product. The justification of choosing the value of c as the starting point for the determination of the value of the year's product is given by the fact that (1) we need a starting point and (2) that starting point itself can be explained by the same principles which explain the phenomena of which c is the starting point. The opposite view would make the study of any social phenomenon (inasmuch as it is an historical phenomenon) methodologically impossible, i.e. arbitrary. Not only the study of history but science itself would become an endless quest for the origin. The backwards *ad infinitum* argument is a measure of Marx's critics' proficiency in methodological questions. On this point they score rather low. In fact, they not only fail to look at the methodological nature of their objection but they fail also to see that its application would make science impossible. If there is anything backward here, it is Marx's critics' understanding of his method and theory.

How should we then interpret Marx' computations as exemplified in table 1 above? It is a basic misunderstanding of Marx's method to consider his mathematical computations as the 'solution' to the transformation problem. Those examples only depict the *computational specificity* of the transformation problem and can acquire their proper significance only when immersed in their proper methodological context. Only when the method and the purpose of the numerical examples have been properly understood, can those examples be seen for what they are, not as examples of a redistribution of already realized value functional for the equilibrium conditions of simple or expanded reproduction, not as an input-output table but – once it has been understood that we deal with that particular moment in which realization and redistribution of value and surplus value coincide chronologically – as examples of how surplus value must be redistributed if the possibility for competitive capitalism to function, i.e. for capital to accumulate, must be accounted for theoretically.

Once the transformation problem is posed in its proper problematic and solved, it can be seen that:

(1) in Marx's numerical examples there is no inconsistency. These examples depict the computational specificity of the transformation problem (not its solution).
(2) these examples are also correct in the sense that, if individual values realize themselves as prices of production, as social values, there must be equality between the total sum of individual and social values of the commodities produced and realized in a certain period, and that total surplus value must be equal to the total sum of profits (assuming, of course, that no surplus value is appropriated by other, unproductive, capitalists, by the state as taxes, etc.).
(3) the objection that the condition of equilibrium (simple or expanded) are violated becomes irrelevant, since the transformation problem has nothing to do with the reproduction schemes and with the conditions of equilibrium they are supposed to explicate.

From von Bortkiewicz on, the transformation problem has been dealt with on the terrain of the ideological opponent, a problem of dialectical logic has been debased to one of mathematical computtation implicitly immersed into an alien problematic. Even within the Marxist camp, the validity of Bortkiewicz' objection has been and is still accepted almost unanimously. As B. Rowthorn puts it, 'Marxists still find themselves trapped within a debate whose terms of reference were laid down by vulgar economists such as Böhm-Bawerk, on the one hand, and neo-Ricardians such as Bortkiewicz on the other' (1979, p. 75). Nor is there anything to be gained in choosing the Sraffian path which is based on the consideration that 'since both inputs including labour power, and outputs have to be transformed into price-terms, and hence in all probability the rate of profits will be affected, these have all to be determined simultaneously and interdependently, i.e. by solving a set of simultaneous equations' (Dobb, 1973, pp. 159–160). This approach too rests on the false assumption that the values of both c and *a* as outputs realize themselves simultaneously. This erroneous conception bars the study of technical progress so that not by chance the neo-Ricardian model of the capitalist economy assumes no technical change.[11] This is one of the many features which indicate the width of the gulf which separates Marx from Sraffa (so that the Sraffa-based critique cannot be thought of as immanent to Marx's theory) as well as the lack of realism which characterizes the Sraffian model. All mathematical 'improvements' of the Bortkiewicz-Winternitz-Seton-and further type or of the Sraffa type[12] are mathematical expressions of a logic alien to Marx's. The transformation problem has to be re-defined, in terms of the logic inherent in Marx's theoretical construction, before it can be solved.[13] When this is done, the Ricardian transformation problem turns out to be like the character of a play who, after having wandered in a world of papier mâché, finds out that he does not exist.

Notes

* This is a shorter version of Carchedi, 1983d. Copies of it can be requested to the author, Department of Economics, University of Amsterdam, Jodenbreestraat 23, Amsterdam. The Netherlands.

1. For a very good discussion of Böhm-Bawerk, see G. Kay, 1975, pp. 46–67.

2. Historically, the formation of prices of production requires a 'higher development of capitalist production' than the formation of market values. (Marx, 1967c, p. 180). In my opinion, whether this is so or not, is irrelevant for the explanation of the mechanism through which values appear as prices. Historical and logical explanations are related but different aspects of the explanatory scheme. The former helps, but does not provide the key for the understanding of the latter. For a different view, see R. Murray, 1977.

3. Marx, 1967c, p. 179. It should be noted that for Marx the transformation problem is the problem of the transformation of individual values into market prices through market values and prices of production and not one of the transformation of values into prices of production (as it is usually assumed). Thus, to deal with the transformation problem means at the same time to deal with the Marxian theory of prices, or at least with a facet of it. (For a different interpretation, see G. Dostaler, 1982). However, in what follows, I will deal only with the transformation of individual values into prices of production, in order to counter the most commonly accepted objections to Marx's procedure. The analysis of the formation of market prices as well as their manifestation in money terms is subsequent to the solution of the formation of prices of production and is not the specific topic of this paper. In a companion article to this one, I shall deal with the mechanism through which values realize themselves as international market prices through international prices of production. But, for the purposes of the present article, it is the relation between values and prices of production which must be analyzed.

4. Two points deserve to be mentioned here summarily, for lack of space. *First*, table 1 does not depict the *process* of the equalization of the rate of profit. It depicts neither the increase in the number of use values produced as a result of the introduction of more efficient techniques (and which, by being sold at a price of production higher than their individual value, allow an appropriation of surplus value through unequal exchange, thus generating a hierarchy of rates of profit) nor the incessant movements of capitals from the less to the more efficient techniques and/or branches (which works towards the equalization of these different rates since capital inflows increase supply, decrease prices of production and thus the surplus value appropriated). The movement towards a hierarchy of rates of profit is the counter-tendency, the movement towards the equalization of the different rates is the tendency. Table 1 does not depict the interplay of technological innovation and of capital movement, nor the succession of tendency and counter-tendency but gives, and is meant to give, only a static and incomplete view of the real

process: it is meant to show the unequal exchange inherent in the formation of the prices of production under tendencial conditions. More specifically, we should distinguish between two levels of analysis in order to assess correctly the theoretical status of table 1. When only production is considered (i.e. when exchange is not allowed to exert any influence), the assumption is made that tendencially the value produced is equal to the value appropriated. Under these assumptions, the only way the rate of profit can be equalized is through an equalization of the organic compositions. The tendency is thus towards an equalization of the rates of profit through an equalization of the organic compositions (due to capital movements) and the countertendency is towards a hierarchy of rates of profit through a hierarchy of organic compositions (due to technological innovations). The price mechanism here explains how different capitals get a uniform rate of profit under tendencial conditions (i.e. when the organic compositions are equal) through *equal* exchange. When exchange is considered, the assumption is made that tendencially the value produced differs from the value appropriated. Under these conditions we have to assume unequal exchange and thus different organic compositions of capital. In other words, we assume a tendency towards a hierarchy of organic compositions (clustered around an average) such that each organic composition gets the average rate of profit. The counter-tendency is the upsetting of this condition through the introduction of new (i.e. higher organic composition) techniques which allow the appropriation of a higher than average rate of profit. Capital movements will tend to restore that hierarchy in which all capitals will get the average rate of profit. On the basis of these considerations we can now understand correctly the nature of table 1. Table 1 is, of course, at the level of abstraction considering both production and exchange. However, it does not depict the succession of tendency (the equalization of the rate of profit on the basis of a hierarchy of organic compositions brought to this tendencial state through capital movements) and countertendency (the upsetting of this hierarchy due to technological innovations). Better said, this table does not depict the movement towards a tendencial state (which only by chance realizes itself) through the constant realization of a series of counter-tendencial moments. Table 1 gives only a static picture, that of the tendency, in order to isolate the cause of *unequal* exchange, the difference in the organic compositions. In other words, table 1 shows the unequal exchange inherent in the formation of the prices of production when the cause of unequal exchange (the difference in organic compositions) is isolated for analysis. Or, table 1 shows how the price mechanism rewards the high composition capitals and penalizes the low composition ones under tendencial conditions, when all capitals get the average rate of profit (through the price mechanism) so that there is no need for capital movements. *Secondly*, table 1 shows that there must be unequal exchange among capitals with different organic compositions. This does not contradict the basic notion that, to understand the production of surplus value and thus capital accumulation, we must assume that commodities (and thus also labour power) must exchange at their value. In fact, *equal* exchange must be assumed at the highest level of abstraction in order to explain the production of surplus value (the excess value above the value of labour power); *unequal* exchange must be assumed at a more concrete level of abstraction to explain the realization of surplus value through exchange. As Dobb (1973) correctly points out, the origin of surplus value must be analyzed before we can explain how that surplus value is realized/distributed due to differences in organic compositions. At the highest levels of abstraction (that of *Capital I*) exchange is not considered explicitly but is *inherent* in the theory of production since the equality of the organic compositions is implicitely assumed. At the lower level of abstraction (that of *Capital III*) exchange is considered explicitly by developing what is inherent in *Capital I*, i.e. by modifying the assumption of equal organic compositions. There is thus no need to choose between equal and unequal exchange as B. Bradby (1975), for example, does. For a more detailed treatment of these points, see Carchedi, 1983d.

5. For a discussion of the conditions under which both equalities hold, see P. Salama, 1975, p. 159.

6. 1975. Fine and Harris claim that 'Seton's difference from neo-Ricardianism arises because he does transform values into prices of production without reference to the technical relations of production which are so fundamental to neo-Ricardianism. This is simply done by setting up simultaneous equations between the price rate of profit and the ratios of prices of production to values. This involves correcting Marx's failure to transform the original costs of production from values into prices of production.' I disagree. Seton sets up his system of simultaneous equations by multiplying cost inputs by prices. Seton's cost inputs are the amount of product of industry j 'reckoned in terms of labour value' going into industry i. These cost inputs are then multiplied by p_j, or the price of industry j's product (per unit of labour value). Now, one of the two. Either the cost inputs K_{ij} are the individual value in terms of labour time, i.e. the labour which has actually been expended to produce the amount of j going into the production of i (which is in all probability Seton's view) and in this case prices reflect individual values. This is *not* Marx's transformation problem which deals with the transformation of individual values into prices of production as expressions of social necessary labour time. For Marx, the price of production is the expression of this latter, not of the former. This is a mistake made also by the neo-Ricardians. Or the k_{ij}'s are already social values, and in this case the controversial aspect of the transformation problem is left behind. But it is precisely this aspect which Seton's (as well as other's) contribution is meant to solve.

7. Among the many reactions to the von Bortkiewicz critique and approach, four deserve special mention. The first correctly stresses that the transformation problem has nothing to do with the reproduction schemes or with the input-output tables but ends up by assuming (instead of showing) that c and v are already transformed values. See, e.g., D. Yaffe, 1975, p. 46. The second stresses correctly the causal relation between values and prices but plays down the importance of the quantitative relation between them, thus in fact giving up that relation. See W. Baumol, 1974, pp. 53–54. See also I.I. Rubin, 1977, pp. 236–7. The third correctly stresses that 'the conception of that-which-has-to-be-calculated' must come before calculation and develops an ingenious procedure (the iterative one) but fails in its own terms. In fact, that procedure is alien to the Marxian one so that implicitly a dialectic solution is reduced to a numerical one which, moreover, shares with the von Bortkietwiczian solution the disadvantage of having to break the quantitative relation between surplus value and profits. See A. Shaikh, 1977, pp. 106–139. The fourth makes a more definite attempt to re-discover Marx's problematic but it too does not manage to break away from the temptation to look for a numerical solution starting from the premise of the validity of von Bortkiewicz' critique. See I. Gernstein, 1976, p. 254. For a more detailed discussion of these authors, see Carchedi, 1983d. After this article had been submitted and accepted for publication, I saw B. Fine, 1983. His note supports some of the arguments to be submitted below and adds the

interesting point that Marx's critics fail to distinguish between the organic and the value composition of capital: this failure is the cause of their mistaken formulation of the transformation problem. Fine's note, however, offers no adequate answer to the circularity and infinite regression critiques.

8. See Carchedi, 1983a, ch. 1. Two shorter presentations can be found in Carchedi, 1983b, pp. 347–366 and Carchedi, 1983c, pp. 110–126.

9. For example, according to B. Fine and L. Harris 'this Marx recognizes for he observes that the value of capital advanced may diverge from the price of production of that capital, but he makes no effort to correct this discrepancy' (1979, p. 25). Marx's text reads 'We have seen how a deviation in prices of production from values arises from . . . the price of production, which so deviates from the value of a commodity, entering into the cost price of other commodities as one of its elements, so that the cost price of a commodity may already contain a deviation from value in those means of production consumed by it, quite aside from a deviation of its own which may arise through a difference between the average profit and the surplus value. It is therefore possible that even the cost price of a commodity produced by capitals of average composition may differ from the sum of the values of the elements which make up this component of their price of production.' (1967c, pp. 206–7).

10. The relation between mathematical and dialectical logic is a complex one and cannot be dealt with here for lack of space. For a treatment of this problem, see Carchedi, 1983a.

11. J.R. Ernst correctly emphasizes the lack of chronological sequence of different production periods in the neo-Ricardian model and the significance for this of their theorization of an economy in which technical change is absent (1982, pp. 85–94). However, Ernst thinks that this is admissible if the conditions of production do not change from period to period. I, on the other hand, argue that the simultaneous determination of values in the neo-Ricardian scheme is incorrect to depict even the case of an economy with no technical progress. In fact, the determination of the value of c as an output must always be separated chronologically from that of *a* as an output. In case of no technical change, the value of c as an input will remain the same as the value it had (in the previous period) as an output, but this does not justify the theoretical mistake of collapsing the two production periods and moments of realization into just one.

12. In this paper, I have considered the Sraffa-based critique of the transformation problem only inasmuch as it is a variation of the circularity critique. According to I. Steedman, Marx assumes that by dividing the surplus value by the sum of the constant and variable capital (all value terms) we get the rate of profit, 'but then derives the result that prices diverge from values, which means precisely, in general, that S/(C + V) is *not* the rate of profit' (1977, p. 31). This paper disposes, I believe, of this critique. The same author mentions also two further objections. First, the transformation problem is deemed to be a pseudo-problem and a redundant one. There is, in fact, so runs the argument, no need to derive profits from surplus value because the rate of profit and the prices of production can be computed once the technical conditions of production and the real wages, both specified in physical quantities, are known. Values can be determined if the physical data relating to methods of production are known, but such a determination is redundant. A reply to this objection would show that the Sraffian prices refer to individual, embodied, labour time rather than to socially necessary labour time and that this is the source of inconsistency, circularity, and a simplistic

(rather than a simplifying) model of the capitalist economy. Secondly, there is the objection that in case of joint production the calculation of value can give either indeterminate (Sraffa) or negative (Steedman) results. In Sraffa's view, indeterminacy results from the fact that joint production implies more products (and thus prices to be determined) than there are processes (and thus equations) to determine them. Negative values result – in Steedman's view – because positive profits can coexist with negative surplus value. The answer to this objection would show both that it is possible to determine the value of the individual components of a joint product within Marx's theory of value and that the Sraffa-based treatment of joint production is one of the weakest spots in the Sraffian system, the one point where the logic of the assumptions takes on the most water. There is another approach which claims superiority upon Marx's theory of prices: the post-Keynesian. (See, e.g., Robinson and Eatwell, 1973; A. S. Eichner, 1979; A.S. Eichner, 1976). A discussion of this approach would stress that post-Keynesian theory is not exempt from the charge of being circular, indeterminate, and of depicting the price behaviour of the individual firm (i.e. the procedure followed by individual firms in setting the price *ex-ante*) rather than the social mechanism through which prices realize themselves independently of the will (and thus of the computations) of the individual firms. For reasons of space, the discussion of these points must await another occasion.

13. No doubt, many neo-Ricardians will have great difficulties in understanding this article. They will charge it with 'juggling' with dialectics, with hanging on an unnecessary, cumbersome body of theory (value analysis), with 'defining away' the transformation problem as they understand it, etc. In other words, they will follow their usual procedure of criticizing Marxism by applying their own theoretical categories to Marxist analysis, thus 'showing' inconsistencies, redundancies, circularities, etc. The neo-Ricardian/Sraffian school has yet to provide a methodologically valid critique of Marxism (either by carrying out an *immanent* critique of it or by challenging its presuppositions) for the simple reason that it is not equipped for such a task.

References

Baumol, W. (1974) 'What Marx "Really" Meant', *Journal of Economic Literature*, March.

Bradby, B. (1975) 'Equal Exchange and the Imperialism of Trade', *Bulletin of the Conference of Socialist Economists*, October.

Carchedi, G. (1983a) *Problems in Class Analysis. Production, Knowledge and the Function of Capital*, Routledge & Kegan Paul.

Carchedi, G. (1983b) 'Class Analysis and the Study of Social Forms', in **Morgan, G.** (ed.) *Beyond Method. Strategies for Social Research*, Sage Publications.

Carchedi, G. (1983c) 'Dialektik und Gessellschaftliche Gesetze', in

Carchedi, G. (1983d) *The Logic of Prices as Values*, Research Memorandum 8320, Department of Economics, University of Amsterdam, Amsterdam, the Netherlands.

Dobb, M. (1973) *Theories of Value and Distribution since Adam Smith*, Cambridge University Press.

Dostaler, G. (1982) 'Marx's Theory of Value and the Transformation Problem: Some Lessons from a Debate', *Studies in Political Economy*, Fall, No. 9.

Eichner, A.S. (1976) *The Megacorp and Ologopoly*, Cambridge University Press.

Eichner, A.S. (ed.) (1979) *A Guide to Post-Keynesian Economics*, Macmillan.

Ernst, J.R. (1982) 'Simultaneous Valuation Extirpated', *The Review of Radical Political Economics*, Vol. 14, No. 2.

Fine, B. (1983) 'A Dissenting Note on the Transformation Problem', *Economy and Society*, Vol. 12, No. 4, November, pp. 520–525.

Fine, B. and Harris, L. (1976) 'Controversial Issues in Marxist Economic Theory', *The Socialist Register*, London.

Fine, B. and Harris, L. (1979) *Re-reading Capital*, Macmillan.

Gernstein, I. (1976) 'Production, Circula-

tion and Value', *Economy and Society*, Vol. 5, No. 3, August.
Hilferding, R. (1973) 'Bohm-Bawerk's Criticism of Marx', in **Sweezy, P.** (ed.) *Karl Marx and the Close of his System*, A.M. Kelley.
Kay, G. (1975) 'Why Labour Is the Starting Point of Capital', in **Elson, D.** (ed.), *Value, the Representation of Labour Under Capitalism*, CSE Books.
Kimmerle, H. (Hg) *Dialektik Heute*, Germinal Verlag Bochum.
Marx, K. (1967a) *Capital*, Vol. I, International Publishers.
Marx, K. (1967b) *Capital*, Vol. II, International Publishers.
Marx, K. (1967c) *Capital*, Vol. III, International Publishers.
Murray, R. (1977) 'Value and Theory of Rent', *Capital and Class*, Nos 3 and 4.
Nichols, T. (ed.) (1980) *Capital and Labour*, Fontana.
Robinson, J. (1972) 'Ideology and Analysis', in **Schwartz, J.** (ed.) *A Critique of Economic Theory*, Penguin Books.
Robinson, J. and Eatwell, J. (1973) *An Introduction to Modern Economics*, McGraw-Hill.
Rothorn, B. (1979) 'Neo-Classicism, Neo-Ricardianism and Marxism', *New Left Review*, No. 80, July–August.
Rubin, I.I. (1972) *Essays on Marx's Theory of Value*, Black and Red, Detriot.
Salama, P. (1975) *Sur la Valeur*, Maspero.
Seton, F. (1957) 'The Transformation Problem', *Review of Economic Studies*.
Shaikh, A. (1977) 'Marx's Transformation of Value and the "Transformation Problem" ', in **Schwartz, J.** (ed.) *The Subtle Anatomy of Capitalism*, Goodyear Publishing Company.
Steedman, I. (1977) *Marx After Sraffa*, New Left Books.
Sweezy, P. (1968) *The Theory of Capitalist Development*, New York, Monthly Review Press.
von Böhm-Bawerk, E. (1973) 'Karl Marx and the Close of his System', in **Sweezy, P.** (ed.) *Karl Marx and the Close of his System*, A.M. Kelley.
von Bortkiewicz, S. (1973) 'On the Correction of Marx's Theoretical Construction in the Third Volume of Capital', in **Sweezy, P.** (ed.) *Karl Marx and the Close of his System*, A.M. Kelley.
Winternitz, J. (1948) 'Values and Prices: A Solution to the So-Called Transformation Problem', *The Economic Journal*.
Yaffe, D. (1975) 'Values and Prices in Marx's Capital', *Revolutionary Communist*, No. 1, Second Edition.

For Product Safety Concerns and Information please contact our EU
representative GPSR@taylorandfrancis.com
Taylor & Francis Verlag GmbH, Kaufingerstraße 24, 80331 München, Germany

www.ingramcontent.com/pod-product-compliance
Ingram Content Group UK Ltd.
Pitfield, Milton Keynes, MK11 3LW, UK
UKHW022133190926
475702UK00013B/1782

* 9 7 8 0 4 1 5 8 3 8 5 3 5 *